INTERMEDIATE CHINESE CHARACTERS

Learn 300 Mandarin Chinese Characters and 1200 Words

Haohsiang Liao and Kang Zhou

TUTTLE Publishing

Tokyo | Rutland, Vermont | Singapore

"Books to Span the East and West"

Tuttle Publishing was founded in 1832 in the small New England town of Rutland, Vermont [USA]. Our core values remain as strong today as they were then—to publish best-in-class books which bring people together one page at a time. In 1948, we established a publishing office in Japan—and Tuttle is now a leader in publishing English-language books about the arts, languages and cultures of Asia. The world has become a much smaller place today and Asia's economic and cultural influence has grown. Yet the need for meaningful dialogue and information about this diverse region has never been greater. Over the past seven decades, Tuttle has published thousands of books on subjects ranging from martial arts and paper crafts to language learning and literature— and our talented authors, illustrators, designers and photographers have won many prestigious awards. We welcome you to explore the wealth of information available on Asia at **www.tuttlepublishing.com**.

Published by Tuttle Publishing, an imprint of
Periplus Editions (HK) Ltd

www.tuttlepublishing.com

Copyright © 2021 Periplus Editions (HK) Ltd
PHOTOS Front cover AZemdega/istockphoto.com;
Following from Shutterstock.com
Pages 10 Rawpixel.com; **18** yatate; **27** mavo; **36, 45** Syda Productions; **53** yut548; **54** Twinsterphoto; **63** Andriy Blokhin; **72** animicsgo; **81** Love the wind; **90** jesadaphorn; **99** testing; **108** Elnur; **117** witita leelasutanon; **126** Ivica Drusany; **135** Artisticco; **144** Shutterstock.com; **153** Chinnapong; **162** Roengrit Kongmuang; **171** LightField Studios; **180** gguy

ISBN: 978-0-8048-4663-9

24 23 22 21   10 9 8 7 6 5 4 3 2 1
Printed in Malaysia   2105VP

TUTTLE PUBLISHING® is a registered trademark of Tuttle Publishing, a division of Periplus Editions (HK) Ltd.

Distributed by

North America, Latin America & Europe
Tuttle Publishing
364 Innovation Drive
North Clarendon, VT 05759-9436 U.S.A.
Tel: 1 (802) 773-8930
Fax: 1 (802) 773-6993
info@tuttlepublishing.com
www.tuttlepublishing.com

Japan
Tuttle Publishing
Yaekari Building 3rd Floor
5-4-12 Osaki
Shinagawa-ku
Tokyo 141 0032
Tel: (81) 3 5437-0171
Fax: (81) 3 5437-0755
sales@tuttle.co.jp
www.tuttle.co.jp

Asia Pacific
Berkeley Books Pte. Ltd.
3 Kallang Sector #04-01
Singapore 349278
Tel: (65) 6741-2178
Fax: (65) 6741-2179
inquiries@periplus.com.sg
www.tuttlepublishing.com

To Download or Stream Online Audio and Printable Flashcards.

1. Make sure you have an Internet connection.
2. Type the URL below into your web browser.
https://www.tuttlepublishing.com/intermediate-chinese-characters

For support, you can email us at info@tuttlepublishing.com.

Contents

Learner's Guide

Learning objectives

In this book, you are going to learn 300 useful Chinese characters by theme, spread over 20 lessons. With these 300 characters, you will:

- master the core Chinese characters needed for basic conversations and authentic language situations.
- become familiar with the characters required for the HSK (**Hànyǔ Shuǐpíng Kǎoshì** 汉语水平考试 *Chinese Proficiency Test*) Level 3.

To help you achieve these goals, this book provides a systematic introduction to the basic Chinese characters. Each lesson includes:

- a dialogue to show you how these characters are used by theme.
- each character's pronunciation, meaning, radical, stroke order, and number of strokes.
- example sentences to show how each Chinese character is used in context.
- helpful writing practice guides to teach you how to write each character.
- useful exercises to enhance your ability to use these characters and give you opportunities to practice character recognition, vocabulary usage, and language production.

How to use the materials

Each lesson contains the following components:

- Dialogue
- Vocabulary
- New Characters
- Individual Character Explanation
- Exercises

Below are the step-to-step explanations for each component with illustrations.

LESSON 8

Family Get Togethers 家庭活动

Dialogue provides a narrative to show how the new characters introduced in the lesson are used by theme, followed by two or three comprehension questions.

---

1. Dialogue

Read the dialogue below and answer the questions in characters.

琳达，美国人，刚到北京工作三个月，王云是她的同事。

琳达：	王云，你这周末有什么安排吗？
王云：	这周末我们过节啊，中秋节。你知道中秋节吗？
琳达：	是不是有点儿像美国的"感恩节"？人们都要回家跟家人团聚。
王云：	没错！在我们家，爷爷说中秋节家人必须在一起。爸爸、妈妈、叔叔、阿姨、兄弟姐妹一个都不能少。
琳达：	中秋节还要吃月饼，对吗？
王云：	对！我特别爱吃月饼！你呢？
琳达：	我还没吃过呢！
王云：	那你有没有兴趣跟我们一起过中秋节？
琳达：	当然有！那我到时候买盒月饼带过去吧。

Vocabulary lists the new words and characters covered in the lesson. Each Chinese word is written in simplified characters, accompanied by its pinyin and English equivalent.

2. Vocabulary

	Word	Pinyin	English equivalent
1.	中秋节	**Zhōngqiūjié**	Mid-Autumn Festival
2.	感恩节	**Gǎnēnjié**	Thanksgiving
3.	团聚	**tuánjù**	gather
4.	必须	**bìxū**	must
5.	叔叔	**shūshu**	uncle
6.	阿姨	**āyí**	aunt
7.	兄弟姐妹	**xiōngdì jiěmèi**	siblings
8.	月饼	**yuèbǐng**	mooncake
9.	爱	**ài**	love
10.	兴趣	**xìngqù**	interest
11.	盒	**hé**	box
12.	带	**dài**	bring
13.	已经	**yǐjīng**	already
14.	丈夫	**zhàngfu**	husband
15.	孩子	**háizi**	child
16.	不好意思	**bùhǎoyìsi**	feel embarrassed

New Characters provides a full list of the new fifteen characters introduced in the lesson.

3. New Characters

Fifteen characters are introduced in this lesson. Use the following explanations to help you understand and remember the characters.

孩　丈　夫　爷　叔　阿　姨　兄　已　经　兴　趣　玩　爱　真

Individual Character Explanations provide the following information of each character: (1) the character number for reference, (2) its standard form, (3) its pinyin, (4) its English equivalent, (5) its semantic radical, (6) some useful phrases and sentences in pinyin, characters, and English translations, and (7) its stroke order.

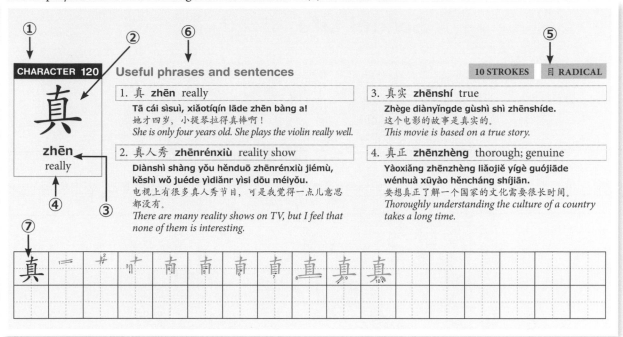

Exercises provide various types of exercises to enhance your ability to use these characters, including (1) fill in the blanks, (2) questions, and (3) improvisation assignments.

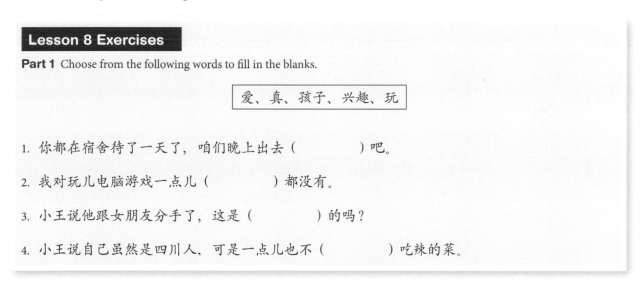

LESSON 1

School Life 学校生活

1. Text

Read the email below and answer the questions in characters.

思明你好:

我今天刚考完试, 所以现在才给你回信, 不好意思!

这个学期我选了四门课, 最喜欢的是中国语言文化。我们班上有三个从中国来的学生, 我很喜欢跟他们讨论问题。不过, 准备这门课的考试要花很多时间, 考试的问题也很难回答。下个星期又要考试了, 我还没开始复习呢。

这个周末我打算请几个好朋友来宿舍, 一起唱唱歌、跳跳舞。我告诉他们可以带一些吃的东西来, 但是不能带酒!

你最近怎么样? 还很忙吗? 我记得你马上要去上海学中文了, 是下个星期吗? 我在上海有几个老朋友, 如果需要帮忙的话, 请告诉我, 不要客气。

祝好!

高山

1. 高山上几门课？他喜欢哪门课？

2. 这个周末高山想做什么？

3. 思明准备去哪儿？他要去做什么？

2. Vocabulary

	Word	Pinyin	English equivalent
1.	完	wán	(resultative ending) finished
2.	才	cái	as late as
3.	信	xìn	letter; mail
4.	选	xuǎn	take (class); choose
5.	班	bān	class; section
6.	讨论	tǎolùn	discuss
7.	准备	zhǔnbèi	prepare
8.	回答	huídá	answer; respond
9.	又	yòu	again
10.	复习	fùxí	review
11.	打算	dǎsuàn	plan
12.	唱歌	chànggē	sing
13.	跳舞	tiàowǔ	dance
14.	一些	yìxiē	some; several
15.	记得	jìdé	remember
16.	马上	mǎshàng	immediately
17.	帮忙	bāngmáng	help; assistance
18.	祝好	zhùhǎo	All the best!

3. New Characters

Fifteen characters are introduced in this lesson. Use the following explanations to help you understand and remember the characters.

选　准　备　回　答　题　跳　舞　班　唱　歌　忙　完　些　帮

CHARACTER 1

选 **xuǎn**
take; choose

9 STROKES 辶 **RADICAL**

Useful phrases and sentences

1. 选择 **xuǎnzé** choose

Zhōngguó xuésheng shàng dàxué yǐqián jiù děi xuǎnzé zhuānyè.
中国学生上大学以前就得选择专业。
College students in China need to choose majors before they matriculate.

2. 选举 **xuǎnjǔ** election

Tā cónglái bù guānxīn xuǎnjǔ zǒngtǒngde shìqing.
他从来不关心选举总统的事情。
He has never been keen about the presidential election.

3. 选修 **xuǎnxiū** take (classes)

Xiànzài, xuǎnxiū zhōngwénde xuésheng yuèláiyuè duōle.
现在，选修中文的学生越来越多了。
More and more students are taking Chinese classes nowadays.

4. 选手 **xuǎnshǒu** contestant

Jīnnián cānjiā shùxué bǐsàide xuǎnshǒu dōu hěn lìhai.
今年参加数学比赛的选手都很厉害！
The contestants in the math competition this year are all great.

选 选

CHARACTER 2

准 **zhǔn**
accurate; to allow

10 STROKES 冫 **RADICAL**

Useful phrases and sentences

1. 准备 **zhǔnbèi** prepare

Nǐde Zhōngwén kǎoshì zhǔnbèide zěnmeyàng le?
你的中文考试准备得怎么样了？
How is your Chinese test preparation going?

2. 标准 **biāozhǔn** accurate; standard

Tā Zhōngwén shuōde hěn liúlì, yě hěn biāozhǔn.
他中文说得很流利，也很标准。
He is fluent and accurate in Chinese.

3. 准时 **zhǔnshí** on time; punctual

Qǐng dàjiā míngtiān zhǔnshí lái kāihuì.
请大家明天准时来开会。
Please attend the meeting tomorrow on time.

4. 准点 **zhǔndiǎn** on time (transportation)

Yīnwèi xià dàyǔ, fēijī bùnéng zhǔndiǎn qǐfēi.
因为下大雨，飞机不能准点起飞。
Flights cannot take off on time due to the heavy rain.

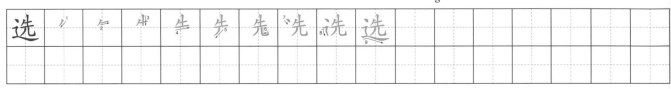

CHARACTER 3

备 **bèi**
prepare

8 STROKES 夂 **RADICAL**

Useful phrases and sentences

1. 具备 **jùbèi** equip; possess

Zài Měiguó dāng lǎoshī xūyào jùbèi shénme tiáojiàn?
在美国当老师需要具备什么条件？
What qualifications are required to become a school teacher in the U.S.A.?

2. 设备 **shèbèi** facility

Zhèjiā gōngchǎngde shèbèi hěnxīn.
这家工厂的设备很新。
This factory's facilities are new.

3. 责备 **zébèi** criticize; blame

Háizi zuòcuòshì yǐjīng hěn nánguòle, bié zébèi tā le.
孩子做错事已经很难过了，别责备他了。
The child already feels sad about the mistakes he made. Do not blame him anymore.

4. 备忘录 **bèiwànglù** memorandum

Tā xíguàn bǎ dàdàxiǎoxiǎode shìqing dōu xiězài bèiwànglù shang.
他习惯把大大小小的事情都写在备忘录上。
He likes to write down all kinds of things in his memo book.

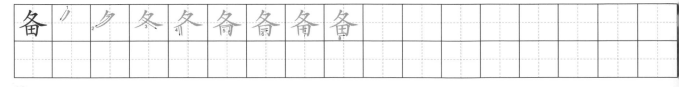

CHARACTER 4

回
huí
return; respond

Useful phrases and sentences

1. 回答 **huídá** to answer

Tā wènwǒ jīnnián duōdà le, wǒ bùxiǎng huídá zhège wèntí.

他问我今年多大了，我不想回答这个问题。

He asked about my age, but I didn't want to answer.

2. 回忆 **huíyì** memory

Duìwǒláishuō, zài Táiběide liúxué shēnghuó shì yíduàn hěn měihǎode huíyì.

对我来说，在台北的留学生活是一段很美好的回忆。

My life studying abroad in Taipei was a beautiful memory for me.

3. 回国 **huíguó** return to one's country

Huíguóde jīpiào nǐ mǎihǎole ma?

回国的机票你买好了吗？

Did you buy your return plane ticket home?

4. 回报 **huíbào** in return

Búyào pà shībài, zhǐyào nǐ nǔlì zǒng yǒu huíbàode.

不要怕失败，只要你努力总有回报的。

Don't be afraid of failure. You always gain something in return as long as you put in effort.

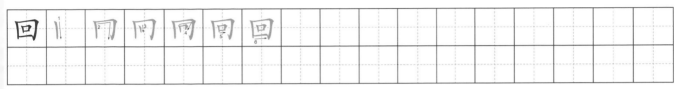

CHARACTER 5

答
dá
answer; reply

Useful phrases and sentences

1. 答案 **dáàn** answer

Shénme shì xìngfú? Wǒ juéde méiyǒu biāozhǔn dáàn.

什么是幸福？我觉得没有标准答案。

What is happiness? I don't think there is a right answer to this.

2. 答谢 **dáxiè** express thanks

Míngtiān wǎnshang liùdiǎn lǎobǎn huì jǔbàn yíge dáxiè jiǔhuì.

明天晚上六点老板会举办一个答谢酒会。

The boss will hold a thank-you banquet tomorrow evening at 6 p.m.

3. 答复 **dáfù** respond; reply

Wǒ shànggeyuè xiěxìn yāoqiú lǎobǎn gěiwǒ jiā yìdiǎn gōngzī, kěshì dào xiànzài háiméi dáfù wǒ.

我上个月写信要求老板给我加一点工资，可是到现在还没答复我。

I wrote to my boss last week to request a salary increase, but still have not received any response.

4. 答应 **dāyìng** promise

Dāyìng biérénde shìqing wǒ yídìng huì zuòdào.

答应别人的事情我一定会做到。

I always keep my promises to people.

CHARACTER 6

题
tí
topic; item

Useful phrases and sentences

1. 难题 **nántí** difficult problem

Jiějué kōngqì wūrǎn shì shìjiè gèguó miànlínde nántí.

解决空气污染是世界各国面临的难题。

Solving air pollution is a tough issue for all the countries in the world.

2. 题目 **tímù** topic

Wǒ zhècì qīzhōng bàogàode tímù shì Zhōngguóde gāokǎo zhìdù.

我这期中报告的题目是中国的高考制度。

The topic of my mid-term report is the gaokao (college entrance examination) system in China.

3. 考题 **kǎotí** test

Zuótiān shùxuékède kǎotí bǐ wǒ xiǎngde róngyì.

昨天数学课的考题比我想的容易。

The math test yesterday was easier than I thought.

4. 主题 **zhǔtí** theme

Zhècì huìyìde zhǔtí shì zěnme bāngzhù dàxuéshēng jiùyè.

这次会议的主题是怎么帮助大学生就业。

The theme for this conference is how to help college students find employment opportunities.

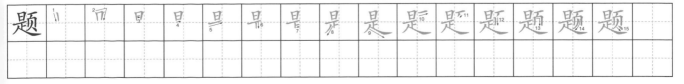

跳

tiào
jump; hop

13 STROKES   足 RADICAL

Useful phrases and sentences

1. 跳舞 **tiàowǔ** dance
   Wǒ měige zhōumò dōu gēn péngyou qù tiàowǔ.
   我每个周末都跟朋友去跳舞。
   I go dancing with my friends every weekend.

2. 跳下来 **tiàoxiàlai** jump down
   Sōngshǔ cóng shùshang tiàoxiàlai zhǎo shíwù.
   松鼠从树上跳下来找食物。
   The squirrel jumped down from the tree to look for food.

3. 跳起来 **tiàoqǐlai** jump up
   Háizi kànjiàn shèngdàn lǎorén gāoxìngde tiàoqǐlai.
   孩子看见圣诞老人高兴地跳起来。
   The children all jumped in excitement when they saw Santa Claus.

4. 跳伞 **tiàosǎn** parachute
   Xiànzài bùshǎo niánqīngrén xǐhuan tiàosǎn zhège yùndòng.
   现在不少年轻人喜欢跳伞这个运动。
   Today, many young people like parachute jumping.

舞

wǔ
dance

14 STROKES   夕 RADICAL

Useful phrases and sentences

1. 舞蹈 **wǔdǎo** dance
   Yúnmén shì Táiwān yíge hěn yǒumíngde wǔdǎotuán.
   "云门"是台湾一个很有名的舞蹈团。
   Yunmen is a famous dance group from Taiwan.

2. 舞会 **wǔhuì** dance party
   Wǒ gēn wǒ xiānsheng shì zài xuéxiàode wǔhuìshang rènshide.
   我跟我先生是在学校的舞会上认识的。
   I met my husband at a school dance.

3. 舞台 **wǔtái** stage
   Xīnde jùchǎng wǔtái hěndà, yě hěn piàoliang.
   新的剧场舞台很大，也很漂亮。
   The new theater's stage is big and pretty.

4. 舞龙 **wǔlóng** Dragon Dance
   Wǔlóng shì Zhōngguórén qìngzhù xīnniánde chuántóng huódòng.
   舞龙是中国人庆祝新年的传统活动。
   The Dragon Dance is a traditional way for Chinese to celebrate the New Year.

班

bān
class; section

10 STROKES   王 RADICAL

Useful phrases and sentences

1. 班级 **bānjí** class
   Zài Zhōngguóde xiǎoxué, yīge bānjí yǒu sìwǔshí rén zuǒyòu.
   在中国的小学，一个班级有四五十人左右。
   There are about forty to fifty students in one class in China.

2. 航班 **hángbān** flight
   Yībānláishuō, zuò wǎnshangde hángbān jīpiào bǐjiào piányi.
   一般来说，坐晚上的航班机票比较便宜。
   In general, night flights are cheaper.

3. 加班 **jiābān** work overtime
   Tā zhōumòde shíhou chángcháng qù bàngōngshì jiābān.
   他周末的时候常常去办公室加班。
   He often works overtime at his office over the weekend.

4. 班车 **bānchē** shuttle bus
   Wǒ měitiān zuò gōngsī bānchē qù shàngbān.
   我每天坐公司班车去上班。
   I go to work every day by a shuttle bus provided by our company.

唱

chàng
sing

Useful phrases and sentences

1. 唱歌 **chànggē** sing; singing

Tā chànggē chàngde hěn hǎotīng.
他唱歌唱得很好听。
He is good at singing.

2. 说唱 **shuōchàng** rap

Shéishì Měiguó zuì yǒumíngde shuōchàng gēshǒu, nǐ zhīdào ma?
谁是美国最有名的说唱歌手，你知道吗？
Do you know who the most famous rapper in the U.S.A. is?

3. 唱片 **chàngpiān** (vinyl) records

Xiànzai mǎi chàngpiànde rén yuè lái yuè shǎo le.
现在买唱片的人越来越少了。
Fewer and fewer people buy (vinyl) records nowadays.

4. 合唱团 **héchàngtuán** choir

Zhège lǎonián héchàngtuán píngjūn niánlìng shì liùshíwǔ suì.
这个老年合唱团平均年龄是六十五岁。
The average age in this senior choir is 65.

歌

gē
song

Useful phrases and sentences

1. 儿歌 **érgē** children's songs; nursery rhymes

Nǐ hái jìde xiǎoshíhou chàngguode érgē ma?
你还记得小时候唱过的儿歌吗？
Do you still remember the kids songs you sang when you were little?

2. 歌剧 **gējù** Western opera

Zhècì lái Wéiyěnà, wǒ hěnxiǎng kàn yìchǎng gējù.
这次来维也纳，我很想看一场歌剧。
I would very much like to see an opera during this visit to Vienna.

3. 歌星 **gēxīng** singer

Tāde mèngxiǎng shì yǐhòu dāng yìmíng gēxīng.
他的梦想是以后当一名歌星。
His dream is to become a singer.

4. 歌迷 **gēmí** fans (of a singer)

Màikèr jiékèxùn zài shìjiè gèdì dōuyǒu hěnduō gēmí.
迈克尔·杰克逊在世界各地都有很多歌迷。
Michael Jackson had many fans worldwide.

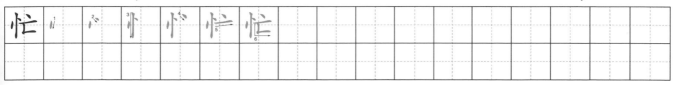

忙

máng
busy

Useful phrases and sentences

1. 忙着 **mángzhe** busy with

Tā zuìjìn mángzhe xiě bìyè lùnwén, měitiān zhǐnéng shuì sānsìge zhōngtóu.
他最近忙着写毕业论文，每天只能睡三四个钟头。
He has been busy with his graduation thesis. He can sleep only three to four hours a day.

2. 忙什么 **mángshénme** busy with what

Nǐ zuìjìn máng shénme ne? Hǎojǐge xīngqī dōu méijiànle!
你最近忙什么呢？好几个星期都没见你了！
What have you been busy with? I haven't seen you for several weeks.

3. 繁忙 **fánmáng** busy; bustling

Fánmángde gōngzuò ràng tā méishíjiān tánliàn'ài.
繁忙的工作让他没时间谈恋爱。
The busy work leaves him no time for romance.

4. 忙乱 **mángluàn** hectic; disorganized

Jīntiān zǎoshang wǒ qǐwǎnle, chūmén yòu wàngle dài qiánbāo, zhēnshì mángluànde yìtiān.
今天早上我起晚了，出门又忘了带钱包，真是忙乱的一天。
I got up late this morning and I forgot my wallet when I went out. What a hectic day!

CHARACTER 13

完

wán
finish; complete

7 STROKES   宀 RADICAL

Useful phrases and sentences

1. 完成 wánchéng finish

Tā yòu méi ànshí wánchéng zuòyè.

他又没按时完成作业。

He did not finish his homework on time again.

2. 完全 wánquán totally; completely

Wǒshì Běijīngrén, wánquán tīngbudǒng shànghǎi fāngyán.

我是北京人，完全听不懂上海方言。

As I am from Beijing, I am totally clueless about the Shanghai dialect.

3. 用完 yòngwán used up; run out

Xǐfàshuǐ kuài yòngwánle, jīntiān děi zài qù mǎi yìpíng.

洗发水快用完了，今天得再去买一瓶。

The shampoo has almost run out. We need to go buy one today.

4. 完美 wánměi perfect

Nǐde jìhuà tài wánměile, women jiù zhème zuòba.

你的计划太完美了，我们就这么做吧。

Your plan sounds perfect. Let's do it.

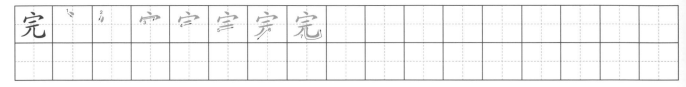

CHARACTER 14

些

xiē
some

8 STROKES   二 RADICAL

Useful phrases and sentences

1. 一些 yìxē some; several

Míngtiān qù péngyou jiā kěyǐ dài yìxiā shuǐguǒ.

明天去朋友家可以带一些水果。

You can bring some fruits to your friends tomorrow.

2. 好些 hǎoxiē a good deal of; a lot of

Shānmíngde hǎoxiē péngyou dōu huì lái cānjiā tāde bìyè diǎnlǐ.

山明的好些朋友都会来参加他的毕业典礼。

A good number of Shanming's friends will attend his commencement ceremony.

3. 早些 zǎoxiē earlier

Zǎoshang bā diǎn jiāotōng hěn bù hǎo, nǐ zuì hǎo zǎoxiē chūfā.

早上八点交通很不好，你最好早些出发。

The traffic is very bad at 8 am. You'd better leave earlier.

4. 有些 yǒuxiē a little bit

Zuìjìn wǒ yǒuxiē máng, děng yǒukòngle zài zhǎo nǐ.

最近我有些忙，等有空了再找你。

I am a little bit busy recently. I'll be in contact when I have time.

CHARACTER 15

帮

bāng
help; assist

9 STROKES   巾 RADICAL

Useful phrases and sentences

1. 帮 bāng help; assist

Wǒ shēntǐ bù shūfu, néng máfan nǐ bāngwǒ mǎidiǎn wǔfàn ma?

我身体不舒服，能麻烦你帮我买点午饭吗？

I am not feeling well. Can you do me a favor and get lunch for me?

2. 帮大忙 bāngdàmáng do (someone) a big favor

Zuótiān nǐ zhēnshi bāngle dàmáng, xièxiè.

昨天你真是帮了大忙，谢谢。

You really did me a big favor yesterday. Thank you!

3. 帮忙 bāngmáng help

Xiǎo Zhāng zhègerén hěn rèxīn, dàjiā yǒu shìqing yě dōu xǐhuan zhǎotā bāngmáng.

小张这个人很热心，大家有事情也都喜欢找他帮忙。

Xiao Zhang is warm-hearted. Everyone likes to reach out to him for help if needed.

4. 帮手 bāngshǒu assistant; helper

Zuòwán zhège huóer děi huā hěnduō shíjiān, nǐ zuìhǎo zhǎoge bāngshǒu.

做完这个活儿得花很多时间，你最好找个帮手。

Finishing this work takes a lot of time. You'd better find an assistant.

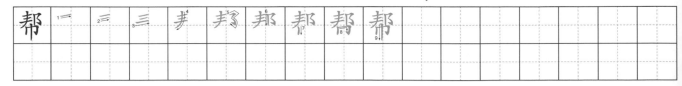

Lesson 1 Exercises

Part 1 Choose from the following words to fill in the blanks.

准备、帮忙、选、回答、忙

1. 这个学期有意思的课太多了，我真不知道（　　　　）什么课好。

2. 明天的考试我已经（　　　　）好了，咱们可以出去玩儿了。

3. 老张，好久不见了，你最近（　　　　）什么呢？

4. 我听说小谢很懂车，你要是买车的话可以找他（　　　　）。

Part 2 Complete the following dialogues using Chinese characters.

1. A: 你最近忙什么呢？

   B: _____。

2. A: 你这个学期上几门课？都是什么课？

   B: _____。

3. A: 你喜欢上什么课？为什么？

   B: _____。

4. A: 你的好朋友是谁？你常常找他帮忙吗？

   B: _____。

5. A: 你喜欢开晚会吗？你去朋友的晚会带什么东西？

   B: _____。

Part 3 学以致用

请你跟朋友说说你的学校生活。

- 你在哪儿上学？
- 你每天都很忙吗？
- 你今年上几门课？你觉得什么课很难，什么课很有意思？
- 不上课的时候，你喜欢跟朋友做什么？

LESSON 2

How Are You Feeling? 你最近身体怎么样?

1. Dialogue

Read the dialogue below and answer the questions in characters.

妈妈:	孩子们, 我们要去 "唱歌" 了。快点儿穿衣服、洗脸、刷牙!
儿子:	妈妈, 我身体不舒服, 眼睛疼、鼻子疼、嘴巴疼、肚子也疼。还有, 最近弹钢琴弹得太多了, 手也疼。
女儿:	我也病了! 我感冒了, 好像还发烧。我觉得从头到脚都疼, 最少有39.5度。
妈妈:	(妈妈笑了)你们是不是耳朵也疼啊? 我刚说的是 "唱歌", 不是 "上课"。
孩子:	啊? 什么? 那......, 我们好点儿了。咱们快走吧!

1. 妈妈要带孩子去哪儿?

_____

2. 儿子和女儿都说他们病了, 为什么呢?

_____

2. Vocabulary

	Word	Pinyin	English equivalent
1.	脸	**liǎn**	face
2.	刷牙	**shuāyá**	brush teeth
3.	身体	**shēntǐ**	body
4.	眼睛	**yǎnjīng**	eye
5.	疼	**téng**	pain
6.	鼻子	**bízi**	nose
7.	肚子	**dùzi**	stomach
8.	嘴巴	**zuǐba**	mouth
9.	弹钢琴	**tángāngqín**	play the piano
10.	手	**shǒu**	hand
11.	病	**bìng**	ill; sick
12.	好像	**hǎoxiàng**	seem
13.	感冒	**gǎnmào**	have a cold
14.	发烧	**fāshāo**	fever
15.	头	**tóu**	head
16.	脚	**jiǎo**	toe; foot
17.	度	**dù**	degree
18.	笑	**xiào**	laugh; smile
19.	耳朵	**ěrduō**	ear
20.	啊	**a**	(indicates surprise; embarrassment)

3. New Characters

Fifteen characters are introduced in this lesson. Use the following explanations to help you understand and remember the characters.

身　体　病　眼　睛　笑　手　头　肚　鼻　耳　烧　度　嘴　脚

身

shēn
body

7 STROKES   身 RADICAL

Useful phrases and sentences

1. 身体 **shēntǐ** body; health

   Lǎogāo, nín zuìjìn shēntǐ zěnmeyàng a?
   老高，您最近身体怎么样啊？
   Lao Gao, how have you been recently?

2. 健身房 **jiànshēnfáng** gym

   Tā bùxǐhuān qù jiànshēnfáng pǎobù, zài wàimian pǎobù gèng shūfu.
   他不喜欢去健身房跑步，在外面跑步更舒服。
   He doesn't like jogging in the gym. He thinks that jogging outside is more comfortable.

3. 身边 **shēnbiān** around

   Xiǎolǐ hěn guānxīn shēnbiān de péngyou.
   小李很关心身边的朋友。
   Xiao Li very much cares about friends around him.

4. 身材 **shēncái** stature; figure

   Wǒde fùqin shēncái gāodà, niánqīngde shíhou shìwèi hěn chūsède lánqiú yùndòngyuán.
   我的父亲身材高大，年轻的时候是位很出色的篮球运动员。
   My father is tall. He was an outstanding basketball player when he was young.

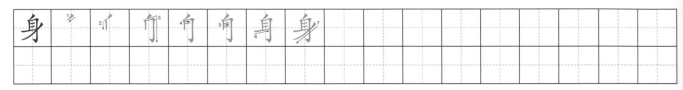

CHARACTER 17

体

tǐ
body; style

7 STROKES   亻 RADICAL

Useful phrases and sentences

1. 体重 **tǐzhòng** body weight

   Zài měiguo, nǐ qiānwàn bié wèn biéren de tǐzhòng.
   在美国，你千万别问别人的体重。
   Don't ask about people's weight in the U.S.A.

2. 集体 **jítǐ** group activity

   Wǒmen gōngsī jīngcháng bàn yìxiē jítǐ huódòng, xīwàng dàjiā néng yǒu gèngduō de jīhuì jiāoliú.
   我们公司经常办一些集体活动，希望大家能有更多的机会交流。
   Our company often holds group activities in the hope that people will have more opportunities to interact.

3. 体验 **tǐyàn** experience

   Wǒ cóngxiǎo zài chéngshì zhǎngdà, hěn xiǎng tǐyànxià nóngcūnde shēnghuó.
   我从小在城市长大，很想体验下农村的生活。
   I grew up in the city and would very much like to experience the rural life.

4. 体育 **tǐyù** physical education

   Tǐyùkè zài Zhōngguó hěnduō dàxué dōushì bìxiūkè.
   体育课在中国很多大学都是必修课。
   Physical education classes are required in many colleges in China.

体 亻 亻 仁 什 体 体 体

CHARACTER 18

病

bìng
illness; disease

10 STROKES   疒 RADICAL

Useful phrases and sentences

1. 疾病 **jíbìng** illness; disease

   Zài dōngtiān, liúgǎn shì zuì chángjiànde jíbìng.
   在冬天，流感是最常见的疾病。
   The flu is a common illness in the winter.

2. 病毒 **bìngdú** virus

   Zhēn zāogāo, wǒde diànnǎo yòu zhòng bìngdúle.
   真糟糕，我的电脑又中了病毒！
   My computer has gotten virus again. How terrible!

3. 毛病 **máobìng** problem; issue

   Nǐde chēzi zěnme yòu chū máobìngle, búshì shànggè lǐbai cái xiūhǎo ma?
   你的车子怎么又出毛病了，不是上个礼拜才修好吗？
   Your car has problems again? Wasn't it fixed last week?

4. 病人 **bìngrén** patient; sick people

   Zài Zhōngguó, qù kàn bìngrénde shíhou yídìng búyào song júhuā.
   在中国，去看病人的时候一定不要送菊花。
   Do not bring chrysanthemums as a gift when you visit a patient in China.

病 丶 亠 广 广 疒 疒 疒 病 病 病

CHARACTER 9

眼

yǎn
eye

Useful phrases and sentences

1. 眼镜 yǎnjìng eyeglasses

Wǒ zěnme zhǎobujiàn yǎnjìngle! Nǐ kànjiànle ma?

我怎么找不见眼镜了！你看见了吗？

How come I can't find my eyeglasses? Have you seen them?

2. 眼熟 yǎnshú familiar

Zhè dìfang wǒmen shìbushì láiguo? Zěnme kànqǐlai zhème yǎnshú?

这地方我们是不是来过？怎么看起来这么眼熟。

Weren't we here before? How come this looks so familiar?

3. 眼泪 yǎnlèi tears

Zhèbu diànyǐng tàiyǒu yìsi le, dàjiā xiàode yǎnlèi dōu liúchūlai le.

这部电影太有意思了，大家笑得眼泪都流出来了。

This movie is marvelous and everyone is crying with laughter.

4. 近视眼 jìnshìyǎn nearsighted

Wǒmen bān wǔshíge rén, chàbuduō rénrén dōushì jìnshìyǎn.

我们班五十个人，差不多人人都是近视眼。

There are fifty people in our class and almost everyone is nearsighted.

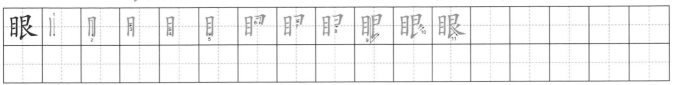

CHARACTER 20

睛

jīng
eyeball

Useful phrases and sentences

1. 眼睛 yǎnjīng eye

Xiǎomíng zuótiān shuìde hěnwǎn, jīntiān kùnde yǎnjīng dōu zhēngbukāi.

小明昨天睡得很晚，今天困得眼睛都睁不开。

Xiaoming went to bed late last night. He is so tired today that he can't even open his eyes.

2. 一双眼睛 yìshuāngyǎnjīng a pair of eyes

Tā yǒu yìshuāng dà yǎnjīng.

他有一双大眼睛。

He has a big pair of eyes.

3. 眨眼睛 zhǎyǎnjīng blink

Érzi zhǎzhe yǎnjīng wèn māma: "Wǒshì cóng nǎli láide?"

儿子眨着眼睛问妈妈：“我是从哪里来的？”

The son blinked his eyes and asked his mother, "Where do I come from?"

4. 目不转睛 mùbùzhuǎnjīng eyes fixed

Tā mùbùzhuǎnjīngde kànzhe qiángshàngde huàr shuō: zhēn měi a!

他目不转睛地看着墙上地画儿说：真美啊！

His eyes fixed on the wall painting, he said, "How pretty!"

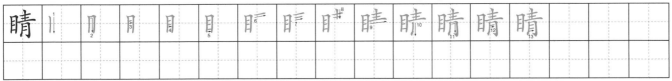

CHARACTER 21

笑

xiáo
smile; laugh

Useful phrases and sentences

1. 笑 xiào to smile

Zhōngguórén cháng shuō "xiàoyixiào, shínián shào", yìsi shì duōxiào huì ràng rén gèng niánqīng.

中国人常说“笑一笑，十年少”，意思是多笑会让人更年轻。

Chinese people often say "xiàoyixiào, shínián shào," which means a smile makes you younger.

2. 笑容 xiàoróng smile

Tāde xiàoróng zǒng ràngrén juéde hěn wēnnuǎn.

她的笑容总让人觉得很温暖。

Her smile always makes people feel warm.

3. 笑声 xiàoshēng laughter

Chuāngwài chuánláile háizimen de xiàoshēng.

窗外传来了孩子们的笑声。

Children's laughter is coming from outside the window.

4. 笑话 xiàohuà joke

Tā xǐhuan gěi dàjiā jiǎng xiàohuà, kěshì tāde xiàohuà yìdiǎnr dōu bùhǎoxiào.

他喜欢给大家讲笑话，可是他的笑话一点儿都不好笑。

He likes telling jokes, but his jokes aren't funny.

CHARACTER 22

手

shǒu
hand

Useful phrases and sentences

1. 手表 **shǒubiǎo** wristwatch

   Yǒule shǒujī yǐhòu, dài shǒubiǎode rén hǎoxiàng yuèláiyuèshǎole.
   有了手机以后，戴手表的人好像越来越少了。
   With smartphones, fewer and fewer people are wearing watches nowadays.

2. 手套 **shǒutào** gloves

   Zhèshuāng shǒutào shì yángmáode, hěn nuǎnhe.
   这双手套是羊毛的，很暖和。
   This pair of wool gloves is warm.

3. 手指 **shǒuzhǐ** finger

   Zuótiān dǎlánqiúde shíhou wǒ bùxiǎoxīn nòngshāngle shǒuzhǐ.
   昨天打篮球的时候我不小心弄伤了手指。
   I hurt my fingers accidentally when playing basketball yesterday.

4. 手术 **shǒushù** surgery

   Hǎopéngyou gang zuòwán shǒushù, wǒ zhǔnbèi míngtiān qù kànkan tā.
   好朋友刚做完手术，我准备明天去看看他。
   Tomorrow, I plan to visit a good friend of mine who just had surgery.

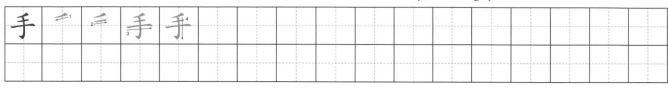

CHARACTER 23

头

tóu
head

Useful phrases and sentences

1. 骨头 **gútou** bones

   Zhōngguó zuìzǎode wénzì kèzài dòngwùde gútoushang.
   中国最早的文字刻在动物的骨头上。
   The earliest Chinese characters were carved on animals' bones.

2. 点头 **diǎntóu** nod

   Zài yǒude guójiā, diǎntóude yìsi shì bùtóngyì huòzhě jùjué.
   在有的国家，点头的意思是不同意或者拒绝。
   Nodding means disagreement or refusal in some countries.

3. 头发 **tóufa** hair

   Nǐde tóufa shì zàinǎr jiǎnde?
   你的头发是在哪儿剪的？
   Where did you have your hair cut?

4. 舌头 **shétou** tongue

   Zhōngyī chángcháng cóng shétoude yánsè pànduàn bìngrénde bìngqíng.
   中医常常从舌头的颜色判断病人的病情。
   Doctors in Traditional Chinese Medicine often tell a patient's condition from the color of his tongue.

CHARACTER 24

肚

dù
stomach

Useful phrases and sentences

1. 肚子 **dùzi** stomach

   Dùzi èle, wǒ děi qù chīfànle.
   肚子饿了，我得去吃饭了。
   I am hungry. I need to go eat.

2. 肚量 **dùliang** generous; tolerant

   Tā zhègerén hényǒu dùliang, cónglái bù gēn biéren jìjiào xiǎoshì.
   他这个人很有肚量，从来不跟别人计较小事。
   He is very generous and never haggles with people over small things.

3. 肚皮舞 **dùpíwǔ** belly dancing

   Xiǎolì zuìjìn zài xué dùpíwǔ, tā shuō hěnyǒu yìsi.
   小丽最近在学肚皮舞，她说很有意思。
   Xiaoli is learning belly dancing. She says it's interesting.

4. 闹肚子 **nàodùzi** stomachache

   Wǒ kěnéng zuótiān chide xīguā bútài xīnxiān, jīntiān yìzhí nào dùzi.
   我可能昨天吃的西瓜不太新鲜，今天一直闹肚子。
   I have a stomachache today. It's probably from the not-so-fresh watermelon I ate yesterday.

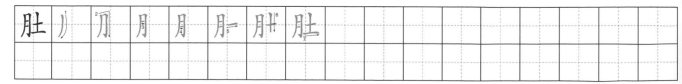

CHARACTER 25

鼻

bí
nose

14 STROKES | 鼻 **RADICAL**

Useful phrases and sentences

1. 鼻子 **bízi** nose

   Zhège hóngbízi xuěrén zhēn kěài.
   这个红鼻子雪人真可爱。
   This red-nosed snowman is adorable.

2. 鼻涕 **bíti** nasal mucus; snot

   Wǒ zhèliǎng tiān déle zhòng gǎnmào, bíti liúge bùtíng.
   我这两天得了重感冒，鼻涕流个不停。
   I have had a bad cold these two days, and snot is flowing nonstop.

3. 鼻炎 **bíyán** sinus infection

   Měinián yídào chūntiān, wǒde guòmǐnxìng bíyán jiùfànle, zhēn nánshòu!
   每年一到春天，我的过敏性鼻炎就犯了，真难受！
   I get a sinus infection every spring. It's awful!

4. 鼻梁 **bíliáng** bridge of the nose

   Tāde bíliáng gāogāode, yǎnjīng dàdàde.
   他的鼻梁高高的，眼睛大大的。
   He has a high-bridged nose and big eyes.

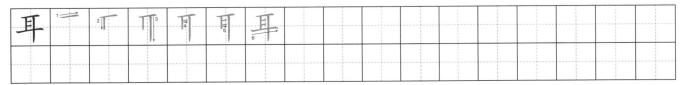

CHARACTER 26

耳

ěr
ear

6 STROKES | 耳 **RADICAL**

Useful phrases and sentences

1. 耳朵 **ěrduō** ear

   Zài Zhōngguó mínjiān, yǒu "ěrduō dà de rén yǒu fúqì" de shuōfa.
   在中国民间，有"耳朵大的人有福气"的说法。
   Chinese folklore believes that big ears bring more luck.

2. 耳环 **ěrhuán** earring

   Nǐ dài lǜsède ěrhuán gèng piàoliàng.
   你戴绿色的耳环更漂亮。
   You look prettier with green earrings.

3. 耳机 **ěrjī** earphone

   Zhèfù ěrjī jiàgé búguì, kěshì yīnzhì hěn hǎo.
   这副耳机价格不贵，可是音质很好。
   This pair of earphones is not expensive and has good sound quality.

4. 耳聋 **ěrlóng** deaf

   Yéye yǐjīng ěrlóng le, wǒ zhǐnéng tōngguò xiězì gēntā jiāoliú.
   爷爷已经耳聋了，我只能通过写字跟他交流。
   My grandfather is deaf. I can communicate with him only through writing.

CHARACTER 27

烧

shāo
burn

10 STROKES | 火 **RADICAL**

Useful phrases and sentences

1. 烧 **shāo** boil; heat up

   Zánmen shāo diǎn rèshuǐ pào chá hē ba.
   咱们烧点热水泡茶喝吧。
   Let's heat up water and make tea.

2. 发烧 **fāshāo** fever

   Háizi zuótiān wǎnshang fāshāole, yíyè méi shuìhǎojiào.
   孩子昨天晚上发烧了，一夜没睡好觉。
   The child had a fever yesterday and didn't sleep well the whole night.

3. 烧伤 **shāoshāng** burn injury

   Nàwèi xiāofángyuán zài jiùhuǒde shíhou shāoshāngle zìjǐ.
   那位消防员在救火的时候烧伤了自己。
   That firefighter got a burn while extinguishing the fire.

4. 烧烤 **shāokǎo** BBQ

   Xiǎo Zhào, jīntiān wǎnshàng péi wǒ qù chī shāokǎo, zěnmeyàng?
   小赵，今天晚上陪我去吃烧烤，怎么样？
   Xiao Zhao, how about going to a BBQ with me tonight?

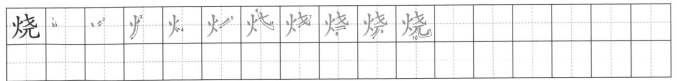

Useful phrases and sentences

9 STROKES | **广 RADICAL**

度
dù
degree

1. 温度 **wēndù** temperature

Tiānqìyùbào shuō jīntiān zuìdī wēndù língxià shídù, nǐ chuān nuǎnhe diǎnr.

天气预报说今天最低温度零下十度，你穿暖和点儿。

The weather forecast says that today's low temperature will be minus ten degrees. Stay warm!

2. 湿度 **shīdù** humidity

Shēnzhènde xiàtiān shīdù tài gāo le, gāng dào zhèlǐde shíhou wǒ hěn bù xíguàn.

深圳的夏天湿度太高了，刚到这里的时候我很不习惯。

The summer humidity in Shenzhen is so high that I was not used to it when I first came here.

3. 角度 **jiǎodù** angle

Měigerén de jīnglì bùtóng, kàn wèntí de jiǎodù yě zìrán bùyíyàng.

每个人的经历不同，看问题的角度也自然不一样。

Everyone looks at things from a different angle because of their own distinct experiences.

4. 制度 **zhìdù** system

Zhōngguó gēn Měiguó zài zhèngzhì zhìdù hé jīngjì zhìdùshang dōu yǒu hěndàde bùtóng.

中国跟美国在政治制度和经济制度上都有很大的不同。

China and the U.S.A. are hugely different in their political and economical systems.

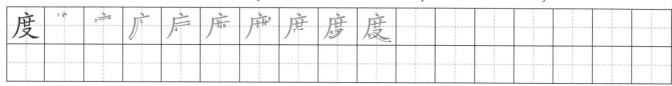

Useful phrases and sentences

16 STROKES | **口 RADICAL**

嘴
zuǐ
mouth

1. 嘴角 **zuǐjiǎo** corner of the mouth

Zuìjìn shànghuǒle, zuǐjiǎo yòugānyòuténg.

最近上火了，嘴角又干又疼。

The corner of my mouth is dry and painful because of the infection.

2. 嘴唇 **zuǐchún** lip

Dìdi yì jǐnzhāng jiù huì yǎo zuǐchún.

弟弟一紧张就会咬嘴唇。

My younger brother always bites his lips when he is nervous.

3. 插嘴 **chāzuǐ** interrupt

Wǒ shuōhuàde shíhou qǐngnǐ búyào chāzuǐ, hǎoma?

我说话的时候请你不要插嘴，好吗？

Please do not interrupt when I talk, okay?

4. 嘴巴 **zuǐbā** mouth

Zài Zhōngwénlǐ, "dàzuǐbā" shuōde shì nàxiē bǎ biéren de mìmi shuōchūqu de rén.

在中文里，"大嘴巴"说的是那些把别人的秘密说出去的人。

In Chinese, "big mouth" refers to a person who cannot keep secrets.

Useful phrases and sentences

11 STROKES | **月 RADICAL**

脚
jiǎo
foot; leg

1. 脚趾头 **jiǎozhǐtóu** toe

Zhèshuāng xīnmǎide xié yǒudiǎnxiǎo, yì zǒulù jiǎozhǐtou téngde yàomìng.

这双新买的鞋有点小，一走路脚趾头疼得要命。

These new shoes are a bit too small. They hurt my toes badly when walking.

2. 脚印 **jiǎoyìn** footprint

Qíguài, zhèbúxiàng shì rén de jiǎoyìn, nándào shénme dòngwù pǎojìnlai le ma?

奇怪，这不像是人的脚印，难道什么动物跑进来了吗？

How strange! These are not human footprints. Could they be animals coming from outside?

3. 跺脚 **duòjiǎo** stamp one's feet

Zuótiān gāngmǎide shǒujī jīntiān jiù bèirén tōule, Xiǎoxiè qìde zhí duòjiǎo.

昨天刚买的手机今天就被人偷了，小谢气得直跺脚。

Xiao Xie was stamping his feet angrily because the cell phone he bought yesterday was stolen.

4. 光脚 **guāngjiǎo** barefoot

Yǒurénshuō guāngjiǎo zǒulù duì jiànkāng yǒu hǎochù.

有人说光脚走路对健康有好处。

Some people believe in the health benefits of walking barefoot.

Lesson 2 Exercises

Part 1 Choose from the following words to fill in the blanks.

> 病、身体、疼、度、笑

1. 他很喜欢（　　　　），好像从来没有不高兴的事情。

2. 爷爷的（　　　　）一天比一天差，我有点儿担心他。

3. 王老师，我昨天（　　　　）了，所以没来上课。

4. 昨天晚上没睡好，今天头（　　　　）得厉害。

Part 2 Complete the following dialogues using Chinese characters.

1. A: 你最近身体怎么样啊？

   B: _____。

2. A: 在你住的地方，要是你生病了，看病方便吗？

   B: _____。

3. A: 一个人要想少生病，应该怎么做？

   B: _____。

4. A: 最近你遇到什么让你"头疼"的事情了吗？

   B: _____。

5. A: 你喜欢不喜欢给朋友讲笑话？

   B: _____。

Part 3 学以致用

你今天病了，很不舒服。请你给高老师写一个电子邮件，告诉她

1) 你身体哪儿不舒服。

2) 你今天不能去上课。

3) 什么时候可以去补课（**bǔkè** make up class）。

To:	gaolaoshi123@gmail.com ⌄

Cc:

Subject: 病假

高老师，您好！

谢谢你！

祝好，

李大明

LESSON 3

Making New Friends 认识新朋友

1. Dialogue

Read the dialogue below and answer the questions in characters.

王丽:	小美，谢谢你上次送我的巧克力蛋糕，真好吃！
小美:	别客气！来美国一个月了，你觉得怎么样？喜欢这里的学习和生活吗？
王丽:	还不错。我希望认识一些新朋友。
小美:	对了，明天下午我要跟一个朋友去喝咖啡，你想一起去吗？我可以介绍你们认识一下。
王丽:	好啊，男生还是女生？你们是怎么认识的？
小美:	男生。你看，这是他的照片！我们是在机场等飞机的时候认识的，他人很好，说话也很幽默。
王丽:	咖啡馆儿叫什么名字，离宿舍远吗？
小美:	叫"好心情咖啡"，从你的宿舍走过去只要十分钟。我一会儿告诉你地址。
王丽:	好的，谢谢！

1. 王丽觉得美国的学习和生活怎么样？ ....

2. 小美明天下午去哪儿，要做什么？ ....

3. 好心情咖啡" 离王丽的宿舍远不远？ ....

2. Vocabulary

	Word	Pinyin	English equivalent
1.	送	**sòng**	give (a gift)
2.	蛋糕	**dàngāo**	cake
3.	巧克力	**qiǎokèlì**	chocolate
4.	希望	**xīwàng**	hope
5.	咖啡	**kāfēi**	coffee
6.	给	**gěi**	to; for
7.	介绍	**jièshào**	introduce
8.	照片	**zhàopiàn**	picture; photo
9.	机场	**jīchǎng**	airport
10.	飞机	**fēijī**	airplane
11.	幽默	**yōumò**	humorous
12.	心情	**xīnqíng**	mood
13.	从	**cóng**	from
14.	只	**zhǐ**	only
15.	一会儿	**yíhuìr**	a while; later
16.	告诉	**gàosù**	tell

3. New Characters

Fifteen characters are introduced in this lesson. Use the following explanations to help you understand and remember the characters.

希　望　告　诉　从　机　场　咖　啡　情　送　片　介　绍　给

希

xī
hope

Useful phrases and sentences

1. 希望 **xīwàng** hope

Fùmǔ xīwàng wǒ yǐhòu dāng yīshēng huòzhě lǎoshī.
父母希望我以后当医生或者老师。
My parents hope that I will become a physician or a teacher.

2. 有希望 **yǒuxīwàng** hopeful

Zhècì tā hěn yǒuxīwàng zài yóuyǒng bǐsàizhōng qǔdé dìyīmíng.
这次他很有希望在游泳比赛中取得第一名。
He is hopeful to win this swimming competition.

3. 没希望 **méixīwàng** no hope

Nǐ měitiān zhǐ shuìjiào bù xuéxí, gēnběn méi xīwàng kǎoshàng Táiwān Dàxué.
你每天只睡觉不学习，根本没希望考上台湾大学！
You just sleep and never study every day. There is no hope that you can go to Taiwan University.

4. 希腊 **Xīlà** Greece

Wǒ yìzhí hěn xiǎng qù Xīlà, tīngshuō nàr de jiànzhù hěn zhídé kàn.
我一直很想去希腊，听说那儿的建筑很值得看。
I've always wanted to go to Greece. I heard that the architecture there is worth seeing.

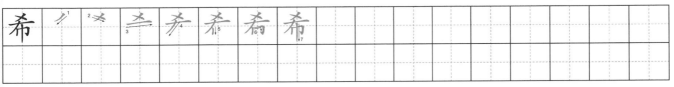

望

wàng
expect; look
towards

Useful phrases and sentences

1. 失望 **shīwàng** disappointing

Zhèjiā xīnkāide jiǔdiàn hěn ràngrén shīwàng, fúwù yìdiǎnr dōu bùhǎo.
这家新开的酒店很让人失望，服务一点儿都不好。
This newly opened hotel is disappointing. Their service is not good at all.

2. 愿望 **yuànwàng** wish

Nǐde xīnnián yuànwàng shì shénme?
你的新年愿望是什么？
What are your New Year wishes?

3. 东张西望 **dōngzhāngxīwàng** look around

Lǎoshīshuō, kǎoshìde shíhou kàn zìjǐde shìjuàn, búyào dōngzhāngxīwàng.
老师说，考试的时候看自己的试卷，不要东张西望。
The teacher says that students should only look at their own test sheets; do not look around.

4. 看望 **kànwàng** visit

Wǒ bàmā měinián xiàtiān huí Zhōngguó kànwàng yéye nǎinai.
我爸妈每年夏天回中国看望爷爷奶奶。
My parents go back to China every summer to visit my grandparents.

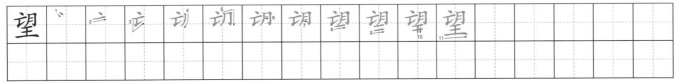

告

gào
tell; report

Useful phrases and sentences

1. 告诉 **gàosù** tell

Wǒ yǒu nánpéngyou le, mǎshànfg jiùyào jiéhūnle. Qǐngnǐ xiān bié gàosù biéren.
我有男朋友了，马上就要结婚了。请你先别告诉别人！
I have a boyfriend and we are getting married soon. Please don't tell other people yet.

2. 广告 **guǎnggào** advertisement

Zài Zhōngguó, dàochù dōunéng kàndào yīngyǔ xuéxíbānde guǎnggào.
在中国，到处都能看到英语学习班的广告。
You can see advertisements for English language classes everywhere in China.

3. 告别 **gàobié** farewell

Míngtiān wǎnshang shì Dàsìxuéshengde gàobié wǎnhuì.
明天晚上是大四学生的告别晚会。
There is a farewell party for college seniors tomorrow evening.

4. 报告 **bàogào** report; presentation

Tāde bàogào jiǎngde shì Xīlà wénzìde lìshǐ, hěnyǒu yìsī.
他的报告讲的是希腊文字的历史，很有意思。
His presentation was about the history of the Greek alphabet. It was very interesting.

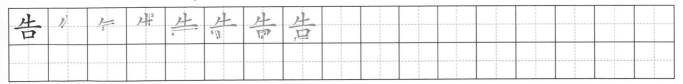

诉
sù
tell; sue;
complain

7 STROKES | **讠 RADICAL**

Useful phrases and sentences

1. 投诉 tóusù complain

Wáng jīnglǐ, yǒu gùkè tóusù women, shuō wǒmen yǒu shípǐn ānquánde wèntí.

王经理，有顾客投诉我们，说我们有食品安全的问题。

Manager, we have received complaints from customers that our food has safety issues.

2. 诉苦 sùkǔ grumble

Nǐ bié zhěngtiān gēnwǒ sùkǔle, měigerén de shēnghuó dōu bù róngyì.

你别整天跟我诉苦了，每个人的生活都不容易。

Don't grumble to me ever day. No one's life is easy.

3. 倾诉 qīngsù talk

Tā gang lílehūn, xīnqíng hěn bùhǎo, zǒng xiǎng zhǎorén qīngsù.

他刚离了婚，心情很不好，总想找人倾诉。

He just got divorced and was in a bad mood. He has been looking for people to talk to.

4. 上诉 shàngsù appeal

Nǐmen gōngsī yàoshì bùdāyìng péicháng, wǒ yídìng huì shàngsùdào fǎyuàn.

你们公司要是不答应赔偿，我一定会上诉到法院。

If your company does not promise compensation, I will definitely appeal to the court.

从
cóng
from

4 STROKES | **人 RADICAL**

Useful phrases and sentences

1. 从来 cónglái at all times

Wǒ cónglái méi kànguo Bǎilǎohuìde biǎoyǎn, hěn xiǎng qù kànkan.

我从来没看过百老汇的表演，很想去看看。

I had never seen any Broadway shows and really wanted to see one.

2. 从此以后 cóngcǐyǐhòu from now on

Yàoshì nǐ zhècì bù bāngwǒ, cóngcǐyǐhòu wǒmen jiù bié zuò péngyou le.

要是你这次不帮我，从此以后我们就别做朋友了。

If you don't help me this time, we will no longer be friends.

3. 从前 cóngqián before

Wǒ jìde tā cóngqián bù xǐhuan shuōhuà, yě bùxǐhuan gēn péngyou chūqù wánr.

我记得他从前不喜欢说话，也不喜欢跟朋友出去玩儿。

I remember he didn't like to talk before. Nor did he like to go out with friends.

4. 从事 cóngshì undertake

Wúlùn cóngshì shénme gōngzuò, zhǐyào zìjǐ xǐhuan jiùxíng.

无论从事什么工作，只要自己喜欢就行。

No matter what kind of job you are undertaking, it will be fine as long as you like it.

机
jī
machine

6 STROKES | **木 RADICAL**

Useful phrases and sentences

1. 手机 shǒujī cell phone

Wǒ bù xǐhuan zài shǒujīshang gēn péngyou liáotiān, háishì jiànmiàn bǐjiàohǎo.

我不喜欢在手机上跟朋友聊天，还是见面比较好。

I don't like to chat with my friends on cell phones. I prefer to meet in person.

2. 计算机 jìsuànjī computer science

Zài wǒmen xuéxiào, xué jìsuànjī zhuānyède xuésheng zuìduō.

在我们学校，学计算机专业的学生最多。

The number of students studying computer science is the largest in our school.

3. 机器人 jīqìrén robot

Zhège jīqìrén búdàn néng tīngdǒng rén shuōde huà, háinéng huídáwèntí, zhēn lìhài!

这个机器人不但能听懂人说得话，还能回答问题，真厉害！

This robot not only understands human languages, it can also answer questions. That's amazing!

4. 机场 jīchǎng airport

Nǐ zuò chūzūchē qù jīchǎng ba, zhǐyào èrshíkuài.

你坐出租出去机场吧，只要二十块。

Why don't you take a taxi to the airport? It costs only 20 kuai.

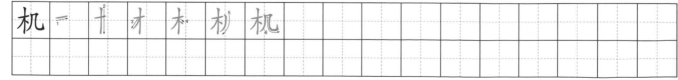

CHARACTER 37

场

chǎng
large space

6 STROKES   土 RADICAL

Useful phrases and sentences

1. 市场 **shìchǎng** market

Xǔdūo wàiguó gōngsī yuèláiyuè zhòngshì Zhōngguó shìchǎng.

许多外国公司越来越重视中国市场。

More and more foreign companies value the Chinese market.

2. 网球场 **wǎngqiúchǎng** tennis court

Xuéxiào xīnjiànde wǎngqiúchǎng hěn dà, kěyǐ zuò yīqiānge guānzhòng.

学校新建的网球场很大，可以坐一千个观众。

The school's newly built tennis court is big. It can seat one thousand people.

3. 场合 **chǎnghé** occasion

Xué wàiyǔ zuì zhòngyàode shì xuéhuì shénme chǎnghé shuō shénme huà.

学外语最重要的是学会什么场合说什么话。

The most important thing about learning a foreign language is to know when to say what.

4. 公共场所 **gōnggòngchǎngsuǒ** public place

Zhèlǐ shì gōnggòng chǎngsuǒ, qǐng búyào xīyān.

这里是公共场所，请不要吸烟。

This is a public place. Please do not smoke.

场 一 圤 圤 场 场 场

CHARACTER 38

咖

kā
coffee

8 STROKES   口 RADICAL

Useful phrases and sentences

1. 咖啡 **kāfēi** coffee

Nǐ búshì dōu hēguo kāfēile ma, zěnme hái zhème kùn?

你不是都喝过咖啡了吗，怎么还这么困？

Didn't you just have coffee? Why are you still so sleepy?

2. 咖啡馆 **kāfēiguǎn** coffee shop

Zánmen zhège zhōumò qù kāfēiguǎn gōngzuò ba!

咱们这个周末去咖啡馆工作吧！

Let's go work in a coffee shop this weekend!

3. 一杯咖啡 **yìbēikāfēi** a cup of coffee

Zài Zhōngguó, yìbēi Xīngbākè de kāfēi yào sìshí duō kuài qián, tài guile!

在中国，一杯星巴克的咖啡要四十多块钱，太贵了！

In China, a cup of Starbucks coffee costs more than forty kuai. It's too expensive.

4. 冰咖啡 **bīngkāfēi** iced coffee

Nǐhǎo, wǒyào yìbēi bīngkāfēi, bùjiā tang.

你好，我要一杯冰咖啡，不加糖。

Hi, I'd like to have a cup of iced coffee with no sugar.

咖 丨 冂 口 叮 叻 咖 咖 咖

CHARACTER 39

啡

fēi
coffee

11 STROKES   口 RADICAL

Useful phrases and sentences

1. 咖啡因 **kāfēiyīn** caffeine

Lǜcházhōng de kāfēiyīn bǐ hóngchá yào shǎo yìxiē.

绿茶中的咖啡因比红茶要少一些。

There is less caffeine in the green tea than in the black tea.

2. 黑咖啡 **hēikāfēi** black coffee

Jùshuō hē hēikāfēi duì jiànkāng hěn yǒu hǎochù.

据说喝黑咖啡对健康很有好处。

It is said that black coffee is good for your health.

3. 咖啡机 **kāfēijī** coffee machine

Qǐngwèn, měishì kāfēijī hé yìshì kāfēijī yǒu shénme bùtóng?

请问，美式咖啡机和意式咖啡机有什么不同？

Excuse me, what is the difference between American coffee machines and Italian coffee machines?

4. 咖啡杯 **kāfēibēi** coffee mug

Zhège kāfēibēi zhēn kěài, nǐshì zài nǎr mǎide?

这个咖啡杯真可爱，你是在哪儿买的？

This coffee mug is so cute. Where did you buy it?

啡 丨 冂 口 叮 叫 叫 叫 唯 唯 啡 啡

CHARACTER 40

情

qíng
feeling; emotion

Useful phrases and sentences

1. 心情 **xīnqíng** mood

   Xīnqíng bùhǎode shíhou, wǒ xǐhuan yígerén qù gōngyuán zǒuzou.

   心情不好的时候，我喜欢一个人去公园走走。

   I like to walk in the park alone when I am in a bad mood.

2. 情况 **qíngkuàng** situation

   Tāmen jiāde jīngjì qíngkuàng bútàihǎo, suǒyǐ tā cónglái bú luàn huāqián.

   他们家的经济情况不太好，所以他从来不乱花钱。

   Their financial situation is not good, so he never spends money carelessly.

3. 情节 **qíngjié** plot

   Zhèbù diànyǐngde qíngjié tài fùzále, hěn nán kàndǒng.

   这部电影的情节太复杂了，很难看懂。

   The plot of this film is too complicated to understand.

4. 情人节 **qíngrénjié** Valentine's Day

   Zhōngguó chuántǒngde qíngrénjié shì měinián nónglì qīyuèqīhào, yějiào qīxī.

   中国传统的情人节是每年农历七月七号，也叫"七夕"。

   Chinese Valentine's Day is on the seventh day of the seventh month. It's also called "Qixi."

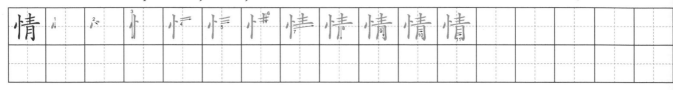

CHARACTER 41

送

sòng
send; give

Useful phrases and sentences

1. 送礼物 **sònglǐwù** give (a gift)

   Zài Zhōngguó, song lǐwù hěnyǒu jiǎngjiū, bǐfāngshuō qiānwàn bùnéng song zhōngbiǎo.

   在中国，送礼物很有讲究，比方说千万不能送钟表。

   Giving gifts has a certain etiquette in China. For instance, you can never give clocks as a gift.

2. 送货 **sònghuò** delivery

   Zhèjiā shāngdiànde sònghuò fúwù hěnhǎo, búdàn kuài, jiàge yě hěn piányi.

   这家商店的送货服务很好，不但快，价格也很便宜。

   The delivery service of this store is very good. It's fast and the price is reasonable.

3. 赠送 **zèngsòng** give presents

   Chūnjié qījiān, hěnduō shāngdiàn dōu huì dǎzhé huòzhě gěi gùkè zèngsòng lǐpǐn.

   春节期间，很多商店都会打折或者给顾客赠送礼品。

   During the Chinese New Year, many shops are having sales or giving presents to their customers.

4. 送（人）**sòng (rén)** see (someone) off

   Jiějie míngtiān jiùyào chūguó liúxuéle, wǒ yào qù jīchǎng sòngtā.

   姐姐明天就要出国留学了，我要去机场送她。

   My older sister is going to study abroad tomorrow. I am going to the airport to see her off.

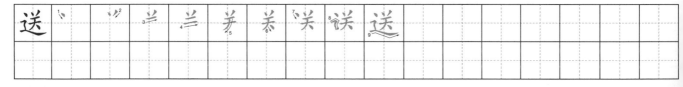

CHARACTER 42

片

piàn
thin piece; film

Useful phrases and sentences

1. 照片 **zhàopiàn** photo

   Zhèzhāng zhàopiàn shì jǐniánqián wǒ zài xiānggǎng pāide.

   这张照片是几年前我在香港拍的。

   I took this photo in Hong Kong several years ago.

2. 名片 **míngpiàn** business card

   Nín hǎo, zhè shì wǒde míngpiàn, hěn gāoxìng rènshi nín.

   您好，这是我的名片，很高兴认识您。

   Hi, this is my business card. Nice to meet you.

3. 动画片 **dònghuàpiàn** animation

   Xiǎoháizi dōu hěn xǐhuan kàn Díshìníde dònghuàpiàn.

   小孩子都很喜欢看迪士尼的动画片。

   All children love Disney's animated films.

4. 卡片 **kǎpiàn** card

   Tā shōudào háizimen zìjǐ zuòde Shèngdàn kǎpiàn, fēicháng kāixīn.

   她收到孩子们自己做的圣诞卡片，非常开心。

   She was exhilarated to receive handmade Christmas cards from her children.

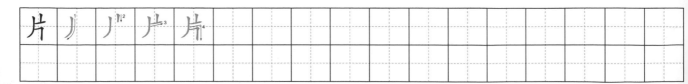

介 jiè
introduce; between

Useful phrases and sentences

4 STROKES   人 RADICAL

1. 中介 **zhōngjiè** intermediary; agent

Zìjǐ zhǎo fángzi tài máfanle, nǐ háishì zhǎo yíge zūfáng zhōngjiè bang nǐ ba.
自己找房子太麻烦了，你还是找一个租房中介帮你吧。
It is so complicated to find a house on your own. It's better for you to reach out to a real estate agent.

2. 简介 **jiǎnjiè** brief introduction

Zhèshì wǒmen gōngsīde jiǎnjiè, yàoshì yǒu rènhé wèntí qǐng gàosù wǒ.
这是我们公司的简介，要是有任何问题请告诉我。
This is a brief introduction of our company. Please let me know if you have any questions.

3. 介意 **jièyì** mind

Tā zhègerén shuōhuà yǒushíhou bǐjiào zhíjiē, qǐng nǐ búyào jièyì.
他这个人说话有时候比较直接，请你不要介意。
Sometimes he talks directly. I hope you don't mind.

4. 介入 **jièrù** intervene

Zhèjiànshì jǐngchá yǐjīng jièrù le, wǒmen jiù děng jǐngchá de diàochá jiéguǒba.
这件事警察已经介入了，我们就等警察的调查结果吧。
The police have intervened in this matter. We just have to wait for their investigative report.

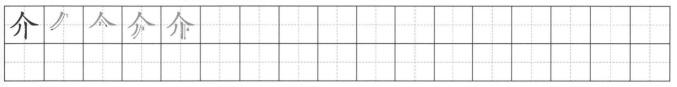

绍 shào
introduce

Useful phrases and sentences

8 STROKES   纟 RADICAL

1. 介绍 **jièshào** introduce

Zìwǒ jièshào yíxià, wǒ jiào Zhāng Xiǎoměi.
自我介绍一下，我叫张小美。
Please allow me to introduce myself. My name is Zhang Xiaomei.

2. 介绍人 **jièshàorén** referral

Wǒ xiǎng shēnqǐng gōngzuò, nín kěyǐ dāng wǒde jièshàorén ma?
我想申请工作，您可以当我的介绍人吗？
I want to apply for a job. Can I list you as my referral?

3. 介绍信 **jièshàoxìn** letter of recommendation

Lǎoshī, kěyǐ máfan nín gěi wǒ xiě yìfēng jièshàoxìn ma?
老师，可以麻烦您给我写一封介绍信吗？
Teacher, could I trouble you to write me a letter of recommendation?

4. 介绍工作 **jièshào gōngzuò** job reference

Rúguǒ nǐ xūyàode huà, wǒ yě yuànyì gěinǐ jièshào gōngzuò.
如果你需要的话，我也愿意给你介绍工作。
If needed, I will also be happy to give you a job reference.

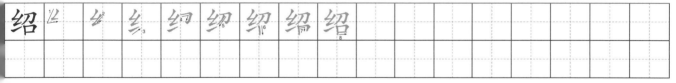

给 gěi
give; to; for

Useful phrases and sentences

9 STROKES   纟 RADICAL

1. 给 **gěi** give

Zuótiān nǐ gěi wǒde nàběnshū, wǒ zěnme zhǎobudào le.
昨天你给我的那本书，我怎么找不到了。
How come I can't find the book you gave me yesterday?

2. 送给 **sònggěi** give to

Qíngrénjié tā sònggěi nǚpéngyǒu yíshùhuā, yìzhāng kǎpiàn.
情人节他送给女朋友一束花，一张卡片。
He gave his girlfriend flowers and a card on Valentine's Day.

3. 拿给 **nágěi** bring

Wǒ gāng zuòhǎole yìxiē bǐnggān. Wǒ nágěi nǐ.
我刚做好了一些饼干。我拿给你。
I just made some cookies. I can bring some over.

4. 给面子 **gěimiànzi** give face

Tā dōu yuēnǐ chīfàn yuēle hǎo jǐcì le, nǐ jiù gěige miànzi, dāyìng tā ba.
他都约你吃饭约了好几次了，你就给个面子，答应他吧。
He has asked you out for dinner several times. Why don't you give him face and say yes?

Part 1 Choose from the following words to fill in the blanks.

介绍、送、希望、告诉、照片

1. 我（ 　　　　 ）我的中文说得越来越好。

2. 听说你的同屋打网球打得很好，能（ 　　　　 ）我认识他吗？

3. 你好，能麻烦您帮我拍一张（ 　　　　 ）吗？

4. 你明天几点的飞机，我想去（ 　　　　 ）一下你。

Part 2 Complete the following dialogues using Chinese characters.

1.　A:　你最近有没有认识新朋友？你们是在哪儿认识的？

　　B: _____ 。

2.　A:　你的朋友常常帮你的忙吗？帮你做什么？

　　B: _____ 。

3.　A:　你喜欢跟朋友见面聊天还是用电脑聊天？

　　B: _____ 。

4.　A:　你觉得什么样的朋友才算是"好朋友？"？

　　B: _____ 。

5.　A:　要是你的朋友做了让你不高兴的事情，你怎么办？

　　B: _____ 。

Part 3 学以致用

你是一名刚到北京的外国留学生。你很想认识一些中国朋友，跟他们聊天，提高自己的中文水平。下面是一个大学生交友的网站，请你在上面介绍一下自己，说说你想找什么样的朋友。

姓名		年龄	国家	
		▼		▼

工作

爱好

你想找什么样的朋友？

LESSON 4

What to Eat Today? 今天吃什么好？

1. Dialogue

Read the dialogue below and answer the questions in characters.

美国留学生安迪（Āndí Andy）在一家中国饭馆儿吃饭。

安迪：	服务员，麻烦拿一下菜单。
服务员：	好，请等一下。
服务员：	您好！以前来这儿吃过吗？
安迪：	没有，第一次来。什么菜好吃？
服务员：	我们家的菜都好吃，您有什么不吃的东西吗？
安迪：	我不吃辣，喜欢吃甜一点儿的。
服务员：	那羊肉、牛肉、猪肉和鱼，您喜欢吃哪一种？
安迪：	猪肉吧。
服务员：	那就来个糖醋里脊，你一定喜欢。
安迪：	"糖醋里脊"不是鸡肉吗？
服务员：	不是，糖醋里脊是猪肉。
安迪：	好的，来一盘吧。再来一碗蛋花汤。
服务员：	那您主食要点儿什么？米饭、面条、还是小笼包？
安迪：	米饭就行。再来一杯西瓜汁。

服务员：	对不起，西瓜汁没有了，珍珠奶茶可以吗？
安迪：	行，少放点儿糖。
服务员：	好的！
安迪：	请问洗手间在哪儿？
服务员：	往前走就到了。
安迪：	谢谢！

1. 安迪喜欢吃辣的吗？他点了什么菜？

2. 安迪吃了什么主食？喝了什么东西？

3. "糖醋里脊"是用什么做的？是什么味道的？

2. Vocabulary

	Word	Pinyin	English equivalent
1.	服务员	fúwùyuán	waiter; waitress
2.	菜单	càidān	menu
3.	菜	cài	dish
4.	辣	là	spicy
5.	甜	tián	sweet
6.	羊肉	yángròu	lamb
7.	牛肉	niúròu	beef
8.	猪肉	zhūròu	pork
9.	鱼	yú	fish
10.	种	zhǒng	kind
11.	糖醋里脊	tángcù lǐjī	sweet and sour pork
12.	鸡肉	jīròu	chicken
13.	盘	pán	plate
14.	碗	wǎn	bowl
15.	蛋花汤	dànhuātāng	egg drop soup
16.	主食	zhǔshí	staple food
17.	米饭	mǐfàn	rice
18.	面条	miàntiáo	noodle
19.	小笼包	xiǎolóngbāo	steamed dumpling (with soup inside)
20.	杯	bēi	glass
21.	西瓜汁	xīguāzhī	watermelon juice
22.	珍珠奶茶	zhēnzhū nǎichá	bubble tea
23.	糖	táng	sugar
24.	洗手间	xǐshǒujiān	restroom

3. New Characters

Fifteen characters are introduced in this lesson. Use the following explanations to help you understand and remember the characters.

牛　奶　鸡　蛋　瓜　羊　肉　鱼　米　条　汤　菜　包　务　员

牛

niú
cow; bull

4 STROKES　　**牛 RADICAL**

Useful phrases and sentences

1. 牛奶 **niúnǎi** milk
   Fúwùyuán, lái yìbēi kāfēi, bùjiā niúnǎi.
   服务员，来一杯咖啡，不加牛奶。
   Excuse me, I like a cup of coffee without milk.

2. 牛肉 **niúròu** beef
   Zhèjiā fànguǎnrde niúròu hěn nèn, wǒmen diǎn yìpán ba.
   这家饭馆儿的牛肉很嫩，我们点一盘吧。
   The beef in this restaurant is very tender. Let's order some.

3. 牛肉面 **niúròu miàn** beef noodles
   Lái Táiwān yídìng yào chī niúròu miàn.
   来台湾一定要吃牛肉面。
   You must try beef noodles in Taiwan.

4. 吹牛 **chuīniú** brag; talk big
   Nàge háizi zhēn néng chuīniú, tā shuō zìjǐ yícì kěyǐ chī sānshíge xiǎolóngbāo.
   那个孩子真能吹牛，他说自己一次可以吃三十个小笼包！
   That child is bragging about his being able to eat thirty steamed dumplings at a time.

CHARACTER 47

奶

nǎi
milk

5 STROKES　　**女 RADICAL**

Useful phrases and sentences

1. 奶茶 **nǎichá** milk tea
   Zhōngguóchéng xīnkāile yìjiā nǎichádiàn, jiào "Gōngfu Nǎichá".
   中国城新开了一家奶茶店，叫"功夫奶茶"。
   There is a new milk tea shop in Chinatown. It's called "Kung Fu Milk Tea."

2. 奶奶 **nǎinai** fraternal grandmother
   Nǎinai yǐjīng qīshísuìle, tā zuìjìn kāishǐ xué Yīngwén le!
   奶奶已经七十岁了，她最近开始学英文了！
   My grandmother is already in her seventies. Recently, she has begun to learn English!

3. 奶酪 **nǎilào** cheese
   Xiǎo Wàn yǐqián bù xǐhuan nǎilào, juéde wénqǐlai yǒudiǎnr chou.
   小万以前不喜欢奶酪，觉得闻起来有点儿臭。
   Xiao Wan didn't like cheese. He felt that it was stinky.

4. 奶油 **nǎiyóu** butter
   Zhège nǎiyóu dàngāo tài tiánle, wǒ chī yíkuài jiù gòu le.
   这个奶油蛋糕太甜了，我吃一块就够了！
   This butter cake is too sugary. One piece is enough for me.

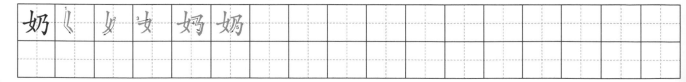

CHARACTER 48

鸡
jī
chicken

7 STROKES   鸟 RADICAL

Useful phrases and sentences

1. 鸡蛋 **jīdàn** egg

   Nǐ xǐhuan chī chǎojīdàn háishì jiānjīdàn?
   你喜欢吃炒鸡蛋还是煎鸡蛋？
   Do you prefer scrambled eggs or eggs sunny side up?

2. 鸡翅 **jīchì** chicken wing

   Míngtiān qù wǒ nàr chī kǎojīchì, nǐ yǒu shíjiān ma?
   明天去我那儿吃烤鸡翅，你有时间吗？
   Do you have time to come to my place to have chicken wings tomorrow?

3. 鸡肉 **jīròu** chicken

   Bùhǎoyìsi, wǒ yàode shì jīròufàn, búshì niúròufàn.
   不好意思，我要的是鸡肉饭，不是牛肉饭。
   Excuse me, I ordered rice with chicken, not beef.

4. 鸡尾酒 **jīwěijiǔ** cocktail

   Āndí měige zhōumò dōu huì tiáo jīwěijiǔ qǐng péngyou hē.
   安迪每个周末都会调鸡尾酒请朋友喝。
   Andy makes cocktails for his friends every weekend.

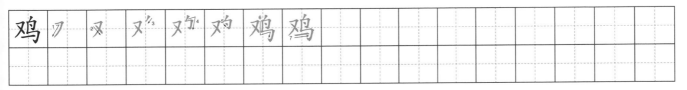

CHARACTER 49

蛋
dàn
egg

11 STROKES   虫 RADICAL

Useful phrases and sentences

1. 蛋糕 **dàngāo** cake

   Míngtiān shì Wáng Jīnglǐde shēngrì, wǒmen gěi tā mǎige shēngrì dàngāo ba.
   明天是王经理的生日，我们给他买个生日蛋糕吧。
   It's Manager Wang's birthday tomorrow. Let's buy him a birthday cake.

2. 蛋花汤 **dànhuātāng** egg drop soup

   Chūguó yǐhòu, wǒ zuì xiǎng hēde jiùshì nǎinai zuòde dànhuātāng.
   出国以后，我最想喝的就是奶奶做的蛋花汤。
   Since I have been abroad, I miss my grandmother's egg drop soup the most.

3. 蛋黄 **dànhuáng** egg yolk

   Nǐ chīguo dànhuáng yuèbǐng ma? Tèbié hǎochī!
   你吃过蛋黄月饼吗？特别好吃！
   Have you had mooncake with an egg yolk inside before? It's so tasty.

4. 蛋炒饭 **dànchǎofàn** fried rice with eggs

   Dànchǎofàn bù nánzuò, kěshì zuòde hǎochī yě bù róngyì.
   蛋炒饭不难做，可是做得好吃也不容易。
   Fried rice with eggs is not difficult to make, but quite hard to make well.

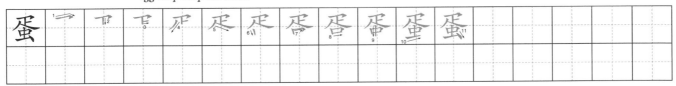

CHARACTER 50

瓜
guā
melon

5 STROKES   瓜 RADICAL

Useful phrases and sentences

1. 南瓜 **nánguā** pumpkin

   Měinián Wànshèngjié wǒ dōu huì zuò yíge nánguādēng.
   每年万圣节我都会做一个南瓜灯。
   I make a pumpkin Jack-o-Lantern every Halloween.

2. 黄瓜 **huángguā** cucumber

   Liángbàn huángguā shì yídào jiāchángcài.
   凉拌黄瓜是一道家常菜。
   Cucumbers in a vinaigrette is a common home-style dish.

3. 瓜果 **guāguǒ** melon and fruit

   Zhèjiā chāoshìde guāguǒ shūcài bú tài xīnxiān.
   这家超市的瓜果蔬菜不太新鲜。
   The melons, fruit, and vegetables in this supermarket are not fresh.

4. 傻瓜 **shǎguā** fool; idiot

   Lǎoshī, wǒde nǚpéngyǒu shuō wǒ shì shǎguā, shǎguā shì shénme guā? Wǒ zěnme cónglái méi chīguò.
   老师，我的女朋友说我是傻瓜，傻瓜是什么瓜？我怎么从来没吃过。
   Teacher, my girlfriend said that I am a shagua. What kind of gua (melon) is it? I've never had it before.

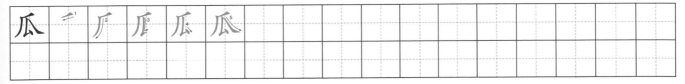

CHARACTER 51

羊

yáng
sheep; goat

6 STROKES | 羊 RADICAL

Useful phrases and sentences

1. 羊肉 **yángròu** mutton

Tā bù xǐhuan chī yángròu, kěshì xǐhuan hē yángròutāng.
他不喜欢吃羊肉，可是喜欢喝羊肉汤。
He doesn't like mutton, but he likes mutton soup.

2. 羊肉串 **yángròuchuàn** lamb skewers

Chī yángròuchuàn yídìng yào hē bīng píjiǔ.
吃羊肉串一定要喝冰啤酒。
You need to have iced beer with lamb skewers.

3. 山羊 **shānyáng** goat

Nàr yǒu jǐzhī shānyáng zhèngzài chī cǎo.
那儿有几只山羊正在吃草。
Several goats are eating grass there.

4. 羊毛 **yángmáo** wool

Zhètiáo wéijīn shì yángmáode, dàiqǐlái hěn nuǎnhe.
这条围巾是羊毛的，戴起来很暖和。
This scarf is wool and warm to wear.

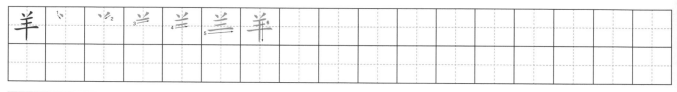

CHARACTER 52

肉

ròu
meat

6 STROKES | 肉 RADICAL

Useful phrases and sentences

1. 猪肉 **zhūròu** pork

Tāshì Huízúrén, qǐng nǐ búyào diǎn zhūròu.
他是回族人，请你不要点猪肉。
Please avoid ordering dishes with pork. He is Muslim.

2. 鸭肉 **yāròu** duck

Měicì lái zhège fànguǎnr wǒu dōu huì diǎn yāròuchǎofàn.
每次来这个饭馆儿我都会点鸭肉炒饭。
I always order the fried rice with duck every time I come to this restaurant.

3. 肉乎乎 **ròuhūhū** with chubby cheeks

Zhège háizide liǎn ròuhūhūde, zhēn kěài.
这个孩子的脸肉乎乎的，真可爱。
This child has chubby cheeks. How cute!

4. 肌肉 **jīròu** muscles

Tā qù jiànshēnfáng búshì wèile liàn jīròu, shì wèile rènshi xīn péngyou.
他去健身房不是为了练肌肉，是为了认识新朋友。
He goes to the gym not for muscles, but for meeting new friends.

CHARACTER 53

鱼

yú
fish

8 STROKES | 鱼 RADICAL

Useful phrases and sentences

1. 鱼 **yú** fish

Zhōngguórén guòniánde shíhou yídìng yào chīyú, nǐ zhīdào wèishénme ma?
中国人过年的时候一定要吃鱼，你知道为什么吗？
Do you know why fish is a must-eat dish during the Chinese New Year?

2. 钓鱼 **diàoyú** fishing

Diàoyú děi yǒu nàixīn, qiānwàn bùnéng zháojí.
钓鱼得有耐心，千万不能着急。
Fishing requires patience. You can't rush.

3. 养鱼 **yǎngyú** keep fish

Tā yǎngde jǐtiáoyú quán bèi māo chīle.
他养的几条鱼全被猫吃了！
The fish he kept were all eaten by the cat.

4. 鲸鱼 **jīnyú** whale

Zhèbù diànyǐng jiǎngdeshì rén bǔshā jīngyúde gùshì.
这部电影讲的是人捕杀鲸鱼的故事。
This movie tells the story of a whale hunt.

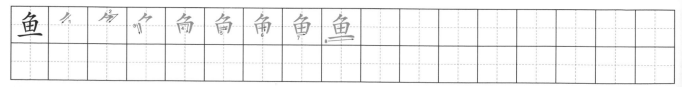

CHARACTER 54

mǐ
rice

Useful phrases and sentences

1. 米饭 mǐfàn rice

Zài Zhōngguó, běifāngrén bǐjiào xǐhuan chī miànshí, nánfāngrén xǐhuan chī mǐfàn.
在中国，北方人比较喜欢吃面食，南方人喜欢吃米饭。
In China, northerners prefer noodles while southerners prefer rice.

2. 玉米 yùmǐ corn

Sōngrényùmǐ shì yídào hěn shòuhuānyíngde cài.
松仁玉米是一道很受欢迎的菜。
Corn with pine nuts is a popular dish.

3. 糙米饭 cāomǐfàn brown rice

Yīshēng jiànyì wǒ duō chī cāomǐfàn.
医生建议我多吃糙米饭。
The doctor advised me to eat more brown rice.

4. 爆米花 bàomǐhuā popcorn

Xièxiānsheng xǐhuan chī xiánde bàomǐhuā, kěshì Xiètàitai xǐhuan chī tiánde.
谢先生喜欢吃咸的爆米花，可是谢太太喜欢吃甜的。
Mr. Xie likes salty popcorn, but Mrs. Xie likes it sweet.

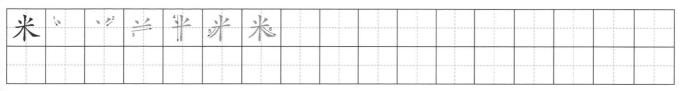

CHARACTER 55

tiáo
measure word for long thin objects

Useful phrases and sentences

1. 一条路 yìtiáolù a road

Zhètiáolù liǎngbiān dōushì shù, qiūtiānde shíhou hěnměi.
这条路两边都是树，秋天的时候很美。
On the two sides of this road are trees. It's pretty in the fall.

2. 条子 tiáozi note

Yàoshì wǒ búzài bàngōngshì, qǐng nǐ gěi wǒ liú yíge tiáozi.
要是我不在办公室，请你给我留一个条子。
Please leave me a note if I am not in my office.

3. 条件 tiáojiàn condition

Zhèsuǒ dàxuéde sùshè tiáojiàn hěn búcuò, měige fángjiān dōu yǒu kōngtiáo.
这所大学的宿舍条件很不错，每个房间都有空调。
The dormitories of this college are in good condition. Every room has an air conditioner.

4. 一条新闻 yìtiáoxīnwén news

Zǎoshang yǒu yìtiáo xīnwénshuō, měitiān shuì qīge xiǎoshí duì shēntǐ zuìhǎo.
早上有一条新闻说，每天睡七个小时对身体最好。
One morning news show says that sleeping seven hours a day is best for your health.

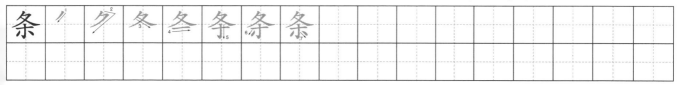

CHARACTER 56

tāng
soup

Useful phrases and sentences

1. 汤 tāng soup

Zhège niúròutāng wénzhe zhēnxiāng!
这个牛肉汤闻着真香！
This beef soup smells so good.

2. 喝汤 hētāng have soup

Zhōngguó nánfāng rén xíguàn xiān hē tāng hòu chīfàn.
中国南方人习惯先喝汤后吃饭。
People in South China like to have soup first, before the meal.

3. 汤圆 tāngyuán glutinous rice balls

"Yuánxiāojié" nàtiān, Zhōngguórén dōu huì chī tāngyuan.
"元宵节"那天，中国人都会吃汤圆。
Chinese people have glutinous rice balls during the Lantern Festival.

4. 泡汤 pàotāng destroy one's hopes

Liú Lǎobǎn méi xiǎngdào zhème hǎode yìbǐ mǎimài jìngrán pàotāngle.
刘老板没想到这么好的一笔买卖竟然泡汤了。
Boss Liu didn't expect that such a good deal would be completely ruined.

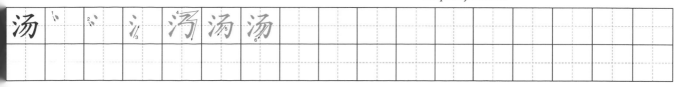

CHARACTER 57

菜

cài
dish; vegetable

11 STROKES ⺿ **RADICAL**

Useful phrases and sentences

1. 炒菜 **chǎocài** cook
   Nǐ chǎocàide shíhou shǎo fang diǎnr yóu.
   你炒菜的时候少放点儿油。
   Use less oil when you cook.

2. 点菜 **diǎncài** to order (food)
   Duì yíge wàiguórén láishuō, qù Zhōngguó fànguǎnr diǎncài hěn bù róngyì.
   对一个外国人来说，去中国饭馆儿点菜很不容易。
   Ordering food at a Chinese restaurant is not easy for foreigners.

3. 家常菜 **jiāchángcài** home-style cooking
   Jīntiān zuòde dōushì jiāchángcài, xīwàng nǐ chideguàn.
   今天做的都是家常菜，希望你吃得惯。
   It's all home-style cooking today. I hope you like it.

4. 菜市场 **càishìchǎng** market
   Lóuxià càishìchǎngde dōngxī jì piányi yòu xīnxiān.
   楼下菜市场的东西既便宜又新鲜。
   Things in the market downstairs are both cheap and fresh.

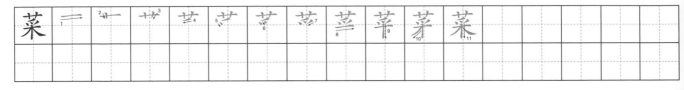

CHARACTER 58

包

bāo
wrap; package

5 STROKES 勹 **RADICAL**

Useful phrases and sentences

1. 面包 **miànbāo** bread
   Mèimei zuìdàde lǐxiǎng shì kāi yìjiā miànbāodiàn.
   妹妹最大的理想是开一家面包店。
   My younger sister's biggest dream is to open a bakery.

2. 包括 **bāokuò** include
   Dàjiā qǐng zhùyì, wǔqiānkuàide lǚxíngfèi bù bāokuò jīpiào.
   大家请注意，五千块的旅行费不包括机票。
   Please note that the five-thousand kuai *travel cost does not include the airfare.*

3. 包饺子 **bāojiǎozi** make dumplings
   Xiàge xīngqī, wǒmende Zhōngwén lǎoshī huì gēn wǒmen yìqǐ bāojiǎozi.
   下个星期，我们的中文老师会跟我们一起包饺子。
   Our Chinese teachers will make dumplings with us next week.

4. 打包 **dǎbāo** wrap up food
   Fúwùyuán, máfan nǐ bǎ zhèliǎngge cài dǎbāo.
   服务员，麻烦你把这两个菜打包。
   Excuse me, please wrap up these two dishes.

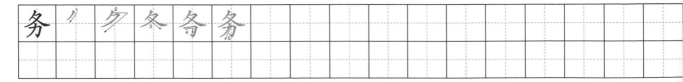

CHARACTER 59

务

wù
business;
by all means

5 STROKES 力 **RADICAL**

Useful phrases and sentences

1. 任务 **rènwù** task; assignment
   Xiǎo Wáng hěn nénggàn, lǎobǎn zǒngshì gěi tā hěnduō rènwù.
   小王很能干，老板总是给她很多任务。
   Xiao Wang is capable. The boss always gives her many tasks.

2. 家务 **jiāwù** household chore
   Dìdi hěn lǎn, zài jiālǐ cónglái bú zuò jiāwù.
   弟弟很懒，在家里从来不做家务。
   My younger brother is very lazy. He never does household chores.

3. 务必 **wùbì** by all means
   Míngtiān zǎoshang bādiǎn kāihuì, qǐng dàjiā wùbì zhǔnshí lái.
   明天早上八点开会，请大家务必准时来。
   We have a meeting at 8 am tomorrow. Please come on time.

4. 义务 **yìwù** duty; responsibility
   Gěi fùmǔ yǎnglǎo shìbushi háizide yìwù?
   给父母养老是不是孩子的义务？
   Is it every child's responsibility to provide an enjoyable retirement life for their parents?

Useful phrases and sentences

员

yuán
staff

1. 售货员 **shòuhuòyuán** salesperson

Xiǎoqián báitiān zài fànguǎnr dǎgōng, wǎnshang qù chāoshì dāng shòuhuòyuán.
小钱白天在饭馆儿打工，晚上去超市当售货员。
Xiao Qian works at a restaurant in the morning and at the supermarket as a salesperson in the evening.

2. 乘务员 **chéngwùyuán** vehicle attendant

Bǎ chēpiào náchūlái, chéngwùyuán lái jiǎnchá piàole.
把车票拿出来，乘务员来检查票了。
The attendant is checking tickets. Take them out.

3. 会员 **huìyuán** member

Wǒ shì zhèjiā jiànshēn zhōngxīnde huìyuán.
我是这家健身中心的会员。
I am a member of this gym.

4. 员工 **yuángōng** staff

Nǐmen gōngsī zhēn búcuò, hái gěi yuángōng tígōng miǎnfèide wǔcān.
你们公司真不错，还给员工提供免费的午餐。
Your company offers free lunch for the staff. How nice!

员	¹丿	²⁄	宀³	尸	咼	员	员				

Lesson 4 Exercises

Part 1 Choose from the following words to fill in the blanks.

鸡蛋、服务、菜单、辣、汤

1. 老师，我昨天去了中国饭馆儿，可是我看不懂（　　　　　）。

2. 这家饭馆儿的（　　　　　）很好，老板很喜欢跟客人聊天。

3. 这道菜看起来很（　　　　　），你真的要吃吗？

4. 我是南方人，我习惯先喝（　　　　　）再吃饭。

Part 2 Complete the following dialogues using Chinese characters.

1. A: 你喜欢吃中国菜吗？哪道菜是你最喜欢吃的？

   B: _____ 。

2. A: 要是你请朋友吃饭，你会带他去哪个饭馆儿？点什么菜？

   B: _____ 。

3. A: 你觉得用中文点菜难不难？为什么？

   B: _____。

4. A: 你喜欢做菜吗？你会做什么菜？

   B: _____。

5. A: 你的早饭、午饭、晚饭常常吃什么？

   B: _____。

Part 3 学以致用

你的朋友请你介绍一家你最喜欢的饭馆儿，请从下面这几个方面说一说。

1. 饭馆儿叫什么名字？
2. 饭馆儿在哪儿？
3. 贵不贵？
4. 什么菜最好吃？
5. 他们的服务怎么样？

LESSON 5

Let's Work Out! 咱们去运动吧!

1. Dialogue

Read the dialogue below and answer the questions in characters.

陈阳:	明天是晴天，我们一起出去运动吧，锻炼一下身体。
李真:	好啊，做什么运动？
陈阳:	踢足球吧。
李真:	踢球太累了，跑得身上都是汗，可能还踢不进一个球，没意思。
陈阳:	那我们打篮球吧。
李真:	你那么高，我这么矮，不跟你打！
陈阳:	那爬山？
李真:	爬山是不错，可是爬完以后腿疼得厉害。
陈阳:	那去游泳？你不总说自己太胖，想瘦一点儿吗？游泳一定能让你瘦下来。
李真:	不去不去！我这么胖，不好意思只穿一条游泳裤。
陈阳:	你啊，总是找借口，根本不想锻炼身体！算了，我自己去吧。

1. 陈阳想叫李真明天跟他去做什么？ ....

2. 李真为什么不想去打篮球、游泳？ ....

3. 最后李真跟陈阳一起去运动了吗？ ....

2. Vocabulary

	Word	Pinyin	English equivalent
1.	晴天	**qíngtiān**	sunny day; clear sky
2.	运动	**yùndòng**	exercise
3.	锻炼	**duànliàn**	work out
4.	踢足球	**tīzúqiú**	play soccer
5.	汗	**hàn**	sweat
6.	半天	**bàntiān**	half a day
7.	打篮球	**dǎ lánqiú**	play basketball
8.	高	**gāo**	tall
9.	矮	**ǎi**	short
10.	爬山	**páshān**	hiking
11.	腿	**tuǐ**	leg
12.	厉害	**lìhai**	tremendously; terribly
13.	游泳	**yóuyǒng**	swim
14.	胖	**pàng**	fat; chubby
15.	瘦	**shòu**	thin; slim
16.	总是	**zǒngshì**	always
17.	借口	**jièkǒu**	excuse

3. New Characters

Fifteen characters are introduced in this lesson. Use the following explanations to help you understand and remember the characters.

晴　踢　足　篮　腿　进　游　泳　汗　高　矮　胖　瘦　锻　炼

CHARACTER 61

晴

qíng
clear

12 STROKES　日 RADICAL

Useful phrases and sentences

1. 晴天 **qíngtiān** clear sky

   Zhèlǐde dōngtiān búdàn cháng, érqiě hěnshǎo néng kàndào qíngtiān.
   这里的冬天不但长，而且很少能看到晴天。
   The winter here is not only long, there are also very few days with a clear sky.

2. 雨过天晴 **yǔguò tiānqíng** clear sky after rain

   Yǔguò tiānqíng, tiānkōng chūxiànle liǎngdào cǎihóng.
   雨过天晴，天空出现了两道彩虹。
   The sky became clear with a double rainbow after the rain.

3. 晴转多云 **qíngzhuǎnduōyún** sunny turns into cloudy

   Tiānqì yùbào shuō míngtiān qíngzhuǎnduōyún.
   天气预报说明天晴转多云。
   The weather forecast says that the sunny day will turn into a cloudy day tomorrow.

4. 晴朗 **qínglǎng** sunny

   Qínglǎngde tiānqì ràngrénde xīnqíng tèbié hǎo.
   晴朗的天气让人的心情特别好。
   Sunny days put people in a good mood.

CHARACTER 62

踢

tī
kick

15 STROKES　足 RADICAL

Useful phrases and sentences

1. 踢 **tī** kick

   Xiǎo Zhào hěn shēngqì, tīkāi mén pǎole chūqu.
   小赵很生气，踢开门跑了出去！
   Zhao Yong was mad. He kicked the door and ran out.

2. 踢足球 **tīzúqiú** play soccer

   Chén Yáng tebié ài tīzúqiú, kěshì tā hǎoxiàng tīde bú tài hǎo.
   陈阳特别爱踢足球，可是他好像踢得不太好。
   Chen Yang likes to play soccer, but he is not good at it.

3. 踢腿 **tītuǐ** stretch legs

   Jīntiān wǔshùkè yào liànxí tītuǐ.
   今天武术课要练习踢腿。
   We are practicing stretching legs in martial arts class today.

4. 踢踏舞 **tītàwǔ** tap dance

   Míngtiān wǎnshang xuéxiào yǒu yíge tītàwǔ biǎoyǎn, nǐ yǒu xìngqù kànkan ma?
   明天晚上学校有一个踢踏舞表演，你有兴趣看看吗？
   There is a tap dance show tomorrow evening at school. Are you interested in going?

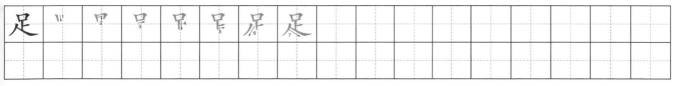

CHARACTER 63

足

zú
foot; sufficient

7 STROKES　足 RADICAL

Useful phrases and sentences

1. 足球 **zúqiú** soccer; football

   Nǐ xǐhuan kàn Yīngshì zúqiú háishì Měishì zúqiú?
   你喜欢看英式足球还是美式足球？
   Which do you like better? British soccer or American football?

2. 足球队 **zúqiúduì** soccer team

   Zhècì bǐsài yígòng yǒu èrshízhī zúqiúduì cānjiā.
   这次比赛一共有二十支足球队参加。
   There are twenty teams in total attending this soccer tournament.

3. 足够 **zúgòu** enough

   Bié jǐnzhāng, míngtiānde kǎoshì zhǔnbèi yíge xiǎoshí zúgòule.
   别紧张，明天的考试准备一个小时足够了。
   Relax. One hour to prepare for tomorrow's test is enough.

4. 充足 **chōngzú** sufficient; plenty of

   Hěnduōrén xǐhuan Jiāzhōu shì yīnwèi nàr yìniánsìjì yángguāng dōu hěn chōngzú.
   很多人喜欢加州是因为那儿一年四季阳光都很充足。
   Many people like California because it has plenty of sunshine all year long.

CHARACTER 64

篮

lán
basket

16 STROKES · 竹 **RADICAL**

Useful phrases and sentences

1. 篮球 **lánqíu** basketball

Yáo Míng kěyǐ shuō shì Zhōngguó zuì yǒumíngde lánqiú yùndòngyuánle.
姚明可以说是中国最有名的篮球运动员了。
Yao Ming is probably the most famous basketball player in China.

2. 篮球队 **lánqiúduì** basketball team

Nàge dàxuéde lánqiúduì zuì lìhài, nǐ zhīdào ma?
哪个大学的篮球队最厉害, 你知道吗?
Do you know which college basketball team is the best?

3. 篮球场 **lánqiúchǎng** basketball court

Zhège lánqiúchǎng yǐjīng yǒu wǔshíduō nián de lìshǐ le.
这个篮球场已经有五十多年的历史了。
This basketball court has a history of more than fifty years.

4. 购物篮 **gòuwùlán** shopping basket

Zhèjiā chāoshì yǒu zhuānmén gěi xiǎopéngyou yòngde gòuwùlán.
这家超市有专门给小朋友用的购物篮。
This supermarket has shopping baskets specially for children.

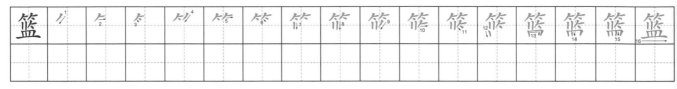

CHARACTER 65

tuǐ
leg

13 STROKES · 月 **RADICAL**

Useful phrases and sentences

1. 腿 **tuǐ** leg

Zuótiān Fāng Lǎoshī dǎlánqiú bùxiǎoxīn nòngshāngle tuǐ.
昨天方老师打篮球不小心弄伤了腿。
Teacher Fang accidentally hurt his knee when playing basketball yesterday.

2. 裤腿 **kùtuǐ** trouser leg

Yǔ tàidàle, wǒde kùtuǐ quán shī le.
雨太大了, 我的裤腿全湿了。
The rain is so heavy that my trouser legs are all wet.

3. 腿脚 **tuǐjiǎo** legs and feet

Zhū lǎo xiānsheng niánjì yǐjīng hěn da le, kěshì tāde tuǐjiǎo hái hěnhǎo, zǒulù yìdiǎnr yě búmàn.
朱老先生年纪已经很大了, 可是他的腿脚还很好, 走路一点儿也不慢。
Mr. Zhu is old but his legs and feet are still strong. He walks fast.

4. 几条腿 **jǐtiáotuǐ** how many legs

Nǐ zhīdao pángxiè yǒu jǐtiáotuǐ ma?
你知道螃蟹有几条腿吗?
Do you know how many legs a crab has?

CHARACTER 66

进

jìn
enter

7 STROKES · 辶 **RADICAL**

Useful phrases and sentences

1. 进来 **jìnlai** enter

Nǐ xiān bié jìnlai, wǒ hái méi huànhǎo yīfu.
你先别进来, 我还没换好衣服。
Please do not enter yet; I am changing clothes.

2. 进行 **jìnxíng** underway; in progress

Bǐsài yǐjīng jìnxíng liǎngge xiǎoshí le, hái méiyǒu jiéshù.
比赛已经进行两个小时了, 还没有结束。
The tournament has been in progress for two hours and is not yet finished.

3. 进去 **jìnqu** go in

Zánmen kuài jìnqu ba, diànyǐng yǐjīng kāishǐ le.
咱们快进去吧, 电影已经开始了。
Let's go in. The movie has already begun.

4. 进口 **jìnkǒu** import

Zài Zhōngguó, yàoshì mǎi yíliàng jìnkǒu qìchē, jiàgé huì fēicháng gāo.
在中国, 要是买一辆进口汽车, 价格会非常高。
Buying an imported car in China is very expensive.

游

yóu
travel; tour

Useful phrases and sentences

1. 游客 **yóukè** tourist

   Ān Huá xǐhuan dōngtiān pá Chángchéng, yīnwèi yóukè bú shì nàme duō.
   安华喜欢冬天爬长城，因为游客不是那么多。
   An Hua likes to go to the Great Wall in the winter because there are fewer tourists.

2. 旅游团 **lǚyóutuán** tour group

   Nǐ xǐhuan zìjǐ qù lǚyóu háishi gēn lǚyóutuán qù?
   你喜欢自己去旅游还是跟旅游团去？
   Do you like to travel on your own or in a tour group?

3. 游乐场 **yóulèchǎng** playground

   Zhège gōngyuánde yóulèchǎng shì miǎnfèide.
   这个公园的游乐场是免费的。
   The playground in this park is free.

4. 导游 **dǎoyóu** tour guide

   Cānguān bówùguǎn háishì qǐng yíge dǎoyóu bǐjiào hǎo, yàobùrán hěnduō dōngxi kànbudǒng.
   参观博物馆还是请一个导游比较好，要不然很多东西看不懂。
   It is better to have a tour guide when visiting a museum. Otherwise, there are many things you won't understand.

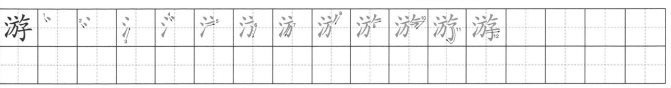

泳

yǒng
swim

Useful phrases and sentences

1. 游泳 **yóuyǒng** swim

   Zhège dàxué yǒu yíge guīdìng, bù huì yóuyǒngde xuésheng bù néng bìyè.
   这个大学有一个规定，不会游泳的学生不能毕业。
   This college requires that all students be able to swim before graduation.

2. 游泳池 **yóuyǒngchí** swimming pool

   Xuéxiào yóuyǒngchíde shuǐ bú tài gānjìng.
   学校游泳池的水不太干净。
   The water of the school's swimming pool is not clean.

3. 蛙泳 **wāyǒng** swim the breaststroke

   Duì wǒ lái shuō, wāyǒng shì zuì róngyì xué de.
   对我来说，蛙泳是最容易学的。
   The breaststroke is the easiest for me to learn.

4. 自由泳 **zìyóuyǒng** freestyle swimming

   Yàoshi nǐ xiǎng yóude kuài, nǐ yīnggāi xué zìyóuyǒng.
   要是你想游得快，你应该学自由泳。
   If you want to swim faster, you should learn freestyle.

汗

hàn
sweat

Useful phrases and sentences

1. 出汗 **chūhàn** to perspire

   Lǐ Zhēn jīntiān zuò bàogàode shíhou jǐnzhāngde dōu chūhànle.
   李真今天做报告的时候紧张得都出汗了。
   Li Zhen was so nervous that he perspired when giving his presentation today.

2. 擦汗 **cāhàn** wipe off sweat

   Nǐ xiūxi yíhuìr ba, cācā hàn, hē diǎnr shuǐ.
   你休息一会儿吧，擦擦汗，喝点儿水。
   Take a break. Wipe off your sweat and have some water.

3. 汗衫 **hànshān** shirt

   Zhè zhǒng hànshān chuānqǐlai jì liángkuài yòu shūfu.
   这种汗衫穿起来既凉快又舒服。
   This shirt is cool and comfortable to wear.

4. 汗珠 **hànzhū** sweat

   Lǎo Mǎ shēngbìngle, tóushangde hànzhū yìzhí wǎng xià liú.
   老马生病了，头上的汗珠一直往下流。
   Lao Ma is sick. Sweat keeps running off his head.

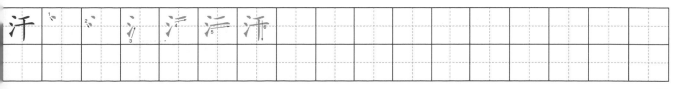

高

gāo
tall; high

10 STROKES | 高 RADICAL

1. 高 **gāo** tall

Cài Xiānsheng yìjiārén dōu hěn gāo.
蔡先生一家人都很高。
The Cai's family is tall.

2. 高级 **gāojí** upscale

Zhèshì yíge gāojí gōngyù, yǒu yóuyǒngchí hé jiànshēnfáng.
这是一个高级公寓，有游泳池和健身房。
This is an upscale apartment complex with a swimming pool and a gym.

3. 高兴 **gāoxìng** happy

Xuéxiàode zúqiúduì yíngle bǐsài, dàjiā dōu hěn gāoxìng.
学校的足球队赢了比赛，大家都很高兴。
Everyone was so happy that the school soccer team won the game.

4. 提高 **tígāo** advance; enhance; increase

Zhāng Lǎoshī, zěnme néng kuài yìdiǎnr tígāo wǒde Zhōngwén shuǐpíng ne?
张老师，怎么能快一点儿提高我的中文水平呢？
Teacher Zhang, how can I increase my Chinese language proficiency more quickly?

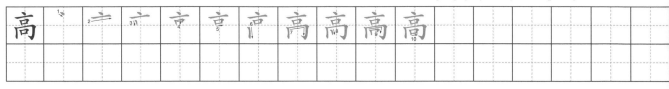

矮

ǎi
short

13 STROKES | 矢 RADICAL

1. 矮 **ǎi** short

Xià Jiàoliàn, wǒ gèzi yǒudiǎnr ǎi, néng cānjiā lánqiúduì ma?
夏教练，我个子有点儿矮，能参加篮球队吗？
Coach Xia, I am a bit short. Can I still join the basketball team?

2. 矮个子 **ǎigèzi** short in height

Nàge ǎigèzi nánshēng shì wǒmen bān yīngwén shuōde zuìhǎode.
那个矮个子男生是我们班英文说得最好的。
That short male student's spoken English is the best in our class.

3. 矮小 **ǎixiǎo** short and small

Wǒ xiǎng shuō "tā hěn àixiào", kěshì shuōchéngle "tā hěn ǎixiǎo".
我想说"他很爱笑"，可是说成了"他很矮小"。
I wanted to say "He likes laughing," but I said "He is short."

4. 低矮 **dī'ǎi** low; short

Nàpái dī'ǎide fángwú míngnián huì bèi chāidiào.
那排低矮的房屋明年会被拆掉。
That row of low, small houses will be torn down next year.

胖

pàng
fat; chubby

9 STROKES | 月 RADICAL

1. 胖 **pàng** fat

Zhōngguórén jiànmiànde shíhou, yǒushíhou huì shuō duìfāng pàngle huòzhě shòule.
中国人见面的时候，有时候会说对方胖了或者瘦了。
When Chinese people meet, sometimes they say "you've gotten fatter" or "slimmer."

2. 胖乎乎 **pànghūhū** chubby

Máo Tàitai jiālǐ yǎngde māo pànghūhūde, zhēn hǎowánr.
毛太太家里养的猫胖乎乎的，真好玩儿。
Mrs. Mao has a chubby cat in her house. She is so cute.

3. 胖瘦 **pàngshòu** fat or slim

Yǒu yánjiū zhèngmíng, yǐngxiǎng rén pàngshòu de zhǔyào yuányīn shì jīyīn.
有研究证明，影响人胖瘦的主要原因是基因。
Research shows that people have genetic reasons for being fat or slim.

4. 肥胖 **féipàng** obesity

Zài hěnduō guójiā, xiǎoháizi de féipàng wèntí yuè lái yuè yánzhòng.
在很多国家，小孩子的肥胖问题越来越严重。
Child obesity has worsened in many countries.

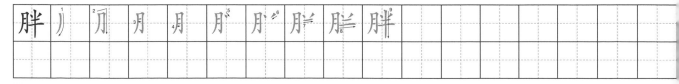

瘦
shòu
thin; slim

14 STROKES | 广 **RADICAL**

Useful phrases and sentences

1. 瘦 **shòu** thin; slim

   Liǎngge xīngqī méijiàn, nǐ zěnme shòule zhème duō?
   两个星期没见，你怎么瘦了这么多？
   I haven't seen you for only two weeks. How come you have become so thin?

2. 瘦小 **shòuxiǎo** thin and small

   Tā suīrán kànqǐlai hěn shòuxiǎo, dànshì lìqi hěn dà.
   他虽然看起来很瘦小，但是力气很大。
   Although he looks thin and small, he is quite strong.

3. 瘦身 **shòushēn** lose weight

   Wèile néng shòushēn, Zhāng Xiǎojiě měitiān wǎnshang dōu bù chīfàn.
   为了能瘦身，张小姐每天晚上都不吃饭。
   In order to lose weight, Ms. Zhang eats nothing every night.

4. 瘦肉 **shòuròu** lean meat

   Zuò gōngbǎo jīdīng zhèdào cài yòng shòuròu bǐjiào hǎo.
   做宫保鸡丁这道菜用瘦肉比较好。
   It is better to make spicy minced chicken with lean meat.

锻
duàn
to forge;
to discipline

14 STROKES | 钅 **RADICAL**

Useful phrases and sentences

1. 锻炼 **duànliàn** exercise; work out

   Zǎoshang qù Běijīngde gōngyuán, dàochù dōu néng kàndào duànliàn shēntǐde rén.
   早上去北京的公园，到处都能看到锻炼身体的人。
   If you go to the park in Beijing, you can see many people working out there in the morning.

2. 多锻炼 **duō duànliàn** exercise more

   Nǐ yīnggāi duō duànliàn shēntǐ, bié zǒng dāi zài fángjiān kàn diànshì.
   你应该多锻炼身体，别总待在房间看电视。
   You should exercise more. Don't just stay home and watch television.

3. 锻炼几次 **duànliàn jǐcì** work out how many times

   Jiàoliàn, nǐ jiànyì yīge xīngqī duànliàn jǐcì?
   教练，你建议一个星期锻炼几次？
   Coach, how many times do you recommend for working out per week?

4. 太少锻炼 **tài shǎo duànliàn** too little exercise

   Érzi, nǐ tài shǎo duànliàn le, zǒu méi jǐbù jiù qìchuǎnxūxū.
   儿子，你太少锻炼了，走没几步就气喘吁吁。
   Son, you get too little exercise. You breathe heavily after walking just a few steps.

炼
liàn
to refine

9 STROKES | 火 **RADICAL**

Useful phrases and sentences

1. 锻炼身体 **duànliàn shēntǐ** exercise

   Lǐ Xiàozhǎng shuō xuésheng bùnéng zhǐ dúshū, háiyào zhùyì duànliàn shēntǐ.
   李校长说学生不能只读书，还要注意锻炼身体。
   Principal Li says that students cannot just study; they should also exercise.

2. 锻炼脑力 **duànliàn nǎolì** brain training

   Lǎoshī, yǒu-méiyǒu shénme xiàlìngyíng kěyǐ ràng háizi duànliàn nǎolì?
   老师，有没有什么夏令营可以让孩子锻炼脑力？
   Teacher, is there any summer camp for kids that focuses on brain training?

3. 锻炼能力 **duànliàn nénglì** enhance ability

   Hěnduō dàxuéshēng shǔjià qù shíxí búshì wèile zhèngqián, érshì wèile duànliàn gōngzuò nénglì.
   很多大学生暑假去实习不是为了挣钱，而是为了锻炼工作能力。
   Many college students do internships not for money, but to enhance their ability.

4. 锻炼心智 **duànliàn xīnzhì** train one's mind

   Yújiā shì hěn hǎo duànliàn xīnzhìde yùndòng.
   瑜伽是很好锻炼心智的运动。
   Yoga is a good exercise to train your mind.

Part 1 Choose from the following words to fill in the blanks.

晴、锻炼、踢、瘦、出汗

1. 香港的气候太湿热了，一出门就（　　　　），很不舒服。

2. 老同学叫我下周末去（　　　　）足球，可是我有事不能去。

3. 他最近忙工作，常常没时间吃饭，一个月下来（　　　　）了不少。

4. 这儿的天气真奇怪，刚才还下大雨，现在又（　　　　）了。

Part 2 Complete the following dialogues using Chinese characters.

1. A: 你喜欢运动吗？喜欢做什么运动？

   B: ＿＿＿＿＿＿＿＿＿＿＿＿＿＿＿＿＿＿＿＿＿＿＿＿＿＿＿。

2. A: 你喜欢自己去运动还是跟朋友一起去？

   B: ＿＿＿＿＿＿＿＿＿＿＿＿＿＿＿＿＿＿＿＿＿＿＿＿＿＿＿。

3. A: 你喜欢在外面运动还是去健身房（**jiànshēnfáng** gym）？

   B: ＿＿＿＿＿＿＿＿＿＿＿＿＿＿＿＿＿＿＿＿＿＿＿＿＿＿＿。

4. A: 你经常看球赛吗？你最喜欢的球队是哪个？

   B: ＿＿＿＿＿＿＿＿＿＿＿＿＿＿＿＿＿＿＿＿＿＿＿＿＿＿＿。

5. A: 在你的国家，能不能对别人说"你胖了"或者"你瘦了"？

   B: ＿＿＿＿＿＿＿＿＿＿＿＿＿＿＿＿＿＿＿＿＿＿＿＿＿＿＿。

从下面的运动中选两个你最喜欢的。说说你是从什么时候开始喜欢这两个运动的？你每个星期运动多长时间？你为什喜欢这两个运动？

LESSON 6

Let's Travel! 我们去旅游吧！

1. Dialogue

Read the dialogue below and answer the questions in characters.

凯文：	喂！朱莉，在家忙什么呢？
朱莉：	收拾行李呢。我后天就要去北京旅游了！
凯文：	啊，我差点儿忘了。后天几点出发？
朱莉：	早上八点的飞机。
凯文：	除了北京以外，你还会去哪些地方？
朱莉：	还会去杭州，都说杭州的风景特别美，就像画儿一样。
凯文：	真羡慕你！我也很想去杭州。
朱莉：	我最近每天都忙着在网上订宾馆，买火车票和汽车票，累死了！
凯文：	我前几天看报纸上说中国的高铁服务特别好。对了，你怎么去机场？有几个箱子？需要我送你吗？
朱莉：	不用了，我刚才给出租车公司打电话叫了一辆车。
凯文：	你这次去多少天？几号回美国？
朱莉：	一共十五天，下个月二号回来。
凯文：	到时候我去机场接你。祝你在中国玩儿得开心！
朱莉：	谢谢,等我回来给你电话！

1. 朱莉要去中国哪些城市？ ....

2. 凯文在报纸上看到了什么？ ....

3. 朱莉这次去中国一共玩儿多少天？ ....

2. Vocabulary

	Word	Pinyin	English equivalent
1.	收拾	**shōushi**	pack
2.	行李	**xínglǐ**	luggage
3.	旅游	**lǚyóu**	travel
4.	忘	**wàng**	forget
5.	出发	**chūfā**	depart
6.	飞机	**fēijī**	airplane
7.	纽约	**Niǔyuē**	New York
8.	除了	**chúle**	beside; in addition to
9.	杭州	**Hángzhōu**	Hangzhou
10.	画儿	**huàr**	painting
11.	羡慕	**xiànmù**	envy
12.	网上	**wǎngshang**	on the internet
13.	订	**dìng**	reserve
14.	火车	**huǒchē**	train
15.	票	**piào**	ticket
16.	汽车	**qìchē**	car; automobile
17.	累	**lèi**	tiring
18.	报纸	**bàozhǐ**	newspaper
19.	高铁	**gāotiě**	high-speed train
20.	特别	**tèbié**	especially; particularly
21.	箱子	**xiāngzi**	box
22.	出租车	**chūzūchē**	taxi
23.	公司	**gōngsī**	company
24.	一辆车	**yíliàngchē**	one car
25.	接	**jiē**	pick up

3. New Characters

Fifteen characters are introduced in this lesson. Use the following explanations to help you understand and remember the characters.

旅　非　累　共　汽　箱　火　飞　长　司　号　票　报　纸　别

CHARACTER 76

旅

lǚ
travel; journey

Useful phrases and sentences

1. 旅游 **lǚyóu** travel

   Nǎge jìjié qù Běijīng lǚyóu bǐjiào hǎo?
   哪个季节去北京旅游比较好？
   What is the best season to travel to Beijing?

2. 旅行社 **lǚxíngshè** travel agency

   Zhèjiā lǚxíngshè jiàgé bú guì, dànshì fúwù hěn zhōudào.
   这家旅行社价格不贵，但是服务很周到。
   This travel agency is not expensive and their service is quite good.

3. 毕业旅行 **bìyè lǚxíng** graduation tour

   Dàsìde xuésheng zhèngzài jìhuà yíge bìyè lǚxíng.
   大四的学生正在计划一个毕业旅行。
   The college seniors are organizing their graduation tour.

4. 旅客 **lǚkè** traveler; passenger

   Gèwèi lǚkè qǐng zhùyì, huǒchē mǎshang dàole, qǐng shōushi hǎo zìjǐde xínglǐ.
   各位旅客请注意，火车马上到了，请收拾好自己的行李。
   Attention, passengers. The train is approaching the terminal station. Please take all your belongings.

CHARACTER 77

非

fēi
not; un-

Useful phrases and sentences

1. 除非 **chúfēi** unless; only if …

   Chúfēi nǐ jīntiān wǎnshang bú shuìjiào, yàoburán nǐ kěndìng xiěbuwán bàogào.
   除非你今天晚上不睡觉，要不然你肯定写不完报告。
   You will not be able to finish your report unless you don't sleep tonight.

2. 非法 **fēifǎ** unlawful; illegal

   Zài Měiguó, bǎ xiǎo háizi yíge rén liú zài jiālǐ shì fēifǎ de.
   在美国，把小孩子一个人留在家里是非法的。
   It is unlawful to leave your child alone at home in the U.S.A.

3. 是非 **shìfēi** right and wrong

   Xiǎowén cónglái bú zài lǎobǎn miànqián shuō tóngshìde shìfēi.
   小文从来不在老板面前说同事的是非。
   Xiaowen never talks about her colleagues' rights and wrongs in front of her supervisor.

4. 非要 **fēiyào** only; nothing other than

   Wǎngshàng mǎi gèng piányi, nǐ wèishénme fēi yào qù shāngdiàn mǎi ne?
   网上买更便宜，你为什么非要去商店买呢？
   It is cheaper to purchase online. Why do you only want to go to shops?

CHARACTER 78

累

lèi
tired; fatigued

Useful phrases and sentences

1. 累 **lèi** tired; fatigued

   Lèile yìtiān le, nǐ zǎodiǎn xiūxi ba.
   累了一天了，你早点休息吧。
   It has been a tiring day. Get an early rest.

2. 劳累 **láolèi** exhausting

   Zhège zhōumò nǐ zěnme yòu yào chūchāi, shízài tài láolèile.
   这个周末你怎么又要出差，实在太劳累了。
   How come you are on a business trip again this weekend? How exhausting!

3. 积累 **jīlěi** accumulate

   Kǎiwén měige xiàtiān dōu qù shíxí, xīwàng néng duō jīlěi yìxiē gōngzuò jīngyàn.
   凯文每个夏天都去实习，希望能多积累一些工作经验。
   Kevin interns every summer in hope of accumulating more experience.

4. 累计 **lěijì** in accumulation

   Tā cānjiā shèqū fúwù yǐjīng lěijì sānbǎige xiǎoshí le.
   他参加社区服务已经累计三百个小时了。
   His community service has accumulated to three hundred hours.

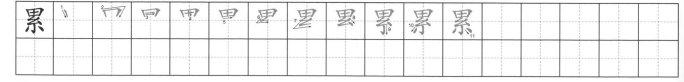

共

gòng
together; total

6 STROKES **八 RADICAL**

Useful phrases and sentences

1. 共事 **gòngshì** work with

Wǒ suīrán méi jīhuì gēn Wú Shuāng gòngshì, dàn tīngshuō tā rén hěn rèxīn.
我虽然没机会跟吴双共事，但听说他人很热心。
Although I did not have the opportunity to work with Wu Shuang, I heard that he's warm-hearted.

2. 共同 **gòngtóng** common

Nǐmen jiārén yǒu shénme gòngtóngde àihào ma?
你们家人有什么共同的爱好吗？
Is there any common hobby in your family?

3. 总共 **zǒnggòng** in total

Xīngbākè kāfēiguǎnr zài Zhōngguó zǒnggòng yǒu sānqiānduō jiā.
星巴克咖啡馆儿在中国总共有三千多家。
There are in total more than three thousand Starbucks in China.

4. 一共 **yígòng** in total

Zhào Jīnglǐ, zhège yuè wǒmen gōngsī yígòng zhuànle duōshǎo qián?
赵经理，这个月我们公司一共赚了多少钱？
Manager Zhao, how much money in total did our company make this month?

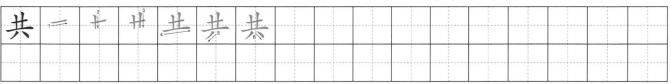

汽

qì
gas; steam

7 STROKES **氵 RADICAL**

Useful phrases and sentences

1. 汽车 **qìchē** car

Nǐ xǐhuan Déguóde qìchē háishì Rìběnde qìchē?
你喜欢德国的汽车还是日本的汽车？
Do you prefer German cars or Japanese cars?

2. 汽车旅馆 **qìchē lǚguǎn** motel

Lái zhèjiā qìchē lǚguǎnde dàduōshì xǐhuan yáogǔnde niánqīngrén.
来这家汽车旅馆的大多是喜欢摇滚的年轻人。
The majority of people coming to this motel are young people who love rock and roll.

3. 汽油 **qìyóu** gas

Qìyóu zěnme yòu zhǎngjiàle! Kuài kāibuqǐ chē le!
汽油怎么又涨价了！快开不起车了！
How come the gas price have increased again! I almost can't afford to drive a car.

4. 汽车站 **qìchē zhàn** bus stop

Qìchē zhàn jiù zài qiánmian, zài zǒu liǎngsānfēnzhōng jiù dào le.
汽车站就在前面，再走两三分钟就到了。
The bus stop is in the front. You'll get there in two or three minutes on foot.

箱

xiāng
box

15 STROKES **竹 RADICAL**

Useful phrases and sentences

1. 冰箱 **bīngxiāng** refrigerator

Bīngxiāngli shénme cài dōu méiyou le, zánmen děi qù chāoshì le.
冰箱里什么菜都没有了，咱们得去超市了。
There is nothing left in the fridge. We need to go to the supermarket.

2. 行李箱 **xínglǐxiāng** baggage; luggage

Qǐngwèn, guójì hángbān zuìduō kěyǐ dài jǐge xínglǐxiāng?
请问，国际航班最多可以带几个行李箱？
Excuse me, how many pieces of baggage are allowed on international flights?

3. 信箱 **xìnxiāng** mailbox

Zhū Lì zài xìnxiānglǐ fāxiàn yíshù huā, bù zhīdào shì shéi sòngde.
朱莉在信箱里发现一束花，不知道是谁送的。
Julie found a bouquet of flowers in the mailbox. I wonder who sent it.

4. 箱子 **xiāngzi** box

Zhège xiāngzi tài zhòngle, nǐ néng bāng wǒ bānyíxià ma?
这个箱子太重了，你能帮我搬一下吗？
This box is too heavy. Can you help me?

huǒ
fire

4 STROKES   火 **RADICAL**

Useful phrases and sentences

1. 火车站 **huǒchē zhàn** train station

   Qǐng wèn, qù huǒchē zhàn zuò jǐlù chē?
   请问，去火车站坐几路车？
   Excuse me, which bus should I take to the train station?

2. 着火 **zháohuǒ** on fire

   Kuàikàn, qiánmian nàdòng fángzi zháohuǒle!
   快看，前面那栋房子着火了！
   Look, the house in the front is on fire!

3. 火鸡 **huǒjī** turkey

   Kǎo huǒjī shì Gǎn'ēnjiéde chuántǒng shíwù.
   烤火鸡是感恩节的传统食物。
   Roasted turkey is a traditional dish on Thanksgiving.

4. 火锅 **huǒguō** hot pot

   Xuéxiào fùjìn xīnkāide huǒguōdiàn zǒngshì jǐmǎnle rén.
   学校附近新开的火锅店总是挤满了人。
   The newly opened hot pot restaurant near school is always packed.

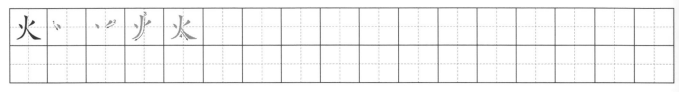

飞

fēi
fly

3 STROKES   飞 **RADICAL**

Useful phrases and sentences

1. 飞机 **fēijī** airplane; flight

   Zāogāo, xiàdàxuěle, fēijī kěnéng huì wǎndiǎn.
   糟糕，下大雪了，飞机可能会晚点。
   Darn, it's snowing right now. The flight may be delayed.

2. 起飞 **qǐfēi** take off

   Duìbuqǐ, fēijī mǎshàng yào qǐfēile, wǒ xiān bù gēn nǐ shuōle.
   对不起，飞机马上要起飞了，我先不跟你说了。
   Sorry, I need to hang up. The plane is taking off soon.

3. 直飞 **zhífēi** direct flight

   Xià Xiānsheng, jīpiào nín yào dìng zhífēide ma?
   夏先生，机票您要订直飞的吗？
   Mr. Xia, do you want to book a direct flight?

4. 飞盘 **fēipán** Frisbee

   Xiǎo shíhou, wǒ gēn gēge zuì xǐhuan wánr fēipán.
   小时候，我跟哥哥最喜欢玩儿飞盘。
   My older brother and I liked to play Frisbee the most when we were little.

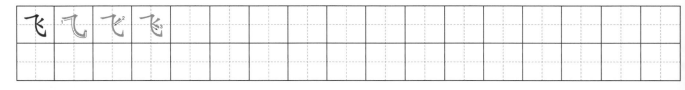

长

cháng / zhǎng
long / grow

4 STROKES   长 **RADICAL**

Useful phrases and sentences

1. 长方形 **chángfāngxíng** rectangle

   Zhū Tàitai xǐhuan chángfāngxíngde cānzhuō.
   朱太太喜欢长方形的餐桌。
   Mrs. Zhu likes rectangular dining tables.

2. 长短 **chángduǎn** length

   Zhètiáo kùzi yàngzi hěnhǎo, bùzhīdao chángduǎn hé-buhéshì.
   这条裤子样子很好，不知道长短合不合适。
   This pair of pants looks pretty, but I don't know if the length would fit.

3. 长 **zhǎng** grow

   Nǐ mèimei zhǎngde hěn xiàng nǐ, tèbié shì xiàoqǐlaide shíhou.
   你妹妹长得很像你，特别是笑起来的时候。
   Your younger sister looks like you, especially when she smiles.

4. 长大 **zhǎngdà** grow up

   Háizi xiǎode shíhou zǒng xīwàng zìjǐ kuàidiǎn zhǎngdà.
   孩子小的时候总希望自己快点儿长大。
   Children always want to grow up quickly when they are little.

CHARACTER 85

司

sī
take charge of

Useful phrases and sentences

1. 公司 **gōngsī** company

Hěnduō dàxuésheng bìyè yǐhòu dōu dǎsuàn zìjǐ kāi gōngsī.
很多大学生毕业以后都打算自己开公司。
Many college students plan to create their own companies after graduation.

2. 司机 **sījī** driver

Běijīngde chūzūchē sījī hěn xǐhuan gēn kèrén liáotiān.
北京的出租车司机很喜欢跟客人聊天。
Taxi drivers in Beijing like to chat with customers.

3. 司马 **Sīmǎ** Sima (last name)

Tā xìng Sīmǎ, bú xìng Sī, bié gǎocuòle.
他姓司马，不姓司，别搞错了。
His last name is Sima, not Si. Do not get it wrong.

4. 打官司 **dǎ guānsi** file a lawsuit

Wáng Lǜshī hěn hǎo, chángcháng bāng qióngrén miǎnfèi dǎ guānsi.
王律师很好，常常帮穷人免费打官司。
Attorney Wang is a nice person. He often helps poor people file lawsuits free of charge.

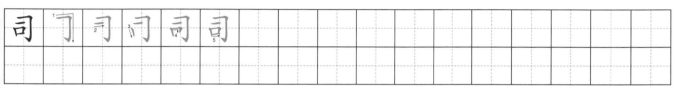

CHARACTER 86

号

hào
number

Useful phrases and sentences

1. 号 **hào** day

Nǐde hūnlǐ shì xiàge yuè jǐhào?
你的婚礼是下个月几号？
What is the date of your wedding next month?

2. 号码 **hàomǎ** number

Xiǎojiě, fāngbiàn gěi wǒ nǐde diànhuà hàomǎ ma?
小姐，方便给我你的电话号码吗？
Miss, may I have your telephone number?

3. 挂号 **guàhào** registration

Zhōngguóde yīyuàn páiduì guàhào yào huā hěn cháng shíjiān.
中国的医院排队挂号要花很长时间。
It takes a long time to register at Chinese hospitals.

4. 信号 **xìnhào** signal

Bàoqiàn, nínde diànhuà xìnhào hǎoxiàng bú tài hǎo, wǒ tīngbuqīngchu.
抱歉，您的电话信号好像不太好，我听不清楚。
I am sorry. Your telephone signal is weak. I can't hear you clearly.

CHARACTER 87

票

piào
ticket

Useful phrases and sentences

1. 门票 **ménpiào** ticket

Zhège bówùguǎn měige xīngqīsān xiàwǔ bú yào ménpiào.
这个博物馆每个星期三下午不要门票。
This museum requires no tickets on Wednesday afternoons.

2. 车票 **chēpiào** train ticket

Chēpiào nǐ yào mǎi wǎngfǎnde háishì dānchéngde?
车票你要买往返的还是单程的？
Regarding the ticket, do you want one-way or round trip?

3. 票价 **piàojià** ticket price

Kuàidào Shèngdànjié le, fēijīde piàojià bǐ píngshí guì yíbèi.
快到圣诞节了，飞机的票价比平时贵一倍。
Christmas is approaching. The airfare is double its regular price.

4. 邮票 **yóupiào** (postage) stamps

Tā kàndào piàoliangde yóupiào dōu huì shōujíqǐlai.
他看到漂亮的邮票都会收集起来。
He collects pretty postage stamps whenever he sees them.

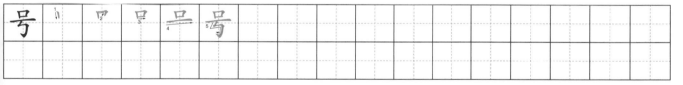

CHARACTER 88

bào
newspaper;
report

7 STROKES   扌 **RADICAL**

Useful phrases and sentences

1. 报纸 **bàozhǐ** newspaper
   Bái Xiānsheng xíguàn měitiān zuò dìtiěde shíhou kàn bàozhǐ.
   白先生习惯每天坐地铁的时候看报纸。
   Mr. Bai likes to read newspapers on the subway every day.

2. 报名 **bàomíng** sign up
   Wǒ dǎsuàn bàomíng cānjiā xiàzhōude mǎlāsōng bǐsài.
   我打算报名参加下周的马拉松比赛。
   I plan to sign up for the marathon next week.

3. 报警 **bàojǐng** report to police
   Zài Zhōngguó, bàojǐng diànhuà shì 110, nǐ yào jìzhù.
   在中国，报警电话是110，你要记住。
   Remember that 110 is the number to call the police in China.

4. 预报 **yùbào** forecast
   Tiānqì yùbào shuō xiàwǔ sāndiǎn kāishǐ xiàxuě.
   天气预报说下午三点开始下雪。
   The weather forecast says that it will start snowing at 3 pm.

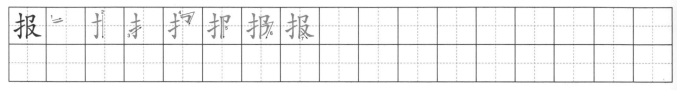

CHARACTER 89

zhǐ
paper

7 STROKES   纟 **RADICAL**

Useful phrases and sentences

1. 纸 **zhǐ** paper
   Zhèxiē zhǐ kěyǐ huíshōu, qǐng bú yào luàn rēng.
   这些纸可以回收，请不要乱扔。
   This paper is recyclable. Don't throw it away.

2. 餐巾纸 **cānjīnzhǐ** napkin
   Fúwùyuán, máfan nín ná jǐzhāng cānjīnzhǐ.
   服务员，麻烦您拿几张餐巾纸。
   Excuse me, can I have more napkins?

3. 纸币 **zhǐbì** bank note
   Zhè shì Qīngcháode zhǐbì, zhēn yǒu yìsi.
   这是清朝的纸币，真有意思。
   This is a bank note from the Qing Dynasty. How interesting!

4. 纸袋 **zhǐdài** paper bag
   Cóng xiàge yuè kāishǐ, chāoshìde zhǐdài kāishǐ shōufèile.
   从下个月开始，超市的纸袋开始收费了。
   Starting next month, they will begin to charge for paper bags at supermarkets.

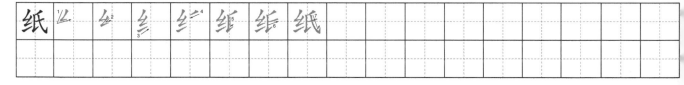

CHARACTER 90

别

bié
other; do not

7 STROKES   刂 **RADICAL**

Useful phrases and sentences

1. 别人 **biérén** other people
   Zuò zìjǐ xǐhuande shìqing, bú yào guǎn biérénde kànfǎ.
   做自己喜欢的事情，不要管别人的看法。
   Do whatever you like; there is no need to care about what other people think.

2. 特别 **tèbié** unique; special
   Zhèdào càide wèidào hěn tèbié, nǐ yào-buyào chángchang?
   这道菜的味道很特别，你要不要尝尝？
   This dish has a special taste. Do you want to try it?

3. 别 **bié** do not
   Tóngxuémen, zhèshì Zhōngwénkè, qǐng nǐmen bié shuō Yīngwén.
   同学们，这是中文课，请你们别说英文。
   Students, this is a Chinese class. Do not speak English.

4. 别管 **bié guǎn** don't worry about
   Bàba, wǒde shìqing nín yǐhou bié guǎnle, wǒ kěyǐ zìjǐ juédìng.
   爸爸，我的事情您以后别管了，我可以自己决定。
   Dad, from now on don't worry about me. I can decide on my own.

Lesson 6 Exercises

Part 1 Choose from the following words to fill in the blanks.

报纸、票、旅游、飞机、号

1. 你决定几（　　　　　）回国了吗？

2. 小张每年都要出国（　　　　　）好几次，他去过很多国家。

3. 现在买（　　　　　）的人比以前少多了，人们更习惯在手机或电脑上看新闻。

4. 我有两张音乐会的门（　　　　　），你有没有兴趣去听？

Part 2 Complete the following dialogues using Chinese characters.

1.　A: 在你旅游过的城市，你最喜欢什么地方？

　　B: _____ 。

2.　A: 你觉得自己旅游好还是跟旅行团好？

　　B: _____ 。

3.　A: 你的老家在哪儿？几月去那旅游比较好？

　　B: _____ 。

4.　A: 以后有机会，你还想去哪儿旅游？为什么？

　　B: _____ 。

5.　A: 你觉得旅游的时候，最麻烦的事情是什么？

　　B: _____ 。

Part 3 学以致用

你是一个中国旅行社的导游，请你给外国朋友介绍一个中国的旅游城市。

1.	去旅游的城市叫什么名字？

2.	这个城市在中国什么地方？

3.	去这个城市可以参观什么？

4.	什么季节去比较舒服？

5.	去几天比较好？大概要花多少钱？

Finding Rooms to Rent 找房子

1. Dialogue

Read the dialogue below and answer the questions in characters.

晓静:	您好！请问是房东吗？我刚才在报纸上看到了您的租房广告，不知道房子租出去了吗？
房东:	还没有，你进来看看吧。来，这是卧室，卫生间在那边，厨房在这边。
晓静:	这儿洗衣服方便吗？
房东:	方便，楼下就是洗衣房。
晓静:	我特别怕吵，不知道你们这儿……？
房东:	这儿很安静。隔壁张老先生家有只狗，可是那只狗吃饱了就睡，也没什么声音。
晓静:	啊，我特别喜欢狗。那要是东西坏了怎么办？
房东:	给我打电话，我让人来换新的。
晓静:	地铁站离这儿远吗？
房东:	不远，就在街道对面。
晓静:	那请问房租一个月多少钱呢？
房东:	一千五百块，包括水电费。每个月的第一天交房租。
晓静:	我挺喜欢这个房子的，不过，房租还能低点儿吗？我还是一个学生，实在没什么钱。房租还能低点儿吗？一千三行不行？
房东:	好吧，那就一千三。
晓静:	谢谢您！

1. 晓静是在哪儿看到租房广告的？ ....

2. 这是一个什么样的房子？安静不安静？ ....

3. 这个房子一个月多少钱？包括什么费？ ....

2. Vocabulary

	Word	Pinyin	English equivalent
1.	房东	**fángdōng**	landlord
2.	刚才	**gāngcái**	just now
3.	租房	**zūfáng**	rental
4.	广告	**guǎnggào**	advertisement
5.	卧室	**wòshì**	bedroom
6.	卫生间	**wèishēngjiān**	bathroom
7.	厨房	**chúfáng**	kitchen
8.	怕	**pà**	afraid; fear
9.	吵	**chǎo**	noisy; loud
10.	安静	**ānjìng**	quiet
11.	隔壁	**gébì**	next door
12.	饱	**bǎo**	full
13.	声音	**shēngyīn**	sound; voice
14.	房租	**fángzū**	rent for a room or house
15.	一千	**yìqiān**	one thousand
16.	包括	**bāokuò**	include
17.	水电费	**shuǐdiànfèi**	utility
18.	坏	**huài**	broken
19.	换	**huàn**	change
20.	地铁站	**dìtiězhàn**	subway statioin
21.	街道	**jiēdào**	street
22.	低	**dī**	low

3. New Characters

Fifteen characters are introduced in this lesson. Use the following explanations to help you understand and remember the characters.

租　广　卧　费　交　坏　换　千　让　吵　安　静　洗　卫　厨

CHARACTER 91

租 **zū** to rent

Useful phrases and sentences

1. 租房 **zūfáng** to rent

Yīnwèi fángjià tài gāo, suǒyǐ zūfángde rén yuè lái yuè duō le.
因为房价太高，所以租房的人越来越多了。
Because housing prices are so high, more and more people are choosing to rent.

2. 房租 **fángzū** rent

Xiǎo Wáng, zhège yuède fángzū nǐ kuàidiǎnr jiāo.
小王，这个月的房租你快点儿交。
Xiao Wang, please pay the rent earlier this month.

3. 出租车 **chūzūchē** taxi

Zāogāo, wǒ bǎ diànnǎo wàng zài chūzūchēshàng le.
糟糕，我把电脑忘在出租车上了。
Darn, I left my laptop in the taxi.

4. 租金 **zūjīn** rental fee

Huáxuě shèbèide zūjīn kěndìng bù piányí.
滑雪设备的租金肯定不便宜。
The rental fee for ski equipment will surely not be cheap.

CHARACTER 92

广 **guǎng** wide; to spread

Useful phrases and sentences

1. 广东 **guǎngdōng** Guangdong (a province in China)

Tāde fùmǔ dōu shì Guǎngdōng rén, tāmen shíniánqián yímín dào Jiānádà.
他的父母都是广东人，他们十年前移民到加拿大。
His parents are both from Guangdong. They emigrated to Canada ten years ago.

2. 广场 **guǎngchǎng** square

Míngtiān xiàwǔ liǎngdiǎn zài Hāfó Guǎngchǎng jiànmiàn, xíng-buxíng?
明天下午两点在哈佛广场见面，行不行？
Let's meet at Harvard Square at 2 pm tomorrow, okay?

3. 广播 **guǎngbō** broadcast

Bái Xiānsheng chángcháng yìbiān kāichē yìbiān tīng guǎngbō.
白先生常常一边开车一边听广播。
Mr. Bai often listens to the radio while driving.

4. 推广 **tuīguǎng** promote

Rén Jiàoshòu rènwéi bǎohù fāngyán hé tuīguǎng pǔtōnghuà dōu hěn zhòngyào.
任教授认为保护方言和推广普通话都很重要。
Professor Ren thinks that protecting dialects and promoting putonghua are both important.

CHARACTER 93

卧 **wò** to crouch; to lie

Useful phrases and sentences

1. 卧室 **wòshì** bedroom

Zhège wòshì zǎoshang yángguāng hěn hǎo, fēicháng shūfu.
这个卧室早上阳光很好，非常舒服。
This bedroom has a lot of sunlight in the morning. It's very comfortable.

2. 卧铺 **wòpù** sleeper (on a train)

Cóng Běijīng dào Xī'ān, zuò wòpù bǐjiào shūfu.
从北京到西安，坐卧铺比较舒服。
It is more comfortable to sit in sleeper from Beijing to Xi'an.

3. 软卧 **ruǎnwò** soft sleeper (on a train)

Xiānsheng, hěn bàoqiàn, ruǎnwòpiào yǐjīng màiwánle.
先生，很抱歉，软卧票已经卖完了。
I am sorry, sir, the soft sleeper tickets are sold out.

4. 卧虎藏龙 **Wòhǔ Cánglóng** *Crouching Tiger Hidden Dragon*

"Wòhǔ Cánglóng" shì wǒ fēicháng xǐhuande yíbù Zhōngwén diànyǐng.
《卧虎藏龙》是我非常喜欢的一部中文电影。
Crouching Tiger Hidden Dragon is one of my favorite Chinese films.

费 fèi
cost; fee

1. 费用 **fèiyòng** cost

Nǐ yígeyuè de wǎngluò fèiyòng dàgài yào duōshǎoqián?
你一个月的网络费用大概要多少钱?
How much is your average monthly internet cost?

2. 消费 **xiāofèi** consumption

Gēn yǐqián bǐ, Zhōngguó rénde xiāofèi shuǐpíng yuè lái yuè gāo le.
跟以前比, 中国人的消费水平越来越高了。
Chinese people's consumption level is becoming higher and higher than before.

3. 费力 **fèilì** difficult; spend a great deal of effort

Xiǎojìngde Yīngwén hěn hǎo, dúwán zhèběn shū yìdiǎnr yě bú fèilì.
晓静的英文很好, 读完这本书一点儿也不费力。
Xiaojing's English is very good. Finishing this book is not difficult at all.

4. 小费 **xiǎofèi** tip

Zài Zhōngguóde fànguǎnr, nǐ búyòng gěi fúwùyuán xiǎofèi.
在中国的饭馆儿, 你不用给服务员小费。
Tipping is not necessary at restaurants in China.

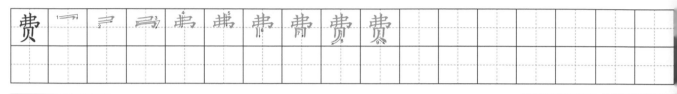

交 jiāo
deliver; exchange

1. 交 **jiāo** hand over; pay

Fángdōng, zhège yuède fángzū kěyǐ wǎn jǐtiān jiāo ma?
房东, 这个月的房租可以晚几天交吗?
Landlord, can I hand in this month's rent a few days late?

2. 交流 **jiāoliú** interact; have social contact

Nǐ jìrán dàole Zhōngguó, jiù yīnggāi duō gēn Zhōngguó rén jiāoliú.
你既然到了中国, 就应该多跟中国人交流。
Now that you have arrived in China, you should interact more with Chinese people.

3. 交通 **jiāotōng** traffic

Xiànzài shì shàngxiàbān shíjiān, jiāotōng fēicháng yōngjǐ.
现在是上下班时间, 交通非常拥挤。
It's rush hour right now. The traffic is quite congested.

4. 打交道 **dǎjiāodào** communicate

Gēn Zhōngguó rén dǎ jiāodaode shíhou yídìng yào gěi duìfāng miànzi.
跟中国人打交道的时候一定要给对方面子。
When communicating with Chinese people, it is important to give them "face."

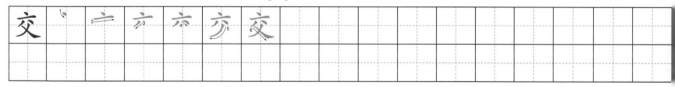

坏 huài
broken; bad

1. 坏 **huài** broken

Xiǎo Lǐ hěn lìhai, shénme dōngxi huàile dōu néng xiūhǎo.
小李很厉害, 什么东西坏了都能修好。
Xiao Li can fix anything broken. He is really good.

2. 弄坏 **nònghuài** to break; to ruin

Shízài bàoqiàn, wǒ bù xiǎoxīn nònghuàile nǐde jíta.
实在抱歉, 我不小心弄坏了你的吉他。
I am really sorry to accidentally break your guitar.

3. 坏事 **huàishì** bad things

Dìdi zài xuéxiào zuòle huàishì, huíjiā bù gǎn gàosù fùmǔ.
弟弟在学校做了坏事, 回家不敢告诉父母。
My younger brother did something bad at school. He didn't dare tell my parents.

4. 破坏 **pòhuài** destroy

Rénlèi bù néng zài jìxù pòhuài dàzìrán le.
人类不能再继续破坏大自然了。
Human beings cannot continue destroying nature any longer.

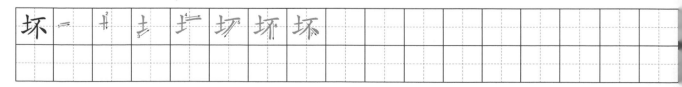

换

huàn
change

Useful phrases and sentences

1. 换 **huàn** change

   Zhège fángjiān tài chǎole, néng gěi wǒ huàn yíge ma?
   这个房间太吵了，能给我换一个吗？
   This room is too loud. Can I change to another one?

2. 换衣服 **huàn yīfu** change clothes

   Nǐ děng yíxia, wǒ huànge yīfu mǎshang jiù lái.
   你等一下，我换个衣服马上就来。
   Wait a second. I am changing clothes and will be right there.

3. 换钱 **huànqián** currency exchange

   Bié dānxīn, jīchǎng jiù yǒu huànqiánde dìfang.
   别担心，机场就有换钱的地方。
   Don't worry. There is currency exchange at the airport.

4. 换车 **huànchē** change to; transfer

   Qǐng wèn, qù Kēxué Bówùguǎn zài nǎr huànchē?
   请问，去科学博物馆在哪儿换车？
   Excuse me, where should I transfer to get to the Science Museum?

换 一 扌 扌 扌 扩 护 换 换 换 换

千

qiān
thousand

Useful phrases and sentences

1. 几千块 **jǐqiānkuài** several thousand *kuai*

   Zhège bāo kànqǐlai hěn pǔtōng, kěshì què yào hǎo jǐqiānkuài.
   这个包看起来很普通，可是却要好几千块。
   This bag looks average but it costs several thousand kuai.

2. 千万 **qiānwàn** by all means

   Xiàxuěle lù hěn huá, kāichē zǒulù qiānwàn yào xiǎoxīn.
   下雪了路很滑，开车走路千万要小心。
   It's snowing and the road is slippery. Be careful when you drive or walk.

3. 千克 **qiānkè** kilogram

   Nǐ zhīdao yìqiānkè děngyú duōshǎo bàng ma?
   你知道一千克等于多少磅吗？
   Do you know how many pounds are equal to one kilogram?

4. 千米 **qiānmǐ** kilometer

   Tā xiàge xīngqī yào cānjiā wǔqiānmǐ chángpǎo bǐsài.
   他下个星期要参加五千米长跑比赛。
   He is competing in a five-kilometer run next week.

千 千 二 千

让

ràng
let

Useful phrases and sentences

1. 让 **ràng** let

   Shàng gāozhōngde shíhou, fùmǔ bú ràng wǒ tánliànài.
   上高中的时候，父母不让我谈恋爱。
   My parents didn't allow me to date in high school.

2. 让位 **ràng wèi** yield one's seat

   Zài chēshàng rúguǒ yǒu lǎorén yīnggāi ràng wèi.
   在车上如果有老人应该让位。
   You should yield your seat to the elderly.

3. 忍让 **rěnràng** endurance

   Yǒude shíhou rěnràng yīxia jiù guòqule.
   有的时候忍让一下就过去了。
   Sometimes bad feelings pass away quickly with just a little endurance.

4. 让步 **ràngbù** give in; concede

   Jīngguò yīge xīngqīde tǎolùn, wǒ tàitai zhōngyú ràngbùle.
   经过一个星期的讨论，我太太终于让步了。
   My wife finally gave in after one week of discussion.

让 讠 讠 让 让

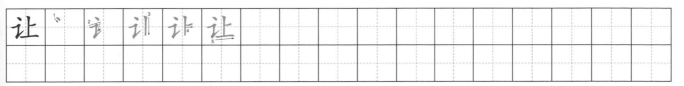

Useful phrases and sentences

7 STROKES   口 RADICAL

吵
chǎo
loud; noisy

1. 吵 **chǎo** loud

Zhù zài gébìde rén měige zhōumò dōu kāi wǎnhuì, tèbié chǎo.

住在隔壁的人每个周末都开晚会，特别吵。

The person next door has parties every weekend. It's so loud.

2. 吵架 **chǎojià** have a fight; quarrel

Wén Xiānsheng gēn tàitai chǎojiàle, tā juédìng jīnwǎn bù huíjiāle.

文先生跟太太吵架了，他决定今晚不回家了。

Mr. Wen haa a fight with his wife. He has decided not to go home tonight.

3. 吵醒 **chǎoxǐng** wake up

Zuówǎn méi shuì hǎo, bànyè sāndiǎn bèi wǒ jiāde māo chǎoxǐngle.

昨晚没睡好，半夜三点被我家的猫吵醒了。

I didn't sleep well last night. I was woken up by our cat at 3 am.

4. 争吵 **zhēngchǎo** argue

Tā shì wǒmende gùkè, jiùsuàn shì tāde cuò, nǐ yě bié hé tā zhēngchǎo.

他是我们的顾客，就算是他的错，你也别和他争吵。

He is our customer. Don't argue with him even if it's his fault.

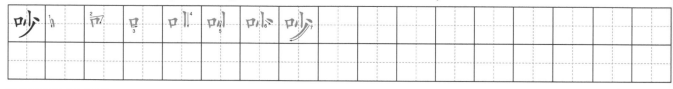

Useful phrases and sentences

6 STROKES   宀 RADICAL

安
ān
peace; safe

1. 安静 **ānjìng** quiet

Zhège gōngyuán rén hěn shǎo, fēicháng ānjìng.

这个公园人很少，非常安静。

There are very few people in this park. It's quiet.

2. 安排 **ānpái** arrangement; engagement

Zhōumò wǒ méiyǒu shénme ānpai, zhǐ xiǎng hǎohao xiūxi yíxia.

周末我没有什么安排，只想好好休息一下。

I have no engagements this weekend. I just want to have a good rest.

3. 安全 **ānquán** safe

Kāichēde shíhou dǎ diànhuà hěn bù ānquán.

开车的时候打电话很不安全。

It's not safe to make phone calls while driving.

4. 安慰 **ānwèi** to comfort

Xiǎo Táng hěn huì ānwèi rén, gēn tā liáowán xīngqíng hǎo duōle.

小唐很会安慰人，跟他聊完心情好多了。

Xiao Tang is good at bringing comfort to people. I feel much better after talking to him.

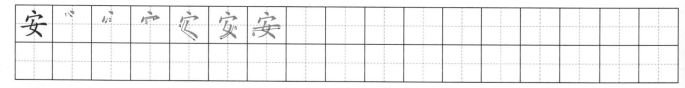

Useful phrases and sentences

14 STROKES   青 RADICAL

静
jìng
calm; serene

1. 静一静 **jìngyijìng** calm down

Bié dānxīn wǒ, wǒ zhǐ shì xūyào zìjǐ jìngyijìng.

别担心我，我只是需要自己静一静。

Don't worry about me. I just need a moment to calm down.

2. 静下来 **jìngxiàlai** calm down

Nǐ xiān bié zháojí, děng jìngxiàlai hǎohao xiǎngxiang, zǒng yǒu bànfa jiějué.

你先别着急，等静下来好好想想，总有办法解决。

Don't worry. You need to calm down and think. There is always a solution.

3. 静音 **jìngyīn** silent mode

Yīnyuèhuì mǎshàng kāishǐ, qǐng dàjiā bǎ shǒujī tiáochéng jìngyīn.

音乐会马上开始，请大家把手机调成静音。

The concert will start momentarily. Please turn your cell phones into silent mode.

4. 动静 **dòngjìng** sound of activity

Nǐ tīng, wàimian hǎoxiàng yǒu shénme dòngjing, yǒu rén lái ma?

你听，外面好像有什么动静，有人来吗？

Listen, there seems to be some sound of activity outside. Anyone out there?

CHARACTER 03

9 STROKES ⟶ **RADICAL**

洗
xǐ
wash

Useful phrases and sentences

1. 洗 **xǐ** wash

Chēzi tài zāngle, wǒmen děi xǐxile.
车子太脏了，我们得洗洗了。
The car is too dirty and requires a wash.

2. 洗手间 **xǐshǒujiān** bathroom; restroom

Zhège sùshède tiáojiàn hěn hǎo, měige xuésheng
dōu yǒu zìjǐde xǐshǒujiān.
这个宿舍的条件很好，每个学生都有自己的洗手间。
*This dormitory is well-equipped. Every student has
their own bathroom.*

3. 洗澡 **xǐzǎo** shower

Nǐ xíguàn zǎoshang xǐzǎo háishi wǎnshang xǐzǎo?
你习惯早上洗澡还是晚上洗澡？
*Do you usually shower in the morning or in the
evening?*

4. 洗衣店 **xǐyīdiàn** laundromat

Duìmiàn nàjiā xǐyīdiàn hěn piányi, xǐ yíjiàn chènyī
zhǐ yào liǎngkuài qián.
对面那家洗衣店很便宜，洗一件衬衣只要两块钱。
*The laundromat across from here is cheap. One shirt
costs only two kuai.*

洗 丶 丶 氵 氵 沪 汼 洗 洗 洗

CHARACTER 04

3 STROKES 卩 **RADICAL**

卫
wèi
to guard;
defend

Useful phrases and sentences

1. 卫生 **wèishēng** hygiene; sanitation

Tā hěn jiǎngjiū wèishēng, měicì chīfàn yǐqián
yídìng yào xǐshǒu.
他很讲究卫生，每次吃饭以前一定要洗手。
*He really cares about hygiene. He always washes his
hands before eating.*

2. 卫生间 **wèishēngjiān** restroom

Zhèdòng gòuwù zhòngxīnde wèishēngjiān zài
èrlóu hé sìlóu jí dìxià yīlóu.
这栋购物中心的卫生间在二楼和四楼及地下一楼。
*The restrooms in this shopping mall are located on
the second and fourth floors, and basement 1.*

3. 卫生纸 **wèishēngzhǐ** toilet paper

Xiǎo Gāo, chūqù máfan mǎi diǎn wèishēngzhǐ.
小高，出去麻烦买点卫生纸。
*Xiao Gao, please buy some toilet paper when you go
out.*

4. 卫冕 **wèimiǎn** defending champion

Gēge shì qùnián quánguó yóuyǒng bǐsàide
guànjūn, xīwàng tā jīnnián kěyǐ wèimiǎn.
哥哥是去年全国游泳比赛的冠军，希望他今年可以
卫冕。
*My older brother was the National Swimming Cham-
pion last year. I hope he will defend his title this year.*

卫 乛 卫 卫

CHARACTER 105

12 STROKES 厂 **RADICAL**

厨
chú
kitchen

Useful phrases and sentences

1. 厨房 **chúfáng** kitchen

Zhèjiān chúfáng yǒudiǎnxiǎo, lián cānzhuō dōu
fàngbúxià.
这间厨房有点小，连餐桌都放不下。
*This kitchen is a bit small. It can't even accommodate
a dining table.*

2. 厨具 **chújù** kitchenware

Zhètào chújù búdàn hǎokàn, érqiě hěn hǎoyòng.
这套厨具不但好看，而且很好用。
*This set of kitchenware is not only pretty, but also
practical.*

3. 厨师 **chúshī** chef

Lǎo Lǐ kāishǐ shì yìmíng chúshī, hòulái zìjǐ kāile
yìjiā fànguǎnr.
老李开始是一名厨师，后来自己开了一家饭馆儿。
*Lao Li started as a chef. He later opened his own
restaurant.*

4. 厨艺 **chúyì** cooking skills

Wǒmen jiā bàbade chúyì zuìhǎo, zuò shénme cài
dōu hǎochī.
我们家爸爸的厨艺最好，做什么菜都好吃。
*My father's cooking skills are the best in our family.
Everything he cooks is tasty.*

厨 一 厂 厂 厈 厨 厨 厨 厨 厨 厨 厨

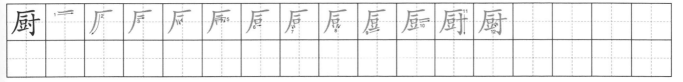

Part 1 Choose from the following words to fill in the blanks.

租、换、让、洗、坏

1. 这里的房费太贵了，我想找朋友跟我一起（　　　　　）房子。

2. 李经理，有一个叫王国生的人（　　　　　）您给他回个电话。

3. 这台电脑已经用了六七年了，太慢了，是应该（　　　　　）一台新的了。

4. 哎！电梯怎么又（　　　　　）了，只好走上去了。

Part 2 Complete the following dialogues using Chinese characters.

1. A: 你租过房子吗？你的房东人怎么样？

    B: _____ 。

2. A: 你喜欢租什么样的房子？你觉得什么最重要？

    B: _____ 。

3. A: 你喜欢自己住还是喜欢跟别人一起住？为什么？

    B: _____ 。

4. A: 你觉得租房好还是买房好？为什么？

    B: _____ 。

5. A: 在你住的城市，租房贵不贵？一个月大概需要多少钱？

    B: _____ 。

Part 3 学以致用

今年夏天，你要去上海实习，需要自己租房子。请你想一想自己需要租一个什么样的房子，然后把自己的要求写下来。

1. 房子的大小（几室几厅？）

2. 你自己租还是跟别人一起租？

3. 一个月可以付多少钱？

4. 房子的位置（希望离哪儿比较近？）

5. 要不要有家具（如果要，希望有什么家具？）

6. 其他问题

LESSON 8

Family Get Togethers 家庭活动

1. Dialogue

Read the dialogue below and answer the questions in characters.

琳达，美国人，刚到北京工作三个月，王云是她的同事。

琳达：	王云，你这周末有什么安排吗？
王云：	这周末我们过节啊，中秋节。你知道中秋节吗？
琳达：	是不是有点儿像美国的"感恩节"？人们都要回家跟家人团聚。
王云：	没错！在我们家，爷爷说中秋节家人必须在一起。爸爸、妈妈、叔叔、阿姨、兄弟姐妹一个都不能少。
琳达：	中秋节还要吃月饼，对吗？
王云：	对！我特别爱吃月饼！你呢？
琳达：	我还没吃过呢！
王云：	那你有没有兴趣跟我们一起过中秋节？
琳达：	当然有！那我到时候买盒月饼带过去吧。
王云：	月饼都已经买好了，你什么都不用买，带上你的丈夫和孩子就行！
琳达：	那多不好意思。
王云：	别这么客气。我们家人看到你来一定会很高兴。那我们周日见吧！
琳达：	好的，周日见！

1. 琳达听说过中国的 "中秋节" 吗？ ....

2. 中国人怎么过中秋节？ ....

3. 王云让琳达带什么去她的家？ ....

2. Vocabulary

	Word	Pinyin	English equivalent
1.	中秋节	**Zhōngqiūjié**	Mid-Autumn Festival
2.	感恩节	**Gǎnēnjié**	Thanksgiving
3.	团聚	**tuánjù**	gather
4.	必须	**bìxū**	must
5.	叔叔	**shūshu**	uncle
6.	阿姨	**āyí**	aunt
7.	兄弟姐妹	**xiōngdì jiěmèi**	siblings
8.	月饼	**yuèbǐng**	mooncake
9.	爱	**ài**	love
10.	兴趣	**xìngqù**	interest
11.	盒	**hé**	box
12.	带	**dài**	bring
13.	已经	**yǐjīng**	already
14.	丈夫	**zhàngfu**	husband
15.	孩子	**háizi**	child
16.	不好意思	**bùhǎoyìsi**	feel embarrassed

3. New Characters

Fifteen characters are introduced in this lesson. Use the following explanations to help you understand and remember the characters.

孩　丈　夫　爷　叔　阿　姨　兄　已　经　兴　趣　玩　爱　真

Useful phrases and sentences

9 STROKES   子 RADICAL

孩

hái
child

1. 小孩子 **xiǎo háizi** child; kid

   Dàgài méiyǒu xiǎo háizi bù xǐhuān táng hé qiǎokèlì ba.
   大概没有小孩子不喜欢糖和巧克力吧。
   Probably all kids like candy and chocolate.

2. 孩童 **háitóng** children

   Měicì xiangqi zìjǐde háitóng shídài, dōu juéde hěn měihǎo.
   每次想起自己的孩童时代，都觉得很美好。
   Whenever I think of my childhood I always feel it's wonderful.

3. 生孩子 **shēng háizi** to have a baby

   Xiànzài bù shēng háizide niánqīng rén yuè lái yuè duō le.
   现在不生孩子的年轻人越来越多了。
   More and more young people choose not to have babies.

4. 几个孩子 **jǐge háizi** how many children

   Nǐjiā yǒu jǐge háizi? Nánháir háishì nǚháir?
   你家有几个孩子？男孩儿还是女孩儿？
   How many children do you have? Boys or girls?

Useful phrases and sentences

3 STROKES   一 RADICAL

丈

zhàng
husband

1. 丈夫 **zhàngfu** husband

   Líndá gēn tāde zhàngfu shì zài péngyou jùhuìshang rènshide.
   琳达跟她的丈夫是在朋友聚会上认识的。
   Linda and her husband met at a friend's gathering.

2. 丈人 **zhàngren** father-in-law

   Huáng Yì dìyīcì jiàn zhàngrende shíhou hěn jǐnzhāng.
   黄逸第一次见丈人的时候很紧张。
   Huang Yi was quite nervous when he met his father-in-law the first time.

3. 丈母娘 **zhàngmǔniáng** wife's mother

   Jiāxìngde zhàngmǔniáng duì tā xiàng zìjǐde érzi yīyàng.
   家兴的丈母娘对他像自己的儿子一样。
   Jiaxing's mother-in-law treats him as her own son.

2. 姑丈 **gūzhàng** husband of paternal aunt

   Wǒ gūzhàng shì Sìchuān rén, 1949 nián dàole Táiwān.
   我姑丈是四川人，一九四九年到了台湾。
   My aunt's husband was from Sichuan. He went to Taiwan in 1949.

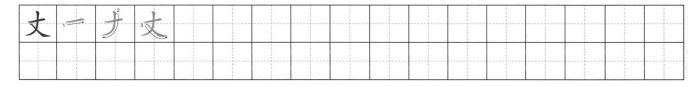

Useful phrases and sentences

4 STROKES   大 RADICAL

夫

fū
man; husband

1. 大夫 **dàifu** doctor

   Zhāng Dàifu, qǐngwèn zhège yào yìtiān chī jǐcì?
   张大夫，请问这个药一天吃几次？
   Dr. Zhang, how many times a day do I need to take this medication?

2. 夫妻 **fūqī** husband and wife; married couple

   Zhèduì lǎo fūqī dōu yǐjīng qīshíduōsuì le, tāmen měinián dōu huì guò Qíngrénjié.
   这对老夫妻都已经七十多岁了，他们每年都会过情人节。
   This old couple is in their seventies. They still celebrate Valentine's Day every year.

3. 夫人 **fūren** wife

   Wǒ gēn fūrén yāoqǐng gèwèi zhōumò lái jiālǐ chī wǎncān.
   我跟夫人邀请各位周末来家里吃晚餐。
   My wife and I invite you all to have dinner in our home this weekend.

4. 功夫 **gōngfu** kungfu; martial art

   Bùshǎo wàiguó rén duì xué Zhōngguó gōngfū hěn gǎn xìngqù.
   不少外国人对学中国功夫很感兴趣。
   Many foreigners are interested in learning Chinese kungfu.

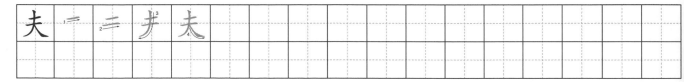

Useful phrases and sentences

6 STROKES **父 RADICAL**

爷

yé

paternal grandfather; old gentleman

1. 爷爷 **yéye** paternal grandfather

Yéye bù xíguàn gēn wǒmen zhù, tā juéde zìjǐ zhù gèng fāngbiàn.

爷爷不习惯跟我们住，他觉得自己住更方便。

My paternal grandfather is not used to living with us. He feels that it's more convenient to live on his own.

2. 爷孙 **yésūn** grandfather and grandchild

Tāmen yésūn gǎnqíng hěn hǎo, ràng rén xiànmù.

他们爷孙感情很好，让人羡慕。

The grandfather and grandchild have a very good relationship. People are envious.

3. 姥爷 **lǎoyé** maternal grandfather

Lǎoyé zhǐ huì shuō Sìchuān huà, bú huì shuō Pǔtōnghuà.

姥爷只会说四川话，不会说普通话。

My maternal grandfather speaks only Sichuanese; he doesn't speak Mandarin.

4. 大爷 **dàye** a respectful term for an old gentleman

Dàye máfan wèn nín yíxia, zhè fùjìn yǒuméiyou yóujú?

大爷麻烦问您一下，这附近有没有邮局？

Excuse me, Sir, is there a post office nearby?

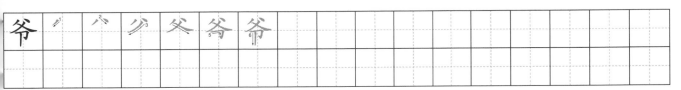

Useful phrases and sentences

8 STROKES **又 RADICAL**

叔

shū

uncle

1. 叔叔 **shūshu** uncle

Wáng Shūshu, xièxie nín sònggěi wǒde lǐwù.

王叔叔，谢谢您送给我的礼物。

Uncle Wang, thank you for the gift you gave me.

2. 叔父 **shūfù** father's younger brother; uncle

"Shūfù" zhǐde shì bàbade dìdi.

"叔父" 指的是爸爸的弟弟。

"Shufu" refers to your father's younger brothers.

3. 大叔 **dàshū** a respectful term for an old gentleman

Dàshū, nín yǒu língqián ma?

大叔，您有零钱吗？

Sir, do you have any change?

4. 叔侄 **shūzhí** uncle and nephew

Tāmen shūzhí liǎ zhǐ chà wǔsuì, kànqǐlái xiàng xiōngdì.

他们叔侄俩只差五岁，看起来像兄弟。

The uncle and his nephew are only five years apart in age. They look like brothers.

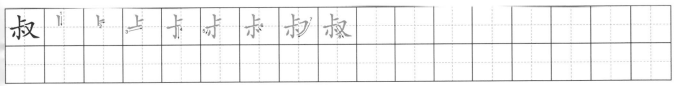

Useful phrases and sentences

7 STROKES **阝 RADICAL**

阿

ā

prefix before names or kinship terms

1. 阿根廷 **Āgēntíng** Argentina

Shìjièbēi zúqiúsài mǎshang kāishǐle, bàba zhīchí Āgēntíng duì, wǒ zhīchí Bāxī duì.

世界杯足球赛马上开始了，爸爸支持阿根廷队，我支持巴西队。

The World Cup soccer game is starting soon. My father supports Argentina and I support Brazil.

2. 阿拉伯 **Ālābó** Arab

Wǒmen xuéxiào míngnián huì kāi Ālābówénde kè.

我们学校明年会开阿拉伯文的课。

Our school will be offering Arabic language classes next year.

3. 阿富汗 **Āfùhàn** Afghanistan

Nǐ duì Āfùhànde liǎojiě yǒu duōshǎo?

你对阿富汗的了解有多少？

How much do you know about Afghanistan?

4. 阿联酋 **Āliánqiú** United Arab Emirates

Tīngshuō Āliánqiú Hángkōngde fúwù tèbié hǎo.

听说阿联酋航空的服务特别好。

I heard that Emirates' service is outstanding.

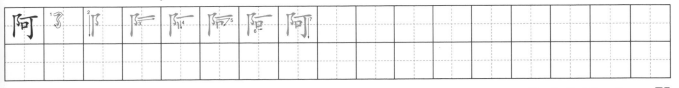

CHARACTER 112

姨

yí
aunt

9 STROKES | **女 RADICAL**

Useful phrases and sentences

1. 阿姨 **āyí** aunt

   Lǐ Āyí, nín néng jiāo wǒ zěnme bāo jiǎozi ma?
   李阿姨，您能教我怎么包饺子吗？
   Aunt Li, can you teach me how to make dumplings?

2. 姨妈 **yímā** mother's sister; aunt

   Māma gēn yímā zhǎngde hěn xiàng, kěshì tāmende xìnggé hěn bù yíyàng.
   妈妈跟姨妈长得很像，可是她们的性格很不一样。
   My mother and my aunt look alike, but their personalities are very different.

3. 姨丈 **yízhàng** husband of mother's sister; uncle

   Yízhàng qù mǎi yīdiǎn dōngxī, mǎshàng huílái.
   姨丈去买一点东西，马上回来。
   Your uncle is going to buy things. He will be right back.

4. 小姨 **xiǎoyí** mother's youngest sister; aunt

   Wǒ xiǎoyí zhùde lí wǒjiā bù yuǎn, shífēnzhōng jiù dàole.
   我小姨住得离我家不远，十分钟就到了。
   My aunt lives not far from us. It's only ten minutes away.

CHARACTER 113

兄

xiōng
older brother

5 STROKES | **儿 RADICAL**

Useful phrases and sentences

1. 兄弟姐妹 **xiōngdì jiěmèi** siblings

   Nǐmen jiā yǒu jǐge xiōngdì jiěmèi?
   你们家有几个兄弟姐妹？
   How many siblings do you have?

2. 兄妹 **xiōngmèi** older brother and younger sister

   Tāmen xiōngmèi liǎ fēicháng dúlì, cháng zìjǐ zuò fàn.
   他们兄妹俩非常独立，常自己做饭。
   The older brother and younger sister are both very independent. They often cook by themselves.

3. 兄长 **xiōngzhǎng** older brother

   "Xiōngzhǎng" jiù shì "gēgede yìsi.
   "兄长"就是"哥哥"的意思。
   "Xiongzhang" means "older brother."

4. 兄嫂 **xiōngsǎo** older brother's wife

   Wǒ xiōngsǎo shì Hánguó rén, Zhōngwén shuōde hěn hǎo.
   我兄嫂是韩国人，中文说得很好。
   My older brother's wife is Korean. Her Chinese is pretty good.

CHARACTER 114

已

yǐ
already

3 STROKES | **己 RADICAL**

Useful phrases and sentences

1. 已经 **yǐjīng** already

   Zhèbù diànyǐng wǒ yǐjīng kànguòle, hěn zhídé kàn.
   这部电影我已经看过了，很值得看。
   I've already seen this movie. It's worth it.

2. 已满 **yǐmǎn** already full

   Bàoqiàn, zhèmén kède rénshù yǐmǎn, bù néng zài bàomíngle.
   抱歉，这门课的人数已满，不能再报名了。
   I am sorry. This class is full and cannot take any new students.

3. 已往 **yǐwǎng** before

   Rújīnde nóngcūn biànhuà hěn dà, gēn yǐwǎng hěn bù yíyàng le.
   如今的农村变化很大，跟已往很不一样了。
   The rural villages have changed a lot and are very different from before.

4. 已婚 **yǐhūn** already married

   Nǐ zhīdao jièzhǐ dài nǎge shǒuzhǐ biǎoshì yǐhūn ma?
   你知道戒指带哪个手指表示已婚吗？
   Do you know which finger with a ring means "already married"?

CHARACTER 15

经

jīng
experience

1. 经过 **jīngguò** pass

Wǒ měitiān shàngbān dōu huì jīngguò yìjiā Rìběn chāoshì.
我每天上班都会经过一家日本超市。
I always pass by a Japanese supermarket on my way to work every day.

2. 经常 **jīngcháng** often; frequently

Wáng Yún bìyè yǐhòu hái jīngcháng huí xuéxiào kàn lǎoshī.
王云毕业以后还经常回学校看老师。
Wang Yun often returned to school to see her teachers after graduation.

3. 经验 **jīngyàn** experience

Bié kàn tā niánlìng xiǎo, kěshì tā gōngzuò jīngyàn hěn fēngfù.
别看他年龄小，可是他工作经验很丰富。
He looks young, but he has a lot of work experience.

4. 经历 **jīnglì** experience

Zài Yīngguó liúxuéde jīnglì zhēn ràng rén nánwàng!
在英国留学的经历真让人难忘！
The experience of studying abroad in the U.K. is unforgettable.

CHARACTER 16

兴

xìng/xīng
excitement/rise

1. 兴趣 **xìngqù** interest

Tā duì xuéxí tiānwénxué hěn yǒu xìngqù.
他对学习天文学很有兴趣。
He is interested in studying astronomy.

2. 兴奋 **xīngfèn** excited

Háizimen tīngdào míngtiān yào qù dòngwùyuán, xīngfènde shuìbuzháo jiào.
孩子们听到明天要去动物园，兴奋得睡不着觉。
When the kids heard that we are going to the zoo tomorrow, they became so excited that they couldn't sleep.

3. 兴隆 **xīnglóng** prosperous; thriving

Wáng Lǎobǎn, zhù nín xīn kāide fànguǎnr shēngyì xīnglóng.
王老板，祝您新开的饭馆儿生意兴隆！
Boss Wang, I wish you great success with your new restaurant.

4. 兴起 **xīngqǐ** rise

Suízhe kējìde jìnbù, wǎngluò xuéxí zhèng zài xīngqǐ.
随着科技的进步，网络学习正在兴起。
Online learning is on the rise with the progress of technology.

CHARACTER 117

趣

qù
interesting

1. 趣味 **qùwèi** interesting

Zhè běn shū dúqǐlái yìdiǎn qùwèi dōu méiyǒu.
这本书读起来一点趣味都没有。
This book is not interesting at all.

2. 趣事 **qùshì** interesting thing

Lǐ Jiàoshòu, nín néng shuō yíjiàn zài guówài shēnghuóde qùshì ma?
李教授，您能说一件在国外生活的趣事吗？
Professor Li, can you share one interesting thing about living abroad?

3. 风趣 **fēngqù** humorous

Mǎ Lǎoshī shuōhuà hěn fēngqù, xuésheng dōu ài tīng tā jiǎngkè.
马老师说话很风趣，学生都爱听他讲课。
Teacher Ma is humorous. Students love to hear him talk.

4. 乐趣 **lèqù** fun; pleasure

Nǐ juéde xuéxí wàiyǔ zuìdàde lèqù shì shénme?
你觉得学习外语最大的乐趣是什么？
What do you think is the most fun about learning foreign languages?

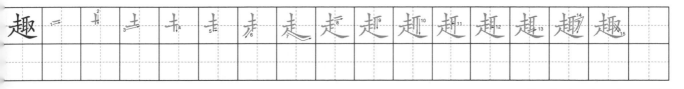

玩 wán
play; have fun

Useful phrases and sentences

1. 玩 **wán** play

   Yǐhòu yǒu kòng jiù cháng lái wǒmen jiā wánr ba.
   以后有空就常来我们家玩儿吧。
   You can come and play in our home when you have time.

2. 开玩笑 **kāi wánxiào** to joke

   Yán Lǎobǎn bù xǐhuān kāi wánxiào, nǐ gēn tā shuōhuà yào xiǎoxīn yīdiǎnr.
   严老板不喜欢开玩笑，你跟他说话要小心一点儿。
   Boss Yan doesn't like to joke. Be cautious when you talk to him.

3. 玩具 **wánjù** toy

   Yéye shuō wǒ xiǎoshíhòu zuì xǐhuānde wánjù shì diàndòng chē.
   爷爷说我小时候最喜欢的玩具是电动车。
   My grandfather said that when I was little my favorite toy was electric cars.

4. 好玩儿 **hǎowánr** for fun; for pleasure

   Zhège xiǎochéng fēngjǐng hěn měi, kěshì méi shénme hǎowánrde dìfāng.
   这个小城风景很美，可是没什么好玩儿的地方。
   The small town's scenery is pretty, but there are no places to have fun.

爱 ài
love; like

Useful phrases and sentences

1. 爱 **ài** like

   Wǒ hěn ài shuō Zhōngwén, dànshì bú ài liànxí hànzì.
   我很爱说中文，但是不爱练习汉字。
   I like to speak Chinese, but I don't like practicing characters.

2. 爱心 **àixīn** kind; compassion

   Xiǎo Ài hěn yǒu àixīn, chángcháng qù dòngwù bǎohù zǔzhī zhàogù xiǎodòngwù.
   小艾很有爱心，常常去动物保护组织照顾小动物。
   Xiao Ai is compassionate. She often goes to the humane society to take care of animals.

3. 爱好 **àihào** hobby

   Mèimei zhǐ yǒu yígè àihào, jiù shì kànshū.
   妹妹只有一个爱好，就是看书。
   My younger sister has only one hobby—reading.

4. 爱情 **àiqíng** romance; love

   "Liáng Shānbó yǔ Zhù Yīngtái" jiǎngde shì yígè gǎnrénde àiqíng gùshì.
   《梁山伯与祝英台》讲的是一个感人的爱情故事。
   "Liang Shanbo and Zhu Yingtai" is a moving love story.

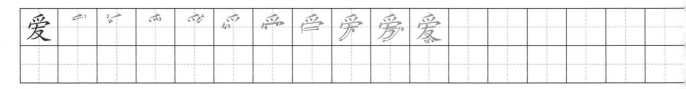

真 zhēn
really

Useful phrases and sentences

1. 真 **zhēn** really

   Tā cái sìsuì, xiǎotíqín lāde zhēn bàng a!
   她才四岁，小提琴拉得真棒啊！
   She is only four years old. She plays the violin really well.

2. 真人秀 **zhēnrénxiù** reality show

   Diànshì shàng yǒu hěnduō zhēnrénxiù jiémù, kěshì wǒ juéde yìdiǎnr yìsi dōu méiyǒu.
   电视上有很多真人秀节目，可是我觉得一点儿意思都没有。
   There are many reality shows on TV, but I feel that none of them is interesting.

3. 真实 **zhēnshí** true

   Zhège diànyǐngde gùshì shì zhēnshíde.
   这个电影的故事是真实的。
   This movie is based on a true story.

4. 真正 **zhēnzhèng** thorough; genuine

   Yàoxiǎng zhēnzhèng liǎojiě yígè guójiāde wénhuà xūyào hěncháng shíjiān.
   要想真正了解一个国家的文化需要很长时间。
   Thoroughly understanding the culture of a country takes a long time.

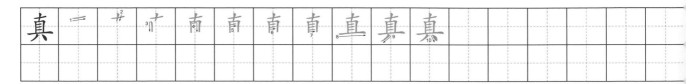

Lesson 8 Exercises

Part 1 Choose from the following words to fill in the blanks.

爱、真、孩子、兴趣、玩

1. 你都在宿舍待了一天了，咱们晚上出去（　　　　　）吧。

2. 我对玩儿电脑游戏一点儿（　　　　　）都没有。

3. 小王说他跟女朋友分手了，这是（　　　　　）的吗？

4. 小王说自己虽然是四川人，可是一点儿也不（　　　　　）吃辣的菜。

Part 2 Complete the following dialogues using Chinese characters.

1.　A: 你有一个大家庭吗？他们都是谁？

　　B: _____ 。

2.　A: 你跟家人会常常见面吗？

　　B: _____ 。

3.　A: 在你们国家，什么节日家人一定要团聚？

　　B: _____ 。

4.　A: 家人团聚的时候，一般会吃什么食物？

　　B: _____ 。

5.　A: 你知道中秋节吗？你吃过月饼吗？

　　B: _____ 。

你准备办一个家庭派对，请给你的亲戚写一个通知，告诉他们聚会在哪儿，什么时间，需要带什么食物，聚会上有什么活动。

时间：	地点：

带什么食物：

有什么活动：

LESSON 9

Can You Do Me a Favor? 你可以帮我一个忙吗?

1. Dialogue

Read the dialogue below and answer the questions in characters.

思明：	任真，你怎么了？
任真：	我后天就要搬到新公寓了，可是这么多东西，怎么办啊？
思明：	这有什么难的，找几个朋友帮忙啊。
任真：	这段时间大家都挺忙的，不太好意思麻烦大家。
思明：	客气什么！朋友不就是应该互相帮助嘛！
任真：	哦，还有，我想换个新床垫，但是不知道旧的应该扔到哪儿。
思明：	可以先放在门口，上面贴一张纸，写上"请带我走"，可能有人会拿去用。
任真：	好！还有，我需要租一辆车，你知道怎么租车吗？
思明：	很方便，租车公司就在"小河超市"的对面，费用是一天五十块。我可以陪你去。
任真：	对了，新公寓的灯好像有点儿问题，你能帮我检查下吗？
思明：	没问题，我特别喜欢修东西。
任真：	有你这个朋友真好！什么都懂，什么问题都有办法解决。等搬完家，一定得请你吃顿饭表示感谢。
思明：	那我就不客气了，我要好好想想吃什么！哈哈！

1. 任真为什么看起来不高兴？ _____

2. 任真的旧床垫会放在哪儿？她怎么去租车？ _____

3. 思明帮任真解决问题了吗？ _____

2. Vocabulary

	Word	Pinyin	English equivalent
1.	搬	**bān**	move
2.	公寓	**gōngyù**	apartment
3.	段	**duàn**	period
4.	麻烦	**máfan**	trouble
5.	应该	**yīnggāi**	should; ought to
6.	互相	**hùxiāng**	each other
7.	帮助	**bāngzhù**	help
8.	床垫	**chuángdiàn**	mattress
9.	旧的	**jiùde**	old ones
10.	放	**fàng**	put
11.	贴	**tiē**	paste
12.	带	**dài**	bring
13.	拿	**ná**	take
14.	河	**hé**	river
15.	超市	**chāoshì**	supermarket
16.	陪	**péi**	accompany
17.	灯	**dēng**	light
18.	检查	**jiǎnchá**	check
19.	修	**xiū**	fix
20.	懂	**dǒng**	know
21.	办法	**bànfǎ**	solution
22.	解决	**jiějué**	solve
23.	表示	**biǎoshì**	express

3. New Characters

Fifteen characters are introduced in this lesson. Use the following explanations to help you understand and remember the characters.

助　应　该　放　拿　带　搬　解　决　办　法　麻　烦　陪　懂

助

zhù
help; assist

Useful phrases and sentences

1. 帮助 bāngzhù help

Nǐ gāng dào zhèr, xūyào shénme bāngzhù suíshí gàosù wǒ.

你刚到这儿，需要什么帮助随时告诉我。

You have just arrived. Let me know if you need any help.

2. 助手 zhùshǒu assistant

Wáng Lǎobǎn duì tāde xīn zhùshǒu hěn mǎnyì.

王老板对他的新助手很满意。

Boss Wang is satisfied with her new assistant.

3. 自助 zìzhù self-serve

Xiànzài, zìzhù chāoshì hé zìzhù fànguǎnr yuè lái yuè duō le.

现在自助超市和自助饭馆儿越来越多了。

There are more and more self-serve supermarkets and self-serve restaurants nowadays.

4. 赞助 zànzhù sponsor

Zhècì mǎlāsōng bǐsài dédào hěn duō jiā gōngsīde zànzhù.

这次马拉松比赛得到很多家公司的赞助。

There are many company sponsors for this marathon.

助 丨 刀 月 日 且 助 助

应

yīng / yìng
should / apply

Useful phrases and sentences

1. 应当 yīngdāng should

Xuǎnzé zhíyè yīngdāng gēnjù zìjǐde xìngqù.

选择职业应当根据自己的兴趣。

You should choose a profession based on your interests.

2. 反应 fǎnyìng reaction

Guānzhòng duì zhèbù diànyǐngde fǎnyìng hěn bùtóng, yǒurén rènwéi hěn gǎndòng, yǒurén juéde méi yìsi.

观众对这部电影的反应很不同，有人认为很感动，有人觉得没意思。

The audience reacts differently to this movie. Some feel that it's touching while others think it's boring.

3. 应用 yīngyòng apply

Yuánzé nǐ dōu zhīdàole, xiàyībù shì zěnme yìngyòng.

原则你都知道了，下一步是怎么应用。

You already know the principles. The next step is how to apply them.

4. 应聘 yìngpìn apply for a position

Lái zhèjiā yóuxì gōngsī yìngpìnde dàduō shì niánqīngrén.

来这家游戏公司应聘的大多是年轻人。

The majority of people applying for jobs at this gaming company are young people.

应 丶 一 广 广 应 应 应

该

gāi
ought to; should

Useful phrases and sentences

1. 该 gāi should

Shíjiān bù zǎole, gāi xiūxile.

时间不早了，该休息了。

It's getting late. You should rest.

2. 应该 yīnggāi should

Lùshang jiāotōng bù hǎo, nǐ yīnggāi zǎodiǎnr chūmén.

路上交通不好，你应该早点儿出门。

The traffic is bad. You should hit the road earlier.

3. 不该 bùgāi should not

Fùmǔ bùgāi zǒng ná zìjǐde háizi gēn qítā háizi bǐ.

父母不该总拿自己的孩子跟其他孩子比。

Parents should not compare their own children with other children.

4. 本该 běngāi should have

Rèn Zhēn běn gāi jīntiān shàngwǔ dào Běijīng, kěshì fēijī wǎndiǎnle.

任真本该今天上午到北京，可是飞机晚点了。

Ren Zhen should have arrived in Beijing this morning, but her flight was delayed.

该 丶 讠 讠 计 讨 该 该 该

放

fàng
put

Useful phrases and sentences

1. 放 **fàng** put

   Wǒ yǐjīng bǎ shū fàngzài nǐde zhuōzi shàng le.
   我已经把书放在你的桌子上了。
   I've put the book on your table.

2. 放假 **fàngjià** on break

   Nǐmen gōngsī shénme shíhou fàngjià.
   你们公司什么时候放假？
   When does your company go on break?

3. 放心 **fàngxīn** rest assured

   Nǐmen fàngxīn, wǒ huì zhùyì hǎo zìjǐde shēntǐ de.
   你们放心，我会注意好自己的身体的。
   Please rest assured. I will take care of my health.

4. 放松 **fàngsōng** relax

   Dǎ Tàijí huòzhě zuò Yújiā dōu hěn ràng rén fàngsōng.
   打太极或者做瑜伽都很让人放松。
   Doing t'ai chi or yoga is very relaxing.

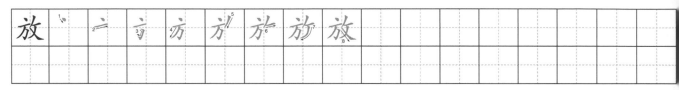

拿

ná
take

Useful phrases and sentences

1. 拿 **ná** take

   Nǐ shǒulǐ názhe shénme dōngxi?
   你手里拿着什么东西？
   What are you taking in your hand?

2. 拿走 **názǒu** take away

   Zhèxiē jiājù dōu búcuò, nǐ xǐhuān de huà dōu kěyǐ názǒu.
   这些家具都不错，你喜欢的话都可以拿走。
   These pieces of furniture are good. You can take them away if you like.

3. 推拿 **Tuīná** tuina (massage in TCM)

   Tuīná hòu wǒde shēntǐ shūfú duōle.
   推拿后我的身体舒服多了。
   My body feels much better after the tuina treatment.

4. 拿主意 **ná zhǔyì** make a decision

   Zhèjiàn shì nǐ děi zìjǐ juédìng, wǒ bù néng bāng nǐ ná zhǔyì.
   这件事你得自己决定，我不能帮你拿主意。
   You need to make a decision on this matter by yourself. I can't help.

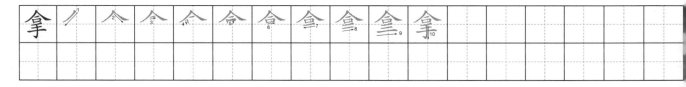

带

dài
bring

Useful phrases and sentences

1. 带 **dài** bring

   Nǐ zěnme dài zhème duō lǐwù! Tài kèqile.
   你怎么带这么多礼物！太客气了。
   Why did you bring so many gifts? You are too kind.

2. 带钱 **dài qián** bring money

   Gāo Zhì'ān zuótiān qǐng péngyou chīfàn, kěshì wàngle dài qián.
   高志安昨天请朋友吃饭，可是忘了带钱。
   Gao Zhi'an invited friends to dinner yesterday, but he forgot to bring money.

3. 携带 **xiédài** bring

   Gèwèi chéngkè, qǐng suíshēn xiédài zìjǐde guìzhòng wùpǐn.
   各位乘客，请随身携带自己的贵重物品。
   Dear passengers, please bring your own personal belongings with you.

4. 领带 **lǐngdài** necktie

   Fùqīnjié nàtiān, Dàhǎi sònggěi bàba yìtiáo lǐngdài.
   父亲节那天，大海送给爸爸一条领带。
   Dahai gave his father a necktie on Father's Day

CHARACTER 127

搬

bān
move

Useful phrases and sentences

1. 搬 **bān** move

Qǐng bǎ zhèzhāng chuáng bāndào lóushangde wòshì.
请把这张床搬到楼上的卧室。
Please move this bed to the bedroom upstairs.

2. 搬家 **bānjiā** move

Nǐ zěnme yòu yào bānjiā le? Zhècì bān dào nǎr ne?
你怎么又要搬家了？这次搬到哪儿呢？
How come you are moving again? Where are you moving to this time?

3. 搬进来 **bānjìnlai** move in

Xīn shìyǒu shuō tā míngtiān xiàwǔ huì bānjìnlai.
新室友说他明天下午会搬进来。
My new roommate said that he will move in tomorrow afternoon.

4. 搬不动 **bānbudòng** unable to move

Nàge shūguì tài zhòngle, liǎngge rén kěndìng bānbudòng.
那个书柜太重了，两个人肯定搬不动。
That bookshelf is too heavy. Two people were unable to move it.

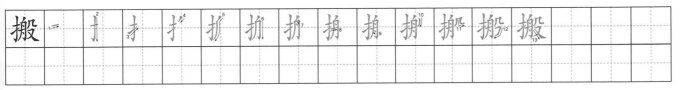

CHARACTER 128

解

jiě
to explain;
to know

Useful phrases and sentences

1. 讲解 **jiǎngjiě** explanation

Zhètào Zhōngwénshū hěn hǎo, tèbié shì yǔfǎ jiǎngjiěde hěn qīngchu.
这套中文书很好，特别是语法讲解得很清楚。
This set of Chinese books is very good. Its grammatical explanations are particularly clear.

2. 了解 **liǎojiě** know

Nǐ liǎojiě Zhōngguó gēn Měiguó Pīngpāng Wàijiāode lìshǐ ma?
你了解中国跟美国"乒乓外交"的历史吗？
Do you know the history of Ping-Pong Diplomacy between China and the U.S.A.?

3. 解释 **jiěshì** explain

Yīnwèi tāde Yīngwén bú tài hǎo, duìfāng jiěshìle bàntiān tā yě méi tīngdǒng.
因为他的英文不太好，对方解释了半天他也没听懂。
Because his English is not good, he doesn't understand even though people explain.

4. 理解 **lǐjiě** understand

Xuéle zhè yíkè yǐhòu, wǒ lǐjiěle Zhōngguó rén wèishénme yào quànjiǔ.
学了这一课以后，我理解了中国人为什么要劝酒。
After this lesson, I understand why Chinese people encourage you to drink in a banquet.

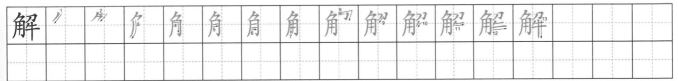

CHARACTER 129

jué
to decide

Useful phrases and sentences

1. 解决 **jiějué** solve

Zhōngguó xūyào jiějué rénkǒu lǎolínghuàde wèntí.
中国需要解决人口老龄化的问题。
China needs to solve the issue of an aging population.

2. 下决心 **xiàjuéxīn** determine

Tā xià juéxīn yào gǎidiào áoyède huài xíguàn.
他下决心要改掉熬夜的坏习惯。
He is determined to get rid of his habit of staying up late.

3. 决定 **juédìng** decide

Tā juédìng shǔjià qù yìjiā Rìběn yīyào gōngsī shíxí.
她决定暑假去一家日本医药公司实习。
She has decided to intern at a Japanese pharmaceutical company in the summer.

4. 决赛 **juésài** final (in a competition)

Jiějie míngtiān yào cānjiā huábīng bǐsài juésài, wǒ yào qù zhīchí tā.
姐姐明天要参加滑冰比赛决赛，我要去支持她。
My sister is having a skating final tomorrow. I am going there to cheer for her.

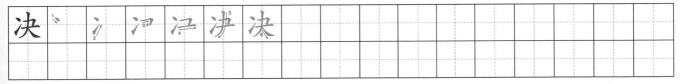

CHARACTER 130

办

bàn
to do; to manage

4 STROKES 力 **RADICAL**

Useful phrases and sentences

1. 办事 **bànshì** handle things; work

   Míngtiān xiàwǔ Zhāng Lǜshī zài wàimiàn bànshì, bú huì zài gōngsī.
   明天下午张律师在外面办事，不会在公司。
   Attorney Zhang is working out of the office tomorrow afternoon. He will not be in.

2. 办法 **bànfǎ** solution

   Bié zháojí, shénme shìqing dōu yǒu bànfǎ jiějué.
   别着急，什么事情都有办法解决。
   Don't worry. There is a solution to everything.

3. 办签证 **bàn qiānzhèng** apply for a visa

   Nǐ shénme shíhou qù Měiguó Dàshǐguǎn bàn qiānzhèng?
   你什么时候去美国大使馆办签证？
   When are you going to the U.S. Embassy to apply for visa?

4. 举办 **jǔbàn** hold; host

   Zhège xīngqī sān xuéxiào huì jǔbàn yíng xīnnián huódòng.
   这个星期三学校会举办迎新年活动。
   The school will hold an event to celebrate the New Year this Wednesday.

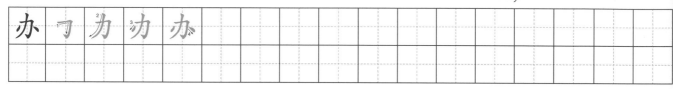

CHARACTER 131

法

fǎ
law; way

8 STROKES 氵 **RADICAL**

Useful phrases and sentences

1. 法律 **fǎlǜ** law

   Tīngshuō xué fǎlǜ zhuānyède xuésheng fēicháng xīnkǔ, zhǎo gōngzuò yě bù róngyì.
   听说学法律专业的学生非常辛苦，找工作也不容易。
   It is said that majoring in law is tough. It's also not easy for students to find a job.

2. 写法 **xiěfǎ** way of writing

   Yǒuxiē Hànzì yǒu jiǎntǐ hé fántǐ liǎngzhǒng xiěfǎ.
   有些汉字有简体和繁体两种写法。
   Some Chinese characters are written in two ways: simplified and traditional.

3. 做法 **zuòfǎ** way of doing

   Yú yǒu hěnduōzhǒng zuòfǎ, wǒ zuì xǐhuānde shì qīngzhēng.
   鱼有很多种做法，我最喜欢的是清蒸。
   There are many ways to cook fish. My favorite is steaming.

4. 看法 **kànfǎ** opinion

   Xuésheng xǐhuān Gù Jiàoshòu shì yīnwèi tā yuànyì tīng xuéshengde kànfǎ.
   学生喜欢顾教授是因为他愿意听学生的看法。
   The reason why students like Professor Gu is because he is willing to listen to their opinions.

CHARACTER 132

麻

má
numb

11 STROKES 麻 **RADICAL**

Useful phrases and sentences

1. 麻 **má** numbing

   Mápó Dòufu yòu má yòu là, chīqǐlái hěn xiāng.
   麻婆豆腐又麻又辣，吃起来很香。
   Mapo dofu is spicy and numbing. It tastes great.

2. 麻烦 **máfan** trouble

   Nín wèi wǒmen zhǔnbèile zhème duō cài, zhēnshì tài máfan nín le.
   您为我们准备了这么多菜，真是太麻烦您了。
   You went to the trouble of preparing so many dishes for us.

3. 麻辣 **málà** hot and numbing

   Huǒguō nǐ xǐhuān chī málàde háishì qīngdàn diǎnrde?
   火锅你喜欢吃麻辣的还是清淡点儿的？
   Regarding hot pot, do you like it hot and numbing or non-spicy?

4. 麻药 **máyào** anesthesia

   Bié pà, dǎle máyào yìdiǎnr dōu bù téng.
   别怕，打了麻药一点儿都不疼。
   Don't be afraid. It's not painful at all with anesthesia.

烦

fán
bother;
annoy

10 STROKES | **火 RADICAL**

Useful phrases and sentences

1. 烦人 fánrén annoying

Tā lǎoshì kāi wǒde wánxiào, zhēn fánrén!
他老是开我的玩笑，真烦人！
He often plays tricks on me. It's really annoying!

2. 烦恼 fánnǎo worry

Měigè rénde shēnghuó dōu yǒu gāoxìngde shì hé fánnǎo de shì.
每个人的生活都有高兴的事和烦恼的事。
Everyone has both happiness and worries in life.

3. 烦心 fánxīn worry

Nǐ zuìjìn kànqǐlai bú tài gāoxìng, pèngdào shénme fánxīn shì le ma?
你最近看起来不太高兴，碰到什么烦心事了吗？
You looked unhappy recently. Is there anything that worries you?

4. 不耐烦 búnàifán impatient

Zhè háizi bùtíngde wèn wǒ wèntí, rang wǒ yǒu diǎnr búnàifán.
这孩子不停地问我问题，让我有点儿不耐烦。
This child asks me questions one after another. I am becoming a bit impatient.

陪

péi
accompany

10 STROKES | **阝 RADICAL**

Useful phrases and sentences

1. 陪 péi accompany

Nǐ zhème bù shūfu, háishì ràng wǒ péi nǐ qù yīyuàn ba.
你这么不舒服，还是让我陪你去医院吧。
You are so ill. Let me accompany you to the hospital.

2. 陪同 péitóng accompany

Sūn Lǎoshī huì péitóng Xiàozhǎng qù cānguān Běijīng Dàxué.
孙老师会陪同校长去参观北京大学。
Teacher Sun will accompany the school president to visit Beijing University.

3. 陪伴 péibàn company

Duì hěnduō lǎorén láishuō, tāmen xūyàode shì érnǚde péibàn.
对很多老人来说，他们需要的是儿女的陪伴。
For many elderly people, what they need is the company of their children.

4. 失陪 shīpéi polite phrase for taking leave

Duìbùqǐ, wǒ xiān zǒule, shīpéile.
对不起，我先走了，失陪了。
I am sorry but I have to go. Please excuse me.

懂

dǒng
know;
understand

15 STROKES | **忄 RADICAL**

Useful phrases and sentences

1. 懂 dǒng understand

Nín kěyǐ zài shuō yíbiàn ma? Wǒ méi dǒng nínde yìsi.
您可以再说一遍吗？我没懂您的意思。
Can you please say it again? I don't understand what you mean.

2. 听懂 tīngdǒng understand (through listening)

Tā jīntiānde kè wánquán méi tīngdǒng.
他今天的课完全没听懂。
He didn't understand today's class at all.

3. 懂事 dǒngshì thoughtful; considerate

Xiǎo Ān shì yíge dǒngshìde háizi, bù xū bàmā dānxīn.
小安是一个懂事的孩子，不需爸妈担心。
Xiao An is very thoughtful. His parents don't need to worry about him.

4. 看懂 kàndǒng understand (through reading)

Zhèjù huàlǐde měige zì wǒ dōu rènshi, kě shì méi kàndǒng shì shénme yìsi.
这句话里的每个字我都认识，可是没看懂是什么意思。
I know every character in this sentence, but I don't know what it means.

Lesson 9 Exercises

Part 1 Choose from the following words to fill in the blanks.

麻烦、帮助、带、陪、办法

我的室友叫安山，他人很好，常常愿意（　　　　）别人。上周五我去饭馆儿吃饭没

（　　　　　）钱，他就跑来给我送钱。这个星期我病了，发高烧、咳嗽，安山就（　　　　　）

我去医院看医生，每天帮我买饭，一点儿也不觉得（　　　　　）。真高兴我有这么好的室友。

Part 2 Complete the following dialogues using Chinese characters.

1. A: 你搬家的时候请朋友帮过忙吗？

   B: _____ 。

2. A: 你会帮你的朋友做什么？

   B: _____ 。

3. A: 要是你的朋友向你借钱，你会帮他吗？

   B: _____ 。

4. A: 你的朋友帮了你的忙，你怎么谢谢他？

   B: _____ 。

5. A: 你碰到什么问题会找家人帮忙解决？

   B: _____ 。

上个星期你生病了。你的室友安山给了你很多帮助，陪你去医院，帮你买饭等等。你准备给他写一张感谢卡。请你在卡片上写几句感谢的话，另外想请他跟你这个周末吃晚饭。

LESSON 10

Is Your Job Hectic? 你最近工作忙不忙？

1. Dialogue

Read the dialogue below and answer the questions in characters.

小牛：	你最近工作忙不忙？
小蔡：	忙死了！昨天几乎没怎么吃饭、喝水，一天下来又饿又渴。
小牛：	你工作一直这么努力，经理对你很满意吧？
小蔡：	别提了！最近总被批评，说我做事粗心，应该再细心一点儿。你工作怎么样？
小牛：	我不怎么忙。可是今年经济情况不好，公司赚不到钱，真害怕哪天关门了。
小蔡：	你也别太担心了，说不定明年经济情况就好起来了呢。
小牛：	算了，咱们不说工作了，说点儿高兴的事情吧！
小蔡：	对了，下个星期乒乓球俱乐部会举行一场比赛，你想参加吗？
小牛：	好啊！星期几？在哪儿？
小蔡：	我还不太清楚，等问好了告诉你。
小牛：	好，那我就等你电话了。
小蔡：	行！

1. 小蔡工作忙不忙？老板对小蔡满意吗？ ....

2. 小牛的公司今年怎么样？小牛担心什么事情？ ....

3. 小蔡跟小牛下个星期要做什么？ ....

2. Vocabulary

	Word	Pinyin	English equivalent
1.	几乎	**jīhū**	almost
2.	饿	**è**	hungry
3.	渴	**kě**	thirsty
4.	一直	**yìzhí**	continuously; all long
5.	努力	**nǔlì**	hardworking
6.	经理	**jīnglǐ**	manager
7.	满意	**mǎnyì**	satisfied; content
8.	被	**bèi**	by (used in the passive)
9.	批评	**pīping**	criticize
10.	粗心	**cūxīn**	careless; reckless
11.	细心	**xìxīn**	careful; attentive
12.	经济	**jīngjì**	economy
13.	情况	**qíngkuàng**	situation
14.	赚	**zhuàn**	make (money)
15.	害怕	**hàipà**	afraid; fcar
16.	担心	**dānxīn**	worry
17.	说不定	**shuōbúdìng**	maybe
18.	算了	**suànle**	forget about it
19.	举行	**jǔxíng**	hold
20.	参加	**cānjiā**	attend; join
21.	清楚	**qīngchǔ**	clear

3. New Characters

Fifteen characters are introduced in this lesson. Use the following explanations to help you understand and remember the characters.

努　力　担　心　满　意　虽　参　加　饿　粗　细　害　怕　算

CHARACTER 136

努

nǔ
to strive

Useful phrases and sentences

1. 努力 **nǔlì** hardworking

   Gēge xuéxí yìzhí hěn nǔlì, zuìhòu kǎoshàngle lǐxiǎngde dàxué.
   哥哥学习一直很努力，最后考上了理想的大学。
   My older brother is hardworking and has matriculated to a good college.

2. 努力学习 **nǔlì xuéxí** study hard

   Cóngxiǎo fùmǔ jiù gàosù wǒ yào nǔlì xuéxí.
   从小父母就告诉我要努力学习。
   My parents have told me to study hard since I was young.

3. 努力工作 **nǔlì gōngzuò** work hard

   Wèile duō zhèng diǎn qián, Yǔjié měitiān nǔlì gōngzuò, yíge rén dǎ liǎngfèn gōng.
   为了多挣点钱，宇杰每天努力工作，一个人打两份工。
   To make more money, Yujie works hard every day. He has two jobs outside of his class time.

4. 共同努力 **gòngtóngnǔyì** joint effort

   Zhècì bǐsài qǔdé dìyīmíng shì dàjiā gòngtóng nǔlìde jiéguǒ.
   这次比赛取得第一名是大家共同努力的结果。
   Winning first prize is the result of a joint effort of everyone.

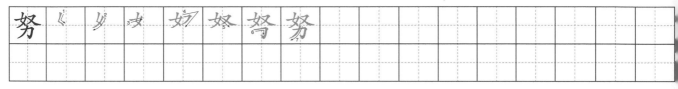

CHARACTER 137

力

lì
power; strength

Useful phrases and sentences

1. 体力 **tǐlì** physical strength

   Zhèzhǒng yǐnliào kěyǐ hěn hǎode bǔchōng tǐlì.
   这种饮料可以很好地补充体力。
   This beverage adequately replenishes your physical strength.

2. 力量 **lìliàng** power

   Zhōngguó zài nǔlì tígāo zìjǐde jīngjì lìliàng.
   中国在努力提高自己的经济力量。
   China is working hard to elevate its economic power.

3. 创造力 **chuàngzàolì** creativity

   Zhèxiē xuésheng búdàn nǔlì, érqiě hái hěn yǒu chuàngzàolì.
   这些学生不但努力，而且还很有创造力。
   These students are not only hardworking, but they are also very creative.

4. 尽力 **jìnlì** do one's best

   Nǐ fàngxīn, wǒ huì jìnlì bāng nǐde máng.
   你放心，我会尽力帮你的忙。
   Please rest assured. I will do my best to help you.

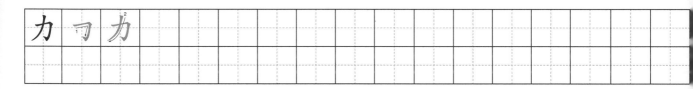

CHARACTER 138

担

dān
to undertake

Useful phrases and sentences

1. 担心 **dānxīn** worried

   Wǒ dānxīn míngtiān huì shuìguòtóu, nǐ kěyǐ jiào yíxià wǒ ma?
   我担心明天会睡过头，你可以叫一下我吗？
   I am worried that I may oversleep tomorrow. Can you wake me up?

2. 担任 **dānrèn** to serve as; to assume the office of

   Dàjiā dōu hěn guānxīn xīn xiàozhǎngde zhíwèi huì yóu shéi dānrèn.
   大家都很关心新校长的职位会由谁担任。
   Everyone is concerned about who is going to assume the office of new school president.

3. 承担 **chéngdān** undertake

   Xiǎo Cài zài gōngsī zǒngshì zhǔdòng chéngdān hěnduō gōngzuò.
   小蔡在公司总是主动承担很多工作。
   Xiao Cai is always actively undertaking many jobs in the company.

4. 负担 **fùdān** afford

   Měiguó dàxuéde xuéfèi hěn guì, hěnduō jiātíng dōu fùdānbùqǐ.
   美国大学的学费很贵，很多家庭都负担不起。
   College tuition in the US is very expensive. Many families cannot afford it.

Useful phrases and sentences

4 STROKES   心 **RADICAL**

心
xīn
heart; mind

1. 关心 **guānxīn** care

Lǎoshī bù yīnggāi zhǐ guānxīn xuéshengde kǎoshì chéngjì.

老师不应该只关心学生的考试成绩。

Teachers shouldn't only care about their students' test grades.

2. 有信心 **yǒuxìnxīn** have confidence

Wǒ duì women gōngsīde fāzhǎn hěnyǒu xìnxīn, dàjiā yào gòngtóng nǔlì.

我对我们公司的发展很有信心，大家要共同努力。

I have great confidence in the development of our company. Everyone needs to work together.

3. 小心 **xiǎoxīn** careful; cautious

Zhèr chē hěnduō, guò mǎlù yào xiǎoxīn yìdiǎnr.

这儿车很多，过马路要小心一点儿。

There are many cars here. Be careful when you cross roads.

4. 伤心 **shāngxīn** sad; heartbroken

Xiǎogǒu sǐle, Xiǎo Niú shāngxīnjíle, sāntiān méiyǒu chīfàn.

小狗死了，小牛伤心极了，三天没有吃饭。

Xiao Niu was heartbroken over his dog's death. He didn't eat for three days.

心 心 心 心

CHARACTER 40

Useful phrases and sentences

13 STROKES   氵 **RADICAL**

满
mǎn
full

1. 满 **mǎn** full

Zhèjiā kāfēiguǎnr zǒngshì zuòmǎnle rén.

这家咖啡馆儿总是坐满了人。

This coffee shop is always full.

2. 满意 **mǎnyì** satisfied

Wǒ yǐjīng jìnlìle, kěshì lǎobǎn duì wǒde gōngzuò háishi bù mǎnyì.

我已经尽力了，可是老板对我的工作还是不满意。

I've done my best, but my boss is still not satisfied with my work.

3. 满口 **mǎnkǒu** a mouthful

Jiāng Píng nàge rén mǎnkǒu huǎnghuà, nǐ qiānwàn bié xiāngxìn tā.

江平那个人满口谎话，你千万别相信他。

Jiang Ping is telling a mouthful of lies. Don't you trust him.

4. 满身 **mǎnshēn** all over

Nǐ shì-bushì hēle hěnduō jiǔ? Zěnme mǎnshēnde jiǔwèir.

你是不是喝了很多酒？怎么满身的酒味儿！

You must have drunk a lot. You smell of alcohol all over.

满 氵 氵 汸 泮 泮 洪 满 满 满 满 满

CHARACTER 141

Useful phrases and sentences

13 STROKES   心 **RADICAL**

意
yì
idea; meaning

1. 同意 **tóngyì** agree

Lǎoshī tóngyì gěi wǒ xiě yìfēng tuījiànxìn.

老师同意给我写一封推荐信。

The teacher has agreed to write me a letter of recommendation.

2. 愿意 **yuànyì** willing

Nǐ yuànyì péi wǒ yìqǐ qù kàn fángzi ma?

你愿意陪我一起去看房子吗？

Are you willing to go and see a house with me?

3. 意思 **yìsi** meaning

Zhōngwénlǐ yíge cí kěnéng yǒu hǎo jǐge yìsi.

中文里一个词可能有好几个意思。

A word may have several meanings in Chinese.

4. 故意 **gùyì** on purpose

Bàoqiàn, wǒ bú shì gùyì bú gàosù nǐde, wǒ shì zhēnde wàngle.

抱歉，我不是故意不告诉你的，我是真的忘了。

I am sorry. It is not that I didn't tell you on purpose. I just forgot.

意 亠 立 音 音 音 音 音 意 意 意

虽

suī
although;
even though

9 STROKES · 虫 RADICAL

Useful phrases and sentences

1. 虽 **suī** though

   Zhètào fángzi suī xiǎo, dànshì zhùqǐlai hěn shūfu.
   这套房子虽小，但是住起来很舒服。
   Though this house is small, it's comfortable to live in.

2. 虽然 **suīrán** although

   Suīrán wǒ bú rènshì nǐ, dànshì wǒ xièxiè nǐ.
   虽然我不认识你，但是我谢谢你。
   Although I don't know you, I thank you.

3. 虽说 **suīshuō** even though

   Nàliàng chē suīshuō jiùdiǎnr, dànshì hěn hǎokāi.
   那辆车虽说旧点儿，但是很好开。
   Even though that car was a bit old, it was fun to drive.

4. 虽是 **suīshì** even if

   Jīnglǐ suīshì zhème shuō, dàn xīnlǐ què bù tóngyì.
   经理虽是这么说，但心里却不同意。
   Even if the manager said so, he actually disagreed.

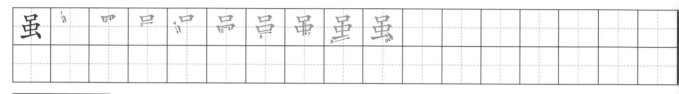

参

cān
join; participate

8 STROKES · 厶 RADICAL

Useful phrases and sentences

1. 参观 **cānguān** visit

   Míngtiān xuéxiào zǔzhī xuésheng qù cānguān yìshù bówùguǎn.
   明天学校组织学生去参观艺术博物馆。
   The school is taking students to visit the art museum tomorrow.

2. 参考 **cānkǎo** refer; reference

   Yàoshì nǐ yánjiū Tángdài lìshǐ, kěyǐ cānkǎo zhèběn shū.
   要是你研究唐代历史，可以参考这本书。
   You can refer to this book if your research is about the history of the Tang Dynasty.

3. 参加 **cānjiā** attend

   Wáng Jiàoshòu sìyuè yào qù Xīyǎtú cānjiā huìyì.
   王教授四月要去西雅图参加会议。
   Professor Wang is attending a conference in Seattle in April.

4. 参与 **cānyù** participate

   Gǎnxiè dàjiā cānyù jīntiānde huódòng.
   感谢大家参与今天的活动。
   Thank you for participating in the event today.

加

jiā
add

5 STROKES · 力 RADICAL

Useful phrases and sentences

1. 加 **jiā** add

   Cài dōu chī wánle, yàobuyào zài jiā liǎngge?
   菜都吃完了，要不要再加两个？
   The food is all gone. Shall we add two more dishes?

2. 增加 **zēngjiā** increase

   Gēn qùnián bǐ, jīnnián xué Zhōngwénde rénshù zēngjiāle wǔshírén.
   跟去年比，今年学中文的人数增加了五十人。
   In comparison to last year, the number of students enrolled for the Chinese class this year has increased by fifty people.

3. 加油 **jiāyóu** a phrase used to cheer somebody on

   Jiāyóu! Jiāyóu! Mǎshang jiù pǎodào zhōngdiǎnle!
   加油！加油！马上就跑到终点了！
   It's almost the finish line! Go, go, go!

4. 更加 **gèngjiā** even more

   Hùliánwǎng ràng rénmende shēnghuó gèngjiā fāngbiàn.
   互联网让人们的生活更加方便。
   The internet makes people's lives even more convenient.

饿

è
hungry

10 STROKES | **饣 RADICAL**

Useful phrases and sentences

1. **饿 è hungry**

   Wǔfàn chide tài duōle, wǒ xiànzài yìdiǎnr yě bú è.
   午饭吃得太多了，我现在一点儿也不饿。
   I ate too much for lunch and am not at all hungry now.

2. **饿死 èsǐ starving**

   Èsǐle! Kuàidiǎnr qù chīfàn ba.
   饿死了！快点儿去吃饭吧。
   I am starving! Let's go eat.

3. **挨饿 ái'è suffer hunger**

   Yéye shuō tā xiǎo shíhou chángcháng ái'è.
   爷爷说他小时候常常挨饿。
   My grandfather said that he often suffered from hunger when he was little.

4. **饿肚子 èdùzi stay hungry**

   Huìpíng jīntiān zǎoshang hěn wǎn qǐchuáng, méi shíjiān chī zǎofàn, zhǐhǎo èdùzi qù shàngbān.
   惠平今天早上很晚起床，没时间吃早饭，只好饿肚子去上班。
   Huiping got up late this morning. She didn't have time for breakfast, so she went to work hungry.

饿 | ⺈ | ⺈ | 饣 | 饣 | 饣 | 伐 | 饿 | 饿 | 饿

粗

cū
thick; careless

11 STROKES | **米 RADICAL**

Useful phrases and sentences

1. **粗 cū thick**

   Zhèzhī máobǐ tài cūle, yǒu xì yìdiǎnde ma?
   这只毛笔太粗了，有细一点的吗？
   This brush is too thick. Do you have a thinner one?

2. **粗心 cūxīn careless**

   Nǐ tài cūxīnle, kǎoshì jìngrán shǎo zuòle hǎojǐdào tí.
   你太粗心了，考试竟然少做了好几道题。
   You are too careless—you missed a few items in the test.

3. **粗鲁 cūlǔ rude**

   Tā shuōhuà hěn cūlǔ, duì biéren fēicháng bù yǒuhǎo.
   他说话很粗鲁，对别人非常不友好。
   He speaks rudely and is very unfriendly to other people.

4. **粗糙 cūcāo rough; coarse**

   Zhège huāpíng zuògōng yǒu diǎnr cūcāo.
   这个花瓶做工有点儿粗糙。
   The workmanship of this vase is a bit rough.

粗 | ` | ⺌ | 二 | 十 | 才 | 米 | 籵 | 籵 | 粗 | 粗 | 粗

细

xì
thin; detailed

8 STROKES | **纟 RADICAL**

Useful phrases and sentences

1. **细 xì thin**

   Nín yào chī xì miàntiáo háishì cū miàntiáo?
   您要吃细面条还是粗面条？
   Do you want thin noodles or thick noodles?

2. **仔细 zǐxì careful**

   Wǒ yǐjīng zǐxì jiǎnchále zhèpiān wénzhāng, bǎozhèng méiyǒu cuòzì.
   我已经仔细检查了这篇文章，保证没有错字。
   I've carefully reviewed this article. I guarantee that there is no error.

3. **详细 xiángxì in detail**

   Jǐngchá xiángxì xúnwènle tā fāshēng chēhuòde jīngguò.
   警察详细询问了他发生车祸的经过。
   The police asked him in detail the cause of the car accident.

4. **细心 xìxīn careful**

   Zhèmeduō nián lái dōu shì tā xìxīn zhàogù nǎinai.
   这么多年来都是她细心照顾奶奶。
   She has been carefully taking care of her grandmother for many years.

细 | 纟 | 纟 | 纟 | 纠 | 细 | 细 | 细 | 细

CHARACTER 148

hài
cause trouble to; harm

Useful phrases and sentences

1. 害怕 **hàipà** afraid
   Dìdi hàipà gǒu, wǒ hàipà māo.
   弟弟害怕狗，我害怕猫。
   My younger brother is afraid of dogs and I am afraid of cats.

2. 害羞 **hàixiū** shy
   Tā xiǎo shíhou hěn hàixiū, zhǎngdà yǐhòu xìnggé hěn kāilǎng.
   他小时候很害羞，长大以后性格很开朗。
   He was shy when he was little, but he is quite outgoing when he grows up.

3. 厉害 **lìhai** terrific; awesome
   Nǐ zhēn lìhai, bànge xiǎoshí jiù zhǔnbèile zhème duō cài.
   你真厉害，半个小时就准备了这么多菜。
   You have prepared so many dishes within just half an hour. You are awesome!

4. 危害 **wēihài** harm
   Xīyān duì rénde shēntǐ jiànkāng yǒu hěn dàde wēihài.
   吸烟对人的身体健康有很大的危害。
   Smoking causes great harm to one's physical health.

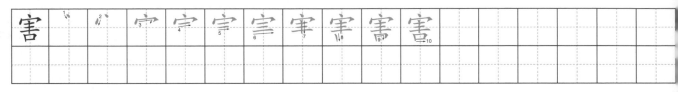

CHARACTER 149

pà
fear; afraid

Useful phrases and sentences

1. 怕 **pà** afraid
   Zài zhème xiàqù, wǒ pà Zhào Míng huì shòubuliǎo.
   再这么下去，我怕赵明会受不了。
   I am afraid that Zhao Ming will not be able to stand it if things continue like this.

2. 恐怕 **kǒngpà** afraid
   Wǒ jīnwǎn yǒu diǎn shì, kǒngpà cānjiābuliǎo nǐmende jùhuì le.
   我今晚有点事，恐怕参加不了你们的聚会了。
   I have engagement tonight. I am afraid that I am not able to join your meeting.

3. 可怕 **kěpà** scary; terrible
   Tài kěpàle! Gāngcái yǒu yíliàng chē chàdiǎnr zhuàngdào wǒ.
   太可怕了！刚才有一辆车差点儿撞到我。
   A car almost hit me just now. How scary!

4. 哪怕 **nǎpà** even if
   Zài wàimiàn zūfáng nǎpà zài guì, wǒ yě bú yuànyì gēn fùmǔ zhù.
   在外面租房哪怕再贵，我也不愿意跟父母住。
   Even if it is expensive to rent a place outside, I am unwilling to stay with my parents.

CHARACTER 150

suàn
count; in the end

Useful phrases and sentences

1. 算 **suàn** count
   Nǐ suànyíxià wǒmen zhècì lǚxíng yígòng huāle duōshǎo qián?
   你算一下我们这次旅游一共花了多少钱？
   Can you add up the total expenses of our trip?

2. 算数 **suànshù** keep one's promise
   Nǐ zěnme shuōhuà bú suànshù? Nǐ shuō lái jiē wǒ, zěnme méi lái?
   你怎么说话不算数？你说来接我，怎么没来？
   How come you did not keep your promise? You said you would come to pick me up, but you didn't.

3. 总算 **zǒngsuàn** finally
   Zǒngsuàn kǎowánshì le, kěyǐ fàngsōngyíxià.
   总算考完试了，可以放松一下。
   The exam is finally over. I can relax a bit.

4. 算了 **suànle** forget about it
   Suànle, cái liǎngkuài qián, bú yòng huángěi wǒ le.
   算了，才两块钱，不用还给我了。
   Forget about it. It's only two kuai. You don't need to give me back.

Lesson 10 Exercises

Part 1 Choose from the following words to fill in the blanks.

参加、努力、害怕、满意、担心

1. 你到家以后一定要给我打个电话，不然我会（　　　　）的。

2. 夏老先生的三个孩子都很懂事，在工作上都很（　　　　）。

3. 妹妹明天要（　　　　）一个钢琴比赛，我要陪她一起去。

4. 今年的学生学习都很认真，我对他们都很（　　　　）。

Part 2 Complete the following dialogues using Chinese characters.

1. A: 你现在做什么工作？

   B: _____ 。

2. A: 最近工作忙不忙？每天睡几个钟头？

   B: _____ 。

3. A: 老板对你的工作满意不满意？

   B: _____ 。

4. A: 你很忙的时候，会做什么让自己放松一点儿？

   B: _____ 。

5. A: 你以后想不想换一个工作？为什么？

   B: _____ 。

Part 3 学以致用

你的朋友想请你去看电影，可是你最近工作实在太忙了，不能陪她去。请你给她写一封电子邮件，告诉她你的情况，希望下次可以跟她一起去。

To: xuezhongwen@cmail.com ﹀

Cc:

Subject:

LESSON 11

City Life 城市生活

1. Dialogue

Read the dialogue below and answer the questions in characters.

许杰:	夏天，在上海住得怎么样？习惯了吗？
夏天:	怎么说呢，有好有坏。好的方面是上海很现代，也很国际化。
许杰:	上海的确是大城市，不过到处都是高楼大厦，我有点儿受不了。你认识新朋友了吗？
夏天:	没呢！这就是不好的方面了。这儿的人好像都特别忙，搬到这儿快一个月了，连邻居都没见过。
许杰:	慢慢来吧。你每天开车还是坐地铁上班？
夏天:	别提了！上下班时间交通不好，汽车就像是乌龟在爬一样。地铁里人也特别多，我现在只好骑自行车。
许杰:	你家离公司远吗？
夏天:	不太远，骑快一点儿二十分钟就到了。
许杰:	那你周末一般做些什么呢？
夏天:	其实也没什么特别的，在家看看喜欢的电视节目，或者跟朋友逛逛街、吃吃东西，我特别喜欢去夜市。哎，但是在大城市，什么都很贵。还好我是单身，生活负担没那么重。
许杰:	你以前不是说去上海先要找个女朋友，好好谈恋爱吗？
夏天:	这个，再等等吧！

1. 夏天喜欢不喜欢上海的生活？ ....

2. 夏天为什么不开车或者坐地铁上班？ ....

3. 夏天周末常常做什么？ ....

2. Vocabulary

	Word	Pinyin	English equivalent
1.	习惯	**xíguàn**	used to; accustomed to
2.	现代	**xiàndài**	modern
3.	国际化	**guójìhuà**	globalize
4.	高楼大厦	**gāolóu dàshà**	hi-rise buildings
5.	受不了	**shòubuliǎo**	cannot endure
6.	邻居	**línjū**	neighbor
7.	地铁	**dìtiě**	subway
8.	像	**xiàng**	like
9.	乌龟	**wūguī**	turtle
10.	爬	**pá**	climb; crawl
11.	骑	**qí**	ride
12.	自行车	**zìxíngchē**	bicycle
13.	离	**lí**	(distant) from
14.	一般	**yìbān**	in general
15.	其实	**qíshí**	actually
16.	节目	**jiémù**	program
17.	逛街	**guàngjiē**	to window shop
18.	夜市	**yèshì**	night market
19.	单身	**dānshēn**	single
20.	负担	**fùdān**	burden
21.	重	**zhòng**	heavy
22.	谈恋爱	**tánliàn'ài**	fall in love; date

3. New Characters

Fifteen characters are introduced in this lesson. Use the following explanations to help you understand and remember the characters.

铁 爬 邻 居 楼 闹 街 负 惯 重 其 实 骑 提 离

CHARACTER 51

铁
tiě
iron

Useful phrases and sentences

1. 地铁 **dìtiě** subway

   Bōshìdùnde dìtiě piào měizhāng chàbuduō sānkuài, bù piányi.
   波士顿的地铁票每张差不多三块，不便宜。
   One one-way ticket on the Boston subway is about three U.S. dollars. It's not cheap.

2. 钢铁 **gāngtiě** steel

   Wáng Shīfu yǐqián zài gāngtiěchǎng gōngzuòguò.
   王师傅以前在钢铁厂工作过。
   Master Wang used to work at a steel factory.

3. 铁公鸡 **tiěgōngjī** stingy person

   Yàoshì shuō yíge rén shì "tiěgōngjī," yìsī shì nàge rén tèbié xiǎoqì.
   要是说一个人是 "铁公鸡"，意思是那个人特别小气。
   If you describe someone as an "iron chicken," that means that person is extremely stingy.

4. 高铁 **gāotiě** hi-speed train

   Zhōngguóde gāotiě hěn fādá, rénmen chūxíng fēicháng fāngbiàn.
   中国的高铁很发达，人们出行非常方便。
   The hi-speech trains in China are well-developed and convenient for people to travel on.

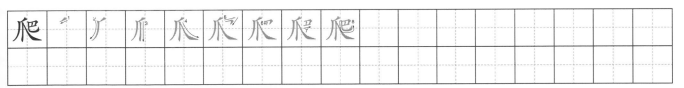

CHARACTER 52

爬
pá
climb; crawl

Useful phrases and sentences

1. 爬楼梯 **pá lóutī** climbing stairs

   Diàntī huàile, zhǐhǎo pá lóutī le.
   电梯坏了，只好爬楼梯了。
   The elevator is broken, so we can only use the stairs.

2. 爬山 **páshān** hiking; mountain climbing

   Xǔ Jié yí dào zhōumò jiù qù páshān.
   许杰一到周末就去爬山。
   Xu Jie always goes hiking on the weekend.

3. 爬起来 **páqǐlái** get up

   Háizi shuāidǎole, māma jiào tā zìjǐ páqǐlái.
   孩子摔倒了，妈妈叫他自己爬起来。
   The kid slipped and fell. His mother told him to get up by himself.

4. 爬行动物 **páxíng dòngwù** reptile

   Dìqiúshàng zuìdàde páxíng dòngwù shì shénme?
   地球上最大的爬行动物是什么？
   What is the biggest reptile on Earth?

CHARACTER 153

邻
lín
neighbor; adjacent

Useful phrases and sentences

1. 邻居 **línjū** neighbor

   Wǒde línjū shì cóng Shāndōng láide, wǒmen hěn tándelái.
   我的邻居是从山东来的，我们很谈得来。
   My neighbor is from Shandong. We get along very well.

2. 邻近 **línjìn** close to; nearby

   Zhèshì yíge gāodàng gōngyù, línjìnde chāoshì hé shāngchǎng dōngxi yě dōu bǐjiào guì.
   这是一个高档公寓，邻近的超市和商场东西也都比较贵。
   This is a high-end apartment. The supermarkets and malls nearby are more expensive.

3. 邻国 **línguó** bordering country

   Yìndù hé Ménggǔ dōu shì Zhōngguóde línguó.
   印度和蒙古都是中国的邻国。
   India and Mongolia are both countries bordering China.

4. 邻省 **línshěng** adjacent province

   Fújiàn shěng hé Guǎngdōng shěng shì línshěng, kěshì zhèliǎngge dìfangde fāngyán hěn bù yíyàng.
   福建省和广东省是邻省，可是这两个地方的方言很不一样。
   Fujian Province and Guangdong Province are adjacent to each other, but the dialects spoken in these two places are very different.

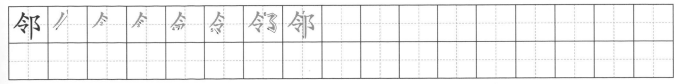

CHARACTER 154

jū
to reside

Useful phrases and sentences

1. 居住 **jūzhù** reside; residence

Zhège xiǎoqūde jūzhù huánjìng hěn hǎo, háiyǒu jiànshēnfáng hé yóuyǒngchí.
这个小区的居住环境很好，还有健身房和游泳池。
The residential environment of this neighborhood is good. It has a gym and a swimming pool.

2. 定居 **dìngjū** settle

Hú Míng dǎsuàn yǐhòu zài Àozhōu dìngjū.
胡明打算以后在澳洲定居。
Hu Ming plans to settle down in Australia.

3. 居然 **jūrán** to one's surprise

Tā shàngge xīngqī xiàng wǒ jièle yìbǎi kuài, kěshì tā jīntiān jūrán shuō bú jìdéle.
他上个星期向我借了一百块，可是他今天居然说不记得了。
He borrowed one hundred kuai from me last week, but to my surprise, he said he didn't remember it today.

4. 新居 **xīnjū** new residence

Gōngxǐ nǐmen qiáoqiān xīnjū!
恭喜你们乔迁新居！
Congratulations on your new residence!

CHARACTER 155

lóu
floor; building

Useful phrases and sentences

1. 楼 **lóu** floor

Lǎoshī, nínde bàngōngshì zài jǐlóu?
老师，您的办公室在几楼？
Teacher, which floor is your office on?

2. 楼上 **lóushang** upstairs

Zhùzài wǒ lóushàngde rén zǒulù shēngyīn hěn dà, tèbié chǎo.
住在我楼上的人走路声音很大，特别吵。
The person living upstairs is loud when he walks. It's noisy.

3. 下楼 **xiàlóu** to go downstairs

Hǎoxiàng yǒu rén qiāomén, nǐ kuài xiàlóu qù kànkan.
好像有人敲门，你快下楼去看看。
It seems that someone is knocking on the door. You should go downstairs to check.

4. 办公楼 **bàngōnglóu** office building

Nà dòng bàngōnglóu lǐ yǒu hěnduō jiā wàiguó gōngsī.
那栋办公楼里有很多家外国公司。
There are many foreign companies in that office building.

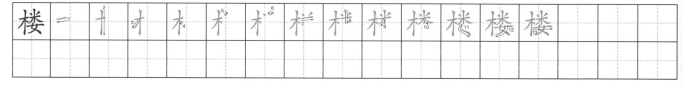

CHARACTER 156

nào
vent; make

Useful phrases and sentences

1. 闹铃 **nàolíng** alarm

Míngtiān nǐ děi zǎoqǐ, bié wàngle shè nàolíng.
明天你得早起，别忘了设闹铃。
You need to get up early tomorrow. Don't forget to set your alarm.

2. 闹矛盾 **nào máodùn** have a quarrel

Nǐ shì-bùshì yòu gēn fùmǔ nào máodùn le?
你是不是又跟父母闹矛盾了？
Are you having a quarrel with your parents again?

3. 闹笑话 **nào xiàohua** a laughingstock

Tāde shēngdiào bú tài hǎo, shuō Zhōngwén chángcháng nào xiàohuà.
她的声调不太好，说中文常常闹笑话。
Her tones are not very good, making her a laughingstock when she speaks Chinese.

4. 热闹 **rènào** lively; hustle and bustle

Nǐ xiǎng zhù zài rènàode shìqū háishì ānjìngde jiāoqū?
你想住在热闹的市区还是安静的郊区？
Do you want to live in the lively downtown or quiet suburbs?

CHARACTER 57

街
jiē
street

12 STROKES 行 RADICAL

Useful phrases and sentences

1. 大街 **dàjiē** avenue

   Píng'ān Lǚxíngshè zài Hépíng Dàjiē wǔhào.
   平安旅行社在和平大街五号。
   The Ping-an Travel Agency is at No. 5 Heping Avenue.

2. 过街 **guòjiē** pass streets

   Nǐ wǎng qián zǒu, guò liǎngtiáo jiē jiù dào dòngwùyuán le.
   你往前走，过两条街就到动物园了。
   Go straight. You will get to the zoo after passing two streets.

3. 逛街 **guàngjiē** window-shop

   Zhū Xiānsheng chángcháng péi tàitai guàngjiē.
   朱先生常常陪太太逛街。
   Mr. Zhu often goes window-shopping with his wife.

4. 华尔街 **Huá'ěrjiē** Wall Street

   Wǒ bìyè hòu xiǎng qù Huá'ěrjiē gōngzuò.
   我毕业后想去华尔街工作。
   I want to work on Wall Street after graduation.

街 ノ 彳 彳 彳 彳 往 往 徍 徍 街 街 街

CHARACTER 58

负
fù
bear; carry

6 STROKES 贝 RADICAL

Useful phrases and sentences

1. 负责 **fùzé** responsible; in charge of

   Zhèjiàn shì wǒ bú fùzé, nǐ kěyǐ zhǎo Chén Zhǔrèn.
   这件事我不负责，你可以找陈主任。
   I am not in charge of this matter. You can go to Director Chen.

2. 负责人 **fùzérén** person in charge

   Qǐng wèn, zhècì juānkuǎn huódòngde fùzérén shì nǎwèi?
   请问，这次捐款活动的负责人是哪位？
   Excuse me, who is the person in charge of this charity event?

3. 欺负 **qīfu** bully

   Wǒ xiǎo shíhou chángcháng bèi tóngxué qīfu.
   我小时候常常被同学欺负。
   I was often bullied by classmates when I was little.

4. 负担 **fùdān** burden

   Wǒ xiǎng gǎnjǐn gōngzuò, jiǎnqīng fùmǔ fùdān.
   我想赶紧工作，减轻父母负担。
   I want to get a job as soon as possible to lessen my parents' burden.

负 ノ 勹 勺 负 负 负

CHARACTER 159

惯
guàn
used to

11 STROKES 忄 RADICAL

Useful phrases and sentences

1. 吃不惯 **chībuguàn** cannot get used to eating something

   Húnán cài nǐ chīdeguàn chībuguàn?
   湖南菜你吃得惯吃不惯？
   Are you used to having Hunan cuisine or not?

2. 惯例 **guànlì** usual practice

   Ànzhào guànlì, xiàozhǎng měinián dōu huì qǐng xuésheng chī Shèngdàn wǎncān.
   按照惯例，校长每年都会请学生吃圣诞晚餐。
   As usual practice, the school president invites students to have Christmas dinner every year.

3. 看不惯 **kànbuguàn** cannot bear to see

   Wǒ zuì kànbuguàn làngfèi shíwùde rén.
   我最看不惯浪费食物的人。
   I cannot bear to see people wasting food.

4. 住不惯 **zhùbuguàn** cannot get used to living somewhere

   Wǒde fùmǔ lái Měiguó hǎoxiàng zhùbuguàn.
   我的父母来美国好像住不惯。
   My parents seem to be not used to living in the U.S.A.

惯 丶 忄 忄 忄 忄 忄 惯 惯 惯 惯 惯

重

zhòng
heavy; serious

9 STROKES | 里 RADICAL

Useful phrases and sentences

1. 重 **zhòng** heavy

Zhèběn shū tài zhòngle, yǒu-méiyǒu diànzǐbǎnde?
这本书太重了，有没有电子版的？
This book is too heavy. Is there an e-book version?

2. 重要 **zhòngyào** important

Jīntiān xiàwǔde huì hěn zhòngyào, měige rén dōu yào lái cānjiā.
今天下午的会很重要，每个人都要来参加。
The meeting this afternoon is very important. Everyone is expected to attend.

3. 严重 **yánzhòng** serious; critical

Xiǎo Yú bìngde hěn yánzhòng, tā yíge xīngqī dōu méi lái shàngbān.
晓雨病得很严重，她一个星期都没来上班。
Xiaoyu is seriously sick. She hasn't come to work for a week.

4. 重点 **zhòngdiǎn** focus; important point

Míngnián wǒmen gōngzuòde zhòngdiǎn shì fāzhǎn hǎiwài shìchǎng.
明年我们工作的重点是发展海外市场。
The focus of our job next year is to expand our market overseas.

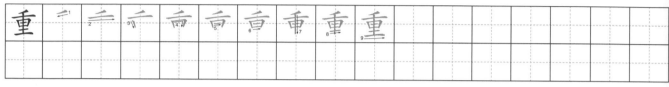

其

qí
that; such

8 STROKES | 八 RADICAL

Useful phrases and sentences

1. 其实 **qíshí** actually

Nǐ bié tài dānxīn wǒ, qíshí wǒ guòde hái kěyǐ.
你别太担心我，其实我过得还可以。
Don't worry too much about me. I am actually fine.

2. 其他 **qítā** other

Yàoshì hái yǒu qítā wèntí, qǐng suíshí dǎ diànhuà.
要是还有其他问题，请随时打电话。
Please call me anytime if you still have any questions.

3. 尤其 **yóuqí** especially

Zhōu Yáng hěn xǐhuan tīng yīnyuè, yóuqí shì bāshí niándàide yáogǔn yīnyuè.
周扬很喜欢听音乐，尤其是八十年代的摇滚音乐。
Zhou Yang likes music, especially 1980's rock and roll.

4. 其中 **qízhōng** among

Tāmen dōu shì wǒde hǎo péngyou, qízhōng liǎngge shì wǒde dàxué tóngxué.
他们都是我的好朋友，其中两个是我的大学同学。
They are all my good friends. Among them, two are my college classmates.

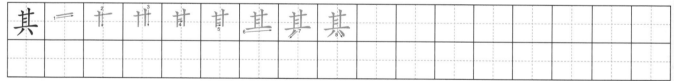

实

shí
real; honest

8 STROKES | 宀 RADICAL

Useful phrases and sentences

1. 确实 **quèshí** indeed

Xué Zhōngwén quèshí bù róngyì, děi huā hěnduō shíjiān.
学中文确实不容易，得花很多时间。
Learning Chinese is indeed not easy; it takes a great amount of time.

2. 实在 **shízài** really

Wǒ chīde shízài tài bǎole, bù néng zài chīle.
我吃得实在太饱了，不能再吃了。
I am really full. I can't eat anymore.

3. 实话 **shíhuà** truth

Shuō shíhuà, zhège diànyǐng bìng méiyǒu wǒ xiǎngde nàme jīngcǎi.
说实话，这个电影并没有我想的那么精彩。
To tell the truth, this movie is not as good as I expected.

4. 诚实 **chéngshí** honest

Chéngshí zuì shàngcè.
诚实最上策。
Honesty is the best policy.

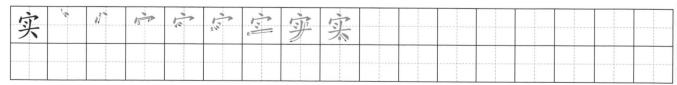

CHARACTER 63

骑

qí
ride

Useful phrases and sentences

1. 骑马 **qímǎ** horse riding
   Yàoshì qù Nèiménggǔ wánr yídìng yào qímǎ.
   要是去内蒙古玩儿一定要骑马。
   You must go horse riding if you go to Inner Mongolia.

2. 骑自行车 **qí zìxíngchē** ride a bicycle
   Zhèlǐde lù tài zhǎile, qí zìxíngchē hěn wēixiǎn.
   这里的路太窄了，骑自行车很危险。
   The roads here are too narrow. It's dangerous to ride bicycles.

3. 骑摩托车 **qí mótuōchē** ride a scooter
   Nǐ huì-búhuì qí mótuōchē?
   你会不会骑摩托车？
   Do you know how to ride a scooter?

4. 骑驴找马 **qí-lǘ-zhǎo-mǎ** keep an option open while looking for something else better (*lit.* ride the donkey while looking for a horse)
   Tā qí-lǘ-zhǎo-mǎ, yìbiān zuòzhe xiànzàide gōngzuò, yìbiān zhǎo xīnde gōngzuò.
   他骑驴找马，一边做着现在的工作，一边找新的工作。
   He is keeping his options open—he is continuing his current job while looking for a new one.

CHARACTER 64

提

tí
carry

Useful phrases and sentences

1. 提 **tí** carry
   Yào-búyào wǒ bāng nǐ tí liǎngge dàizi?
   要不要我帮你提两个袋子？
   Do you want me to carry two bags for you?

2. 提前 **tíqián** in advance
   Tā měitiān dōu tíqián wǔfēnzhōng dào jiàoshì.
   他每天都提前五分钟到教室。
   He arrives at the classroom five minutes early every day.

3. 提问 **tíwèn** Q&A
   Xiànzài shì tíwèn shíjiān, yǒu wèntí qǐng jǔshǒu.
   现在是提问时间，有问题请举手。
   Now it's Q&A. Please raise your hand to ask a question.

4. 提醒 **tíxǐng** remind
   Chēzi méi yóu le, bié wàngle tíxǐng wǒ qù jiāyóu.
   车子没油了，别忘了提醒我去加油。
   The car is out of gas. Do not forget to remind me to add gas.

CHARACTER 165

离

lí
distant from;
leave

Useful phrases and sentences

1. 离 **lí** distant from
   Hé Yīngde jiā lí gōngsī hěn yuǎn, zuò dìtiě yào yíge zhōngtóu zuǒyòu.
   何英的家离公司很远，坐地铁要一个钟头左右。
   He Ying's home is very far from the company. It takes about one hour by subway.

2. 离婚 **líhūn** divorce
   Tīngshuō nàwèi míngxīng shàngge yuè líhūnle.
   听说那位明星上个月离婚了。
   I heard that that celebrity was divorced last month.

3. 距离 **jùlí** distance
   Nǐ juéde wǎngluò ràng rénmende jùlí gèng jìnle ma?
   你觉得网络让人们的距离更近了吗？
   Do you feel that the internet makes people closer?

4. 离开 **líkāi** leave
   Zhège māma yì líkāi háizi jiù kū.
   这个妈妈一离开孩子就哭。
   This kid cries as soon as the mother is away.

Part 1 Choose from the following words to fill in the blanks.

其实、习惯、负担、热闹、离

1. 张先生是广东人，还不太（　　　　　）吃北方菜。

2. 我的宿舍（　　　　　）教室不太远，走路只需要五分钟。

3. 我喜欢（　　　　　）的地方，所以以后大概不会住在农村。

4. 现在年轻人的生活（　　　　　）太重了，买房子、养孩子都太贵了。

Part 2 Complete the following dialogues using Chinese characters.

1. A: 你最喜欢哪个城市？

   B: _____ 。

2. A: 你喜欢住在大城市还是小一点儿的城市？

   B: _____ 。

3. A: 你觉得住在城市有什么好处？有什么坏处？

   B: _____ 。

4. A: 在你生活的城市，交通怎么样？生活负担重吗？

   B: _____ 。

5. A: 你觉得一个不错的城市应该是什么样的？

   B: _____ 。

Part 3 学以致用

你的一个朋友打算搬到你生活的城市，他很想听听你的建议。请你告诉他你的城市是什么样的？比方说气候怎么样？交通好不好？生活负担重不重等等。

LESSON 12

Our Dormitory Room is Messy 宿舍太乱了

1. Dialogue

Read the dialogue below and answer the questions in characters.

小叶:	这个周末，我想在宿舍开一个电影晚会，我们来商量商量吧。
小邱:	什么是电影晚会？
小叶:	就是请朋友一起来看电影，聊天，吃东西，你们有没有兴趣？
小姚:	有！不过，是不是又要收拾房间了？
小叶:	对，宿舍太乱了！卫生间的地板很脏，客厅的桌椅乱七八糟的，特别是厨房，筷子、盘子扔得到处都是。哎，你们怎么不说话？不愿意收拾吗？
小姚:	没有啊！我们在等你说完。
小叶:	对了，小邱，你的衬衫、袜子、帽子怎么都扔在沙发上，请拿回自己的房间。还有小姚，你的狗为什么越来越不听话了，总是把东西弄乱，该管管了。好了，我说完了。等等，还有，那把伞是谁的，怎么一直扔在墙角？
小邱:	好好好，那谁负责买吃的呢？要不要买点水果？还有，我们看什么电影呢？
小叶:	这个我还没想好，等把宿舍打扫干净再说。
小姚:	（小声说）真奇怪，不是说要商量电影晚会吗？
小邱:	小姚，你的狗好像又在咬什么东西了，你快去看看。

1. 小叶准备周末做什么？

2. 小叶的宿舍怎么样？厨房、卫生间都干净吗？

3. 他们最后商量好怎么开电影晚会了吗？

2. Vocabulary

	Word	Pinyin	English equivalent
1.	宿舍	sùshè	dormitory
2.	商量	shāngliang	discuss
3.	乱	luàn	messy
4.	特别	tèbié	especially
5.	脏	zāng	dirty
6.	桌椅	zhuōyǐ	table and chair (seat)
7.	乱七八糟	luàn-qī-bā-zāo	in a mess; in disorder
8.	筷子	kuàizi	chopsticks
9.	盘子	pánzi	plate
10.	衬衫	chènshān	shirt
11.	袜子	wàzi	sock
12.	帽子	màozi	cap; hat
13.	沙发	shāfā	sofa; couch
14.	越	yuè	more
15.	管	guǎn	concern oneself about
16.	伞	sǎn	umbrella
17.	扔	rēng	throw
18.	墙角	qiángjiǎo	wall corner
19.	负责	fùzé	in charge of; responsible
20.	打扫	dǎsǎo	to clean
21.	干净	gānjìng	clean
22.	奇怪	qíguài	strange; odd
23.	咬	yǎo	bite

3. New Characters

Fifteen characters are introduced in this lesson. Use the following explanations to help you understand and remember the characters.

宿　舍　干　净　乱　扫　脏　桌　椅　管　收　拾　越　特　责

Useful phrases and sentences　　　　　**11 STROKES**　｀｀ **RADICAL**

sù
lodge

1. 宿舍　**sùshè**　dormitory
Zhèjiān sùshè zěnme méiyǒu kōngtiáo ne?
这间宿舍怎么没有空调呢？
Why isn't this dormitory air-conditioned?

2. 住宿　**zhùsù**　accommodation; lodging
Hòutiān jiù yào dào Běijīng le, kěshì wǒ hái méi jiějué zhùsù wèntí.
后天就要到北京了，可是我还没解决住宿问题。
I am going to Beijing the day after tomorrow, but I still haven't solved the problem of accommodation.

3. 食宿　**shísù**　room and board
Xuéfèi yǐjīng bāokuò shísùfèi le, bù xūyào lìngwài jiāo.
学费已经包括食宿费了，不需要另外交。
Room and board are already included in the tuition. You don't need to pay separately.

4. 寄宿　**jìsù**　boarding
Zhèsuǒ xuéxiào shì jìsù zhōngxué, xuésheng yíge xīngqī huí yícì jiā.
这所学校是寄宿中学，学生一个星期回一次家。
This is a boarding school. Students go home once a week.

Useful phrases and sentences　　　　　**8 STROKES**　舌 **RADICAL**

shè/shě
residence/
give up

1. 校舍　**xiàoshè**　school building
Wǒmen xuéxiàode xīn xiàoshè fēicháng piàoliang.
我们学校的新校舍非常漂亮。
Our school's new buildings are pretty.

2. 寒舍　**hánshè**　humble abode
Děng yìqíng guòqù zài yāoqǐng dàjiā dào hánshè yíjù.
等疫情过去再邀请大家到寒舍一聚。
I will invite everyone to my humble abode for a get-together when the disease outbreak is over.

3. 舍不得　**shěbudé**　hate to part with
Mǎshang yào huíguóle, wǒ zhēn shěbudé zhèlǐde péngyou.
马上要回国了，我真舍不得这里的朋友。
I am going back to my country soon. It's really hard to say goodbye to friends here.

4. 舍弃　**shěqì**　give up
Hěnduō nǚxìng wèile zhàogù háizi shěqìle zìjǐde gōngzuò.
很多女性为了照顾孩子舍弃了自己的工作。
Many women give up their jobs in order to take care of children.

Useful phrases and sentences　　　　　**3 STROKES**　干 **RADICAL**

gān/gàn
dry/to do

1. 干　**gàn**　to do
Nǐ zài gànshénme ne? Zěnme bǎ jiālǐ nòngde luàn-qī-bā-zāo de?
你在干什么呢？怎么把家里弄得乱七八糟的？
What are you doing? Why do you make the house such a mess?

2. 干燥　**gānzào**　dry
Zài Zhōngguó, běifāngde dōngtiān qìhou hánlěng gānzào.
在中国，北方的冬天气候寒冷干燥。
Winter in northern China is cold and dry.

3. 能干　**nénggàn**　capable
Tā hěn nénggàn, cái gōngzuò yìnián jiù dāngshangle zǒngjīnglǐ.
她很能干，才工作一年就当上了总经理。
She is very capable. She was promoted to manager after only one year of work.

4. 干杯　**gānbēi**　to propose a toast; bottoms up
Lái, ràng wǒmen wèi yǒuyì gānbēi.
来，让我们为友谊干杯！
Let's toast to our friendship!

CHARACTER 69

净

jìng
clean; net

Useful phrases and sentences

1. 干净 **gānjìng** clean

   Dàxuě guòhòu, zhěngge chéngshì hǎoxiàng gānjìngle hěn duō.
   大雪过后，整个城市好像干净了很多。
   The city seems to be much cleaner after the snow.

2. 纯净水 **chúnjìngshuǐ** purified water

   Kǒu kěle, qù mǎi jǐpíng chúnjìngshuǐ ba.
   口渴了，去买几瓶纯净水吧。
   I am thirsty. Let's buy some bottles of purified water.

3. 净化器 **jìnghuàqì** purifier

   Zuìjìn kōngqì hěn bù hǎo, gěi jiālǐ mǎi yìtái kōngqì jìnghuàqì ba.
   最近空气很不好，给家里买一台空气净化器吧。
   The air quality is not good recently. Let's buy an air purifier for the house.

4. 净收入 **jìngshōurù** net income

   Wǒmen zuòde shì xiǎo mǎimài, jìngshōurù méi duōshao.
   我们做的是小买卖，净收入没多少。
   We are running a small business and don't have much net income.

CHARACTER 70

乱

luàn
messy;
randomly

Useful phrases and sentences

1. 乱 **luàn** messy

   Xiǎo Qiū, Xiǎo Yáo, nǐmende fángjiān shízài tài luànle, qù zhěnglǐ yīxià.
   小邱、小姚，你们的房间实在太乱了，去整理一下。
   Xiao Qiu and Xiao Yao, your room is really messy. Go clean it up.

2. 弄乱 **nòngluàn** mess up

   Wǒ gāng zhěnglǐhǎode shūguì, shéi yòu gěi wǒ nòngluànle.
   我刚整理好的书柜，谁又给我弄乱了？
   I just organized the book cabinet. Who messed it up again?

3. 乱停车 **luàn tíngchē** park disorderly

   Zhèr bù néng luàn tíngchē, yàobùrán huì fá liǎngbǎi kuài.
   这儿不能乱停车，要不然会罚两百块。
   Parking disorderly is prohibited here. Otherwise you will be fined two hundred kuai.

4. 乱写 **luànxiě** write randomly

   Qǐng bú yào zài qiángshàng luànxiě luànhuà.
   请不要在墙上乱写乱画。
   Do not write or draw randomly on the wall.

CHARACTER 171

扫

sǎo/sào
sweep

Useful phrases and sentences

1. 扫地 **sǎodì** sweep the floor

   Míngtiān lúndào nǐ sǎodìle, bié wàngle.
   明天轮到你扫地了，别忘了。
   Don't forget that it's your turn to sweep the floor tomorrow.

2. 扫雪 **sǎoxuě** shovel snow

   Dàishàng shǒutào, màozi, wǒmen qù sǎoxuě ba!
   带上手套、帽子，我们去扫雪吧！
   Put on your gloves and hat. Let's go shovel snow.

3. 扫描 **sǎomiáo** scan

   Zhèfèn wénjiàn nǐ néng bāng wǒ sǎomiáo yíxià ma?
   这份文件你能帮我扫描一下吗？
   Can you scan this document for me?

4. 扫帚 **sàozhou** broom

   Sàozhou zài chúfáng guìzide pángbiān.
   扫帚在厨房柜子的旁边。
   The broom is next to the cabinet in the kitchen.

脏

zāng/zàng
dirty/organ

10 STROKES 月 RADICAL

Useful phrases and sentences

1. 脏 **zāng** dirty

   Yīfu quán zāngle, míngtiān shàngbān chuān shénme a?
   衣服全脏了，明天上班穿什么啊？
   All the clothes are dirty. What am I wearing to work tomorrow?

2. 脏乱 **zāngluàn** dirty and disorderly; messy

   Niǔyuē yǒuxiē jiēdào fēicháng zāngluàn.
   纽约有些街道非常脏乱。
   Some streets in New York City are dirty and messy.

3. 心脏 **xīnzàng** heart

   Wǒ bù gǎn qù tiàosǎn, wǒ pà xīnzàng shòubuliǎo.
   我不敢去跳伞，我怕心脏受不了！
   I can't go parachuting. I am afraid that my heart cannot take it.

4. 内脏 **nèizàng** innnards; organs

   Nǐ chīdeguàn dòngwùde nèizàng ma?
   你吃得惯动物的内脏吗？
   Do you eat animals' innards?

脏 丿 刀 月 月 月 肝 肝 胪 胪 脏

桌

zhuō
table; desk

10 STROKES 木 RADICAL

Useful phrases and sentences

1. 书桌 **shūzhuō** desk

   Nǐde shūzhuō tài luànle, gāi shōushi yíxià le.
   你的书桌太乱了，该收拾一下了。
   Your desk is messy. You should tidy up.

2. 桌椅 **zhuōyǐ** table and chair (seats)

   Zhōngwén kèshàng, lǎoshī xǐhuan bǎ zhuōyǐ bǎichéng bànyuánxíng.
   中文课上，老师喜欢把桌椅摆成半圆形。
   The teacher likes to arrange the seats in a semi-circle in Chinese class.

3. 桌球 **zhuōqiú** table tennis

   Xiǎo Yè dǎ zhuōqiú hěn lìhai, shéi dōu yíngbuliǎo tā.
   小叶打桌球很厉害，谁都赢不了他。
   Xiao Ye plays table tennis very well. No one can beat him.

4. 桌面 **zhuōmiàn** desktop; computer desktop

   Wǒde diànnǎo zhuōmiànshang zhìshǎo yǒu sānshíge wénjiànjiā.
   我的电脑桌面上至少有三十个文件夹。
   There are at least thirty folders on my computer desktop.

桌 卜 与 卢 占 占 卓 卓 桌 桌

椅

yǐ
chair

12 STROKES 木 RADICAL

Useful phrases and sentences

1. 一把椅子 **yìbǎ yǐzi** one chair

   Fúwùyuán, kěyǐ zài ná yìbǎ yǐzi guòlái ma?
   服务员，可以再拿一把椅子过来吗？
   Excuse me, can you bring one more chair?

2. 摇椅 **yáoyǐ** rocking chair

   Nàge xiǎo bǎobao tǎng zài yáoyǐshàng shuìzháole.
   那个小宝宝躺在摇椅上睡着了。
   The little baby fell asleep in the rocking chair.

3. 长椅 **chángyǐ** bench

   Gōngyuán nàbiān yǒu yìxiē chángyǐ, wǒmen qù zuò huǐr.
   公园那边有一些长椅，我们去坐会儿。
   There is a bench in the park. Let's go sit there a bit.

4. 轮椅 **lúnyǐ** wheelchair

   Fēijīchǎng yǒu miǎnfèi lúnyǐde fúwù.
   飞机场有免费轮椅的服务。
   There is free wheelchair service at the airport.

椅 一 十 扌 木 机 杧 杧 桥 椅 椅 椅 椅

管
guǎn
concern oneself about

14 STROKES   竹 RADICAL

Useful phrases and sentences

1. 管 guǎn concern oneself about

Wǒde shìqing nǐ jiù bié guǎnle.
我的事情你就别管了。
Don't concern yourself with my things.

2. 尽管 jǐnguǎn even though

Jǐnguǎn tā hěn yǒu qián, kěshì tā cónglái bú luàn huā yìfēn qián.
尽管他很有钱，可是他从来不乱花一分钱。
Even though he is rich, he doesn't do any unnecessary spending.

3. 管理 guǎnlǐ manage

Zhèběn shū jiǎngde shì yīnggāi zěnme guǎnlǐ hǎo shíjiān.
这本书讲的是应该怎么管理好时间。
This book is about how to manage time well.

4. 管用 guǎnyòng effective

Zhège gǎnmàoyào hěn guǎnyòng, chī yícì jiù chàbuduō hǎole.
这个感冒药很管用，吃一次就差不多好了。
The flu medication is very effective. You only need to take one and you will feel much better.

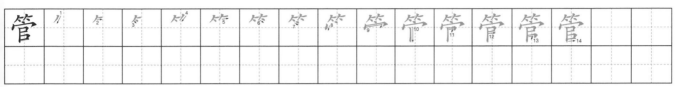

收
shōu
receive

6 STROKES   攵 RADICAL

Useful phrases and sentences

1. 收到 shōudào receive

Yéye, nín shōudào wǒ jìgěi nínde xīnnián lǐwùle ma?
爷爷，您收到我寄给您的新年礼物了吗？
Grandpa, have you received my New Year's gift?

2. 收获 shōuhuò harvest; gain

Zhècì chūguó jiāoliú xuéxí ràng wǒ shōuhuò bù xiǎo.
这次出国交流学习让我收获不小。
I've gained a lot from this overseas exchange program.

3. 收入 shōurù income

Zài nǐde guójiā, néng-bùnéng wèn biéren yìniánde shōurù yǒu duōshao?
在你的国家，能不能问别人一年的收入有多少。
Can you ask people about their annual income in your country?

4. 回收 huíshōu recycle

Nǐ zhīdao huíshōude lājī yīnggāi rēng zài nǎr ma?
你知道回收的垃圾应该扔在哪儿吗？
Do you know where to dispose the trash for recycling?

拾
shí
pick up; arrange

9 STROKES   扌 RADICAL

Useful phrases and sentences

1. 拾 shí pick up

Jīntiān nǚ'ér zài hǎibiān shíle hěnduō cǎisède bèiké.
今天女儿在海边拾了很多彩色的贝壳。
My daughter picked up many colorful shells at the beach today.

2. 收拾 shōushi to clean; to tidy up

Chīwánfàn yǐhòu, shéi yě bù xiǎng shōushi chúfáng.
吃完饭以后，谁也不想收拾厨房。
No one wants to clean the kitchen after dinner.

3. 拾起来 shíqǐlai pick up

Tóngxuémen, líkāi jiàoshì zhīqián qǐng bǎ dìshangde zhǐ shíqǐlai.
同学们，离开教室之前请把地上的纸拾起来。
Students, please pick up the papers on the floor before you leave the classroom.

4. 收拾行李 shōushi xíngli pack (luggage)

Kuài diǎnr shōushi xíngli, hái yǒu sānge xiǎoshí jiù chūfāle.
快点儿收拾行李，还有三个小时就出发了。
Please pack quickly. We are departing in three hours.

CHARACTER 178

越

yuè
more

Useful phrases and sentences

1. 越来越… **yuè lái yuè…** more and more …
   Zuìjìnde qìwēn yuè lái yuè gāo, kànlái chūntiān kuài dàole.
   最近的气温越来越高，看来春天快到了。
   The temperature is getting higher and higher. Spring seems to be on its way.

2. 越南 **Yuènán** Vietnam
   Tā shì Yuènányì Měiguó rén, huì jiǎng Yuènányǔ, Zhōngwén hé Yīngwén.
   她是越南裔美国人，会讲越南语、中文和英文。
   She is Vietnamese-American. She speaks Vietnamese, Chinese and English.

3. 超越 **chāoyuè** surpass
   Màikè'ěr Jiékèxùn zài yīngyuèshàngde chéngjiù hěn nán yǒu rén chāoyuè.
   迈克尔杰克逊在音乐上的成就很难有人超越。
   It's hard for people to surpass Michael Jackson's achievement in music.

4. 越过 **yuèguò** cross; pass
   Yuèguò qiánmiàn nàzuò xiǎoshān jiù dàole.
   越过前面那座小山就到了。
   You'll get there after crossing the hill ahead of you.

越 | 一¹ | 十² | 土³ | 土⁴ | 走⁵ | 走⁶ | 走⁷ | 走⁸ | 起⁹ | 越¹⁰ | 越¹¹ | 越¹²

CHARACTER 179

特

tè
special; unique

Useful phrases and sentences

1. 特殊 **tèshū** special; unusual
   Jīntiān shì tèshū qíngkuàng, yǐhòu bù néng chídàole.
   今天是特殊情况，以后不能迟到了。
   Today is an exception. You can't be late again.

2. 特长 **tècháng** personal strength
   Nǐ yǒu shé me tècháng?
   你有什么特长？
   What is your personal strength?

3. 特色 **tèsè** featured (dish)
   Xī'ān yǒu hěnduō tèsè xiǎochī, nǐ yídìng yào chángchang.
   西安有很多特色小吃，你一定要尝尝。
   There are many featured dishes in Xi'an. You must try them.

4. 特产 **tèchǎn** special local product
   Nǐ tuījiàn nǎge Táiwān tèchǎn?
   你推荐哪个台湾特产？
   Which special local product from Taiwan do you recommend?

特 | ノ¹ | 仁² | 牛³ | 牛⁴ | 牛⁵ | 牛⁶ | 特⁷ | 特⁸ | 特⁹ | 特¹⁰

CHARACTER 180

责

zé
responsibility;
to blame

Useful phrases and sentences

1. 责怪 **zéguài** blame
   Tā yǐjīng zhīdao cuòle, nǐ jiù bié zài zéguàile.
   他已经知道错了，你就别再责怪了。
   He already knew that it's his fault. Don't blame him anymore.

2. 责任心 **zérènxīn** sense of responsibility
   Shí Qí hěn yǒu zérènxīn, jiāogěi tāde gōngzuò měicì dōu wánchéngde hěn hǎo.
   石奇很有责任心，交给他的工作每次都完成得很好。
   Shi Qi has a strong sense of responsibility. Tasks assigned to him are all well taken care of.

3. 自责 **zìzé** self-blame
   Nǐ bú yào zìzéle, shéi dōu huì yǒu zuòcuòde shíhou.
   你不要自责了，谁都会有做错的时候。
   Don't blame yourself. Everyone makes mistakes.

4. 职责 **zhízé** duty; responsibility
   Zhìbìng jiùrén shì yīshēngde zhízé.
   治病救人是医生的职责。
   Curing patients is the duty of doctors.

责 | 一¹ | 二² | 丰³ | 主⁴ | 青⁵ | 青⁶ | 责⁷ | 责⁸

Lesson 12 Exercises

Part 1 Choose from the following words to fill in the blanks.

> 收拾、管、干净、特别、负责

1. 这道菜的味道很（　　　　　　），不知道是怎么做的。

2. 电梯坏了好几天了，怎么没有人（　　　　　　）呢？

3. 今天下午我打算（　　　　　　）一下房间，房间太乱了。

4. 这次活动我（　　　　　　）给大家买食物和水果。

Part 2 Complete the following dialogues using Chinese characters.

1.　A:　你的宿舍住几个人？

　　B: _____ 。

2.　A:　你的房间乱不乱？

　　B: _____ 。

3.　A:　你一般多长时间打扫一次房间？

　　B: _____ 。

4.　A:　周末的时候，你在宿舍开过晚会吗？

　　B: _____ 。

5.　A:　要是在你的宿舍开晚会，你们会不会一起收拾房间？

　　B: _____ 。

Part 3 学以致用

这个星期五，你跟室友想在宿舍开一个晚会。可是你们的房间有点儿乱，请你安排一下，告诉你的几个室友应该怎么收拾宿舍。

客厅：

把桌子放好

卧室：

厨房：

卫生间：

其他：

Grand Opening of a New Restaurant 新餐厅开张了！

1. Text

Read the announcement below and answer the questions in characters.

亲爱的顾客朋友们：

八月八号绿茶餐厅就要开张了！多种主食，各地风味，价格便宜。我们要特别推荐酸菜鱼和麻辣大虾。另外，绿茶味儿的冰激凌和甜品也是我们的一大特色。你也可以上网了解我们的菜单。我们会根据您的口味，做出您最满意的菜。

八月八号到十八号这段时间在绿茶餐厅用餐，我们会送两杯饮料和一些糖果。要是您想坐靠窗的位子，看城市夜景，最好提前打电话。欢迎大家乘电梯到意美大厦六层绿茶餐厅用餐！

绿茶餐厅
8月5号

1. 绿茶餐厅推荐什么菜？

2. 为什么在八月十八号以前去吃饭比较好？

3. 什么时候需要给餐厅打电话订座？

2. Vocabulary

	Word	Pinyin	English equivalent
1.	亲爱	qīn'ài	dear
2.	顾客	gùkè	customer
3.	绿茶	lǜchá	green tea
4.	餐厅	cāntīng	restaurant
5.	开张	kāizhāng	open
6.	风味	fēngwèi	flavor
7.	价格	jiàgé	price
8.	推荐	tuījiàn	recommend
9.	酸	suān	sour
10.	虾	xiā	shrimp
11.	冰激凌	bīngjīlíng	ice cream
12.	甜品	tiánpǐn	dessert
13.	特色	tèsè	specialty
14.	上网	shàngwǎng	go online
15.	根据	gēnjù	according to
16.	用餐	yòngcān	dine; have a meal
17.	饮料	yǐnliào	beverage
18.	糖果	tángguǒ	candy
19.	靠窗	kào chuāng	by the window
20.	位子	wèizi	seat
21.	乘	chéng	take; ride
22.	电梯	diàntī	elevator
23.	层	céng	floor

3. New Characters

Fifteen characters are introduced in this lesson. Use the following explanations to help you understand and remember the characters.

座　位　窗　冰　餐　杯　主　食　酸　甜　品　辣　饮　料　单

座

zuò
seat

Useful phrases and sentences

10 STROKES　广 RADICAL

1. 座位 **zuòwèi** seat

   Qǐng wèn, zhège zuòwèi yǒu rén ma?
   请问，这个座位有人吗？
   Excuse me, is this seat taken?

2. 讲座 **jiǎngzuò** lecture

   Míngtiān xiàwǔ xuéxiào yǒu yìchǎng guānyú xīfāng yìshùshǐde jiǎngzuò.
   明天下午学校有一场关于西方艺术史的讲座。
   There is a lecture on the history of Western art at school tomorrow afternoon.

3. 座 **zuò** measure word for mountains

   Zài nàzuò shānde shāndǐng yǒu yíge sìmiào.
   在那座山的山顶有一个寺庙。
   There is a temple on the top of the mountain.

4. 让座 **ràngzuò** yield one's seat

   Gèwèi chéngkè, qǐng zhǔdòng gěi lǎorén hé értóng ràngzuò.
   各位乘客，请主动给老人和儿童让座。
   Dear passengers, please yield your seat to the elderly and small children.

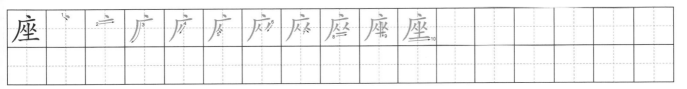

位

wèi
location; place

Useful phrases and sentences

7 STROKES　亻 RADICAL

1. 位 **wèi** measure word for people

   Nàwèi chuān zǐsè yīfude jiù shì wǒmende xīn lǎobǎn.
   那位穿紫色衣服的就是我们的新老板。
   That person in a purple dress is our new boss.

2. 地位 **dìwèi** status

   Zài Rìběn, lǎoshī yǒu hěn gāode shèhuì dìwèi.
   在日本，老师有很高的社会地位。
   Teachers enjoy high social status in Japan.

3. 单位 **dānwèi** work unit; organization

   Bùhǎoyìsi, wǒ wàngle nín zài nǎge dānwèi gōngzuò?
   不好意思，我忘了您在哪个单位工作？
   I am sorry, I forgot which organization you work for.

4. 位置 **wèizhì** location

   Nǐmen gōngsī jùtǐ zài shénme wèizhì?
   你们公司具体在什么位置？
   Where exactly is your company located?

窗

chuāng
window

Useful phrases and sentences

12 STROKES　穴 RADICAL

1. 窗户 **chuānghu** window

   Yào xià dàyǔ le, kuài bǎ chuānghu guānshang.
   要下大雨了！快把窗户关上。
   It's going to rain heavily soon. Close the windows.

2. 窗帘 **chuānglián** curtain

   Fángjiānlǐ méiyǒu chuānglián, nǐ děi zìjǐ mǎi.
   房间里没有窗帘，你得自己买。
   There are no curtains in the room. You need to buy them yourself.

3. 靠窗 **kào chuāng** window seat

   Nǐ xiǎng zuò kào chuāngde wèizi háishì kào zǒudàode wèizi?
   你想坐靠窗的位子还是靠走道的位子？
   Would you like window seat or aisle seat?

4. 窗口 **chuāngkǒu** (service) window

   Xuéxiào cāntīng yǒu hěnduō chuāngkǒu, mài gèdìde shíwù.
   学校餐厅有很多窗口，卖各地的食物。
   There are many service windows at the school's dining hall. They sell food of all varieties.

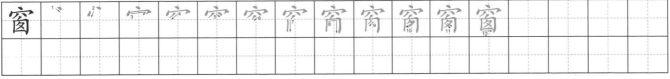

CHARACTER 184

冰
bīng
ice

6 STROKES 〉 RADICAL

Useful phrases and sentences

1. 冰 **bīng** ice
   Wǒ yào yìbēi bīng nátiě, bù jiā nǎiyóu.
   我要一杯冰拿铁，不加奶油。
   I want an iced latte, no whipped cream.

2. 滑冰 **huábīng** ice skating
   Hā'ěrbīn yě jiào "Bīngchéng," tīngshuō nàrde rén hěn xǐhuan huábīng.
   哈尔滨也叫"冰城"，听说那儿的人很喜欢滑冰。
   Harbin is also called the "City of Ice." I heard that people there love ice skating.

3. 冰水 **bīngshuǐ** ice water
   Wǒ lái Měiguó shíjǐnián le, háishì hēbuguàn bīngshuǐ.
   我来美国十几年了，还是喝不惯冰水。
   I've been in the U.S.A. for dozens of years and am still not used to drinking ice water.

4. 冰凉 **bīngliáng** ice cold
   Tiānqì tài lěngle, zài wàimiàn zhàn yíhuìr jiù shǒujiǎo bīngliáng.
   天气太冷了，在外面站一会儿就手脚冰凉。
   It's too cold. You'll easily get cold hands and feet if standing outside.

CHARACTER 185

餐
cān
meal

16 STROKES 食 RADICAL

Useful phrases and sentences

1. 餐厅 **cāntīng** restaurant
   Zhè fùjìn nǎjiā cāntīng zuì shòu huānyíng?
   这附近哪家餐厅最受欢迎？
   Which restaurant nearby is the most popular?

2. 餐具 **cānjù** utensils
   Shěn Tàitai hěn jiǎngjiū yòng shénme cānjù chīfàn.
   沈太太很讲究用什么餐具吃饭。
   Mrs. Shen pays special attention to the dining utensils.

3. 野餐 **yěcān** picnic
   Zhōumò tiānqì hěn hǎo, wǒmen qù gōngyuán yěcān ba.
   周末天气很好，我们去公园野餐吧。
   The weather for the weekend is good. Let's have a picnic in the park.

4. 大餐 **dàcān** a great meal; feast
   Kǎowánshì yǐhòu wǒ yào hǎohǎo chī yídùn dàcān.
   考完试以后我要好好吃一顿大餐。
   I want to have a feast after the test.

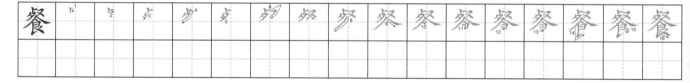

CHARACTER 186

杯
bēi
cup; glass

8 STROKES 木 RADICAL

Useful phrases and sentences

1. 水杯 **shuǐbēi** cup
   Wǒ jīntiān bǎ shuǐbēi wàngzài jiàoshìle.
   我今天把水杯忘在教室了。
   I left my cup in the classroom today.

2. 酒杯 **jiǔbēi** wine glass
   Zhèjǐge jiǔbēi shì nǚ'ér qù Fǎguóde shíhou mǎide.
   这几个酒杯是女儿去法国的时候买的。
   My daughter bought these wine glasses while traveling in France.

3. 奖杯 **jiǎngbēi** trophy
   Wā, nǐ déle zhème duō chángpǎo bǐsàide jiǎngbēi.
   哇，你得了这么多长跑比赛的奖杯。
   Wow, you've won so many long-distance running trophies.

4. 茶杯 **chábēi** tea cup
   Wǒde Rìběn péngyou sònggěi wǒ yítào rìshì chábēi.
   我的日本朋友送给我一套日式茶杯。
   My Japanese friend gave me a set of Japanese tea cups.

主

zhǔ
host; main

5 STROKES ` RADICAL

Useful phrases and sentences

1. 主人 **zhǔrén** host

Lái, dàjiā jìng zhǔrén yìbēi. Nǐmen xīnkǔle!
来，大家敬主人一杯。你们辛苦了！
Let's toast to the host for making such effort.

2. 主要 **zhǔyào** main

Nín zhècì lái chūchāide zhǔyào mùdì shì shénme?
您这次来出差的主要目的是什么？
What is the main purpose of your business trip this time?

3. 主食 **zhǔshí** staple food

Tā bù xǐhuan chī zhǔshí, zhǐ chī cài hé shuǐguǒ.
他不喜欢吃主食，只吃菜和水果。
He doesn't like staple food. He only eats vegetables and fruit.

4. 主意 **zhǔyì** idea

Chūnjià yào qù nǎr wánr, wǒ xiànzài hái méiyǒu zhǔyì.
春假要去哪儿玩儿，我现在还没有主意。
I still have no idea about where to go for spring break.

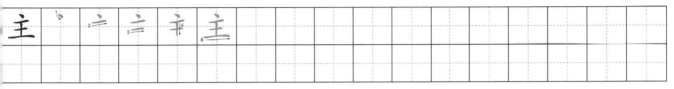

食

shí
food

9 STROKES 食 RADICAL

Useful phrases and sentences

1. 食物 **shíwù** food

Míngtiānde huìyì huì wèi dàjiā zhǔnbèi yìxiē jiǎndānde shíwù.
明天的会议会为大家准备一些简单的食物。
Simple food will be served for tomorrow's meeting.

2. 零食 **língshí** snack

Bié chī tài duō língshí, bú jiànkāng.
别吃太多零食，不健康。
Don't eat too many snacks. It's not healthy.

3. 饮食 **yǐnshí** food and drink; eating

Měigè dìfang dōu yǒu zìjǐde yǐnshí xíguàn.
每个地方都有自己的饮食习惯。
Every place has its own eating customs.

4. 食品 **shípǐn** grocery

Lóuxiàde shípǐndiàn zǎoshang liùdiǎn bàn jiù kāiménle.
楼下的食品店早上六点半就开门了。
The grocery store downstairs opens at 6:30 am.

suān
sour; sore

14 STROKES 酉 RADICAL

Useful phrases and sentences

1. 酸 **suān** sour

Nǐ zuòde tāng tài suānle, wǒ hēbuxiàqù.
你做的汤太酸了，我喝不下去。
The soup you made is too sour. I can't eat it.

2. 酸奶 **suānnǎi** yogurt

Zhè shì dāngdì nóngchǎngde suānnǎi, fēicháng xīnxiān hǎohē.
这是当地农场的酸奶，非常新鲜好喝。
This yogurt is from a local farm. It's fresh and tasty.

3. 心酸 **xīnsuān** sad

Dúwán zhège gùshì ràng rén juéde hěn xīnsuān.
读完这个故事让人觉得很心酸。
This story makes people feel sad.

4. 酸痛 **suāntòng** sore

Zuótiān cái yùndòng bàngè zhōngtóu, méi xiǎngdào jīntiān jīròu suāntòng.
昨天才运动半个钟头，没想到今天肌肉酸痛。
I only worked out half an hour yesterday, but today my muscles are all sore.

Useful phrases and sentences   11 STROKES 甘 RADICAL

tián
sweet

1. 甜 **tián** sweet

Zhège xīguā kě zhēn tián!
这个西瓜可真甜！
This watermelon tastes really sweet.

2. 甜蜜 **tiánmì** sweet; happy

Fùmǔ yuánlái bù tóngyì tāmen jiéhūn, kěshì tāmen xiànzàide shēnghuó hěn tiánmì.
父母原来不同意他们结婚，可是他们现在的生活很甜蜜。
Their parents didn't approve of their marriage, but they are having a happy life now.

3. 甜点 **tiándiǎn** dessert

Zhīshì dàngāo shì wǒ zuì xǐhuande tiándiǎn.
芝士蛋糕是我最喜欢的甜点。
Cheesecake is my favorite dessert.

4. 甜言蜜语 **tián-yán-mì-yǔ** sweet words

Léi Míng nàge rén jiù xǐhuan shuō xiē tián-yán-mì-yǔ, bù zhīdào tā shuōde shì-búshì zhēnxīnhuà.
雷明那个人就喜欢说些甜言蜜语，不知道他说的是不是真心话。
Lei Ming likes to say sweet words, but I am not sure how serious he is.

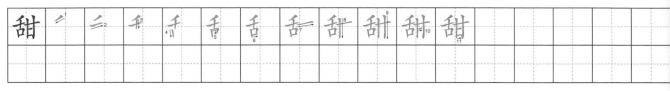

Useful phrases and sentences   9 STROKES 口 RADICAL

pǐn
to sample;
to taste

1. 品尝 **pǐncháng** to sample

Gèwèi gùkè, huānyíng dàjiā miǎnfèi pǐncháng xīnkuǎn dàngāo.
各位顾客，欢迎大家免费品尝新款蛋糕。
Dear customers, you are welcome to sample our new cakes.

2. 品牌 **pǐnpái** brand

Xiǎohuì hǎoxiàng zhǐ mǎi Yìdàlì pǐnpáide xiézi.
小慧好像只买意大利品牌的鞋子。
Xiaohui seems to only buy Italian brand shoes.

3. 商品 **shāngpǐn** commodity

Wàiguó shāngpǐn dàole Zhōngguó dōu biànde fēicháng guì.
外国商品到了中国都变得非常贵。
Foreign commodities have become extremely expensive in China.

4. 品味 **pǐnwèi** good taste (in fashion, etc.)

Tā chuān yīfu hěn yǒu pǐnwèi.
她穿衣服很有品味。
She dresses tastefully.

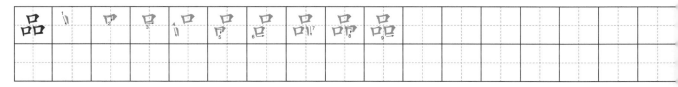

Useful phrases and sentences   14 STROKES 辛 RADICAL

là
hot; spicy

1. 辣 **là** spicy

Nǐ néng chī lade cài ma?
你能吃辣的菜吗？
Do you eat spicy food?

2. 酸辣 **suānlà** spicy and sour

Lái zhèjiā fànguǎnr yídìng yào chángchang suānlàtāng.
来这家饭馆儿一定要尝尝酸辣汤。
You must try the spicy and sour soup in this restaurant.

3. 辣椒 **làjiāo** chili; hot pepper

Lái yífèn chǎo mǐfàn, shǎo fàngdiǎn làjiāo.
来一份炒米饭，少放点辣椒。
I want one fried rice. Please use fewer hot peppers.

4. 酸甜苦辣 **suān-tián-kǔ-là** joys and sorrows of life

Měigè rénde shēnghuólǐ dōu yǒu suān-tián-kǔ-là.
每个人的生活里都有酸甜苦辣。
Everyone's life is full of joys and sorrows.

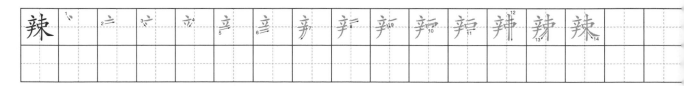

CHARACTER 93

饮

yǐn
to drink

7 STROKES   饣 **RADICAL**

1. 饮水机 **yǐnshuǐjī** water dispenser

Yǐnshuǐjī bú zài zhèr, zài gébìde bàngōngshì.
饮水机不在这儿，在隔壁的办公室。
The water dispenser is not here. It's in the office next door.

2. 热饮 **rèyǐn** hot drink

Nǐmen zhèr yǒu-méiyou rèyǐn? Rè qiǎokèlì, rè chá shénme de.
你们这儿有没有热饮？热巧克力、热茶什么的。
Do you have hot drinks here, such as hot chocolate or hot tea?

3. 餐饮 **cānyǐn** food and beverage

Cóng wǒ yéye kāishǐ, wǒmen jiā jiù cóngshì cānyǐn hángyè.
从我爷爷开始，我们家就从事餐饮行业。
Our family has been in the food and beverage business since my grandfather's time.

4. 饮酒 **yǐnjiǔ** drinking

Yǐnjiǔ guòduō hěn shāng shēntǐ, háishì shǎo hē diǎnr.
饮酒过多很伤身体，还是少喝点儿。
Overdrinking is harmful to your health. You'd better drink less.

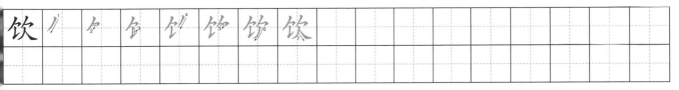

CHARACTER 94

料

liào
material

Useful phrases and sentences

10 STROKES   斗 **RADICAL**

1. 资料 **zīliào** materials

Zhèmén kède zīliào lǎoshī dōu fàngzài wǎngshàng le.
这门课的资料老师都放在网上了。
The teacher has put all the materials for this class online.

2. 原料 **yuánliào** raw materials

Měiguó měinián cóng Zhōngguó jìnkǒu hěnduō huàxué yuánliào.
美国每年从中国进口很多化学原料。
Many chemical raw materials are imported from China to the U.S.A. every year.

3. 材料 **cáiliào** ingredients

Dànchǎofàn xūyàode cáiliào hěn shǎo, dànshì wèidao hěn xiāng.
蛋炒饭需要的材料很少，但是味道很香。
The fried rice with eggs doesn't require many ingredients, but it smells very good.

4. 饮料 **yǐnliào** beverage

Tā bù hē hán táng yǐnliào, zhǐ hē shuǐ.
她不喝含糖饮料，只喝水。
She doesn't drink any beverages with sugar. She only drinks water.

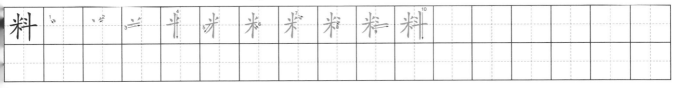

CHARACTER 195

单

dān
bill; sole

Useful phrases and sentences

8 STROKES   十 **RADICAL**

1. 菜单 **càidān** menu

Qǐng wèn, nǐmen yǒu-méiyou Yīngwén càidān?
请问，你们有没有英文菜单？
Excuse me, do you have English menus?

2. 单身 **dānshēn** single (unmarried)

Tā líhūn yǐhòu méi zài jiéguohūn, tā juéde dānshēn shēnghuó hěn hǎo.
她离婚以后没再结过婚，她觉得单身生活很好。
She never remarried after her divorce. She felt that it's good to stay single.

3. 单人间 **dānrénjiān** single room

Wǒ dìngde shì dānrénjiān, bú shì shuāngrénjiān.
我订的是单人间，不是双人间。
I reserved a single room, not double.

4. 简单 **jiǎndān** easy

Jīntiānde kǎoshì hěn jiǎndān, bànge zhōngtóu jiù zuòwánle.
今天的考试很简单，半个钟头就做完了。
The test today was easy. I finished it in thirty minutes.

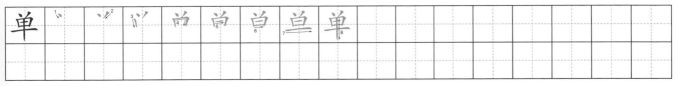

Part 1 Choose from the following words to fill in the blanks.

座位、饮料、杯、酸、主食

1. 除了米饭以外，你们还有什么（　　　　　）？

2. 请问，您旁边的这个（　　　　）有没有人？

3. 服务员，请给我拿一（　　　　）热水和一双筷子。

4. 这道菜吃起来有点儿（　　　　），应该再加点儿糖。

Part 2 Complete the following dialogues using Chinese characters.

1. A: 你常常去饭馆儿吃饭吗？

   B: ＿＿＿＿＿＿＿＿＿＿＿＿＿＿＿＿＿＿＿＿＿＿＿＿＿＿＿。

2. A: 你最喜欢的饭馆儿是什么？

   B: ＿＿＿＿＿＿＿＿＿＿＿＿＿＿＿＿＿＿＿＿＿＿＿＿＿＿＿。

3. A: 你看得懂中文菜单吗？你觉得用中文点菜难不难？

   B: ＿＿＿＿＿＿＿＿＿＿＿＿＿＿＿＿＿＿＿＿＿＿＿＿＿＿＿。

4. A: 你的饮食习惯是什么？能不能吃辣的菜？

   B: ＿＿＿＿＿＿＿＿＿＿＿＿＿＿＿＿＿＿＿＿＿＿＿＿＿＿＿。

5. A: 你知道在中国有很多美国快餐店吗？

   B: ＿＿＿＿＿＿＿＿＿＿＿＿＿＿＿＿＿＿＿＿＿＿＿＿＿＿＿。

Part 3 学以致用

要是请你开一家新饭馆儿，你想开什么样的饭馆儿？请根据下面的内容说说你的想法。

名字：

特色：

风味儿：

厨师推荐的菜：

其他：

LESSON 14

Do You Want to Go to a Hockey Game?
你想去看冰球比赛吗？

1. Dialogue

Read the dialogue below and answer the questions in characters.

李明：	林丽，昨晚给你打了好几个电话，怎么没人接？你去哪儿了？
林丽：	我去学校体育馆看篮球比赛了！当时太吵了，根本没听见手机响。
李明：	哎，联系不上你，真是急死人了！比赛怎么样？
林丽：	我们学校赢了！不过开始的时候一直输球，看得人特别紧张。
李明：	我记得你以前不喜欢看篮球比赛啊？怎么突然有兴趣了？
林丽：	我两个星期以前认识了一个朋友，叫郝 (hǎo) 帅，他是篮球队的，我是去支持他的。我跟你说，他长得特别帅！
李明：	原来是这样。你的嗓子怎么了？不舒服吗？
林丽：	昨晚一边看比赛，一边大声喊他的名字，结果把嗓子喊哑了。
李明：	那你要多喝水。对了，星期五我有一个游泳比赛，你要不要来看？
林丽：	啊，那天下午我跟郝帅约好看音乐会，他说有免费的票。
李明：	那音乐会几点结束？我们的比赛晚上八点一刻才开始，你别迟到了。
林丽：	这个我还不太清楚，不过我们打算看完音乐会一起去吃饭。
李明：	哎，那算了吧。

1. 昨天晚上林丽为什么没有接李明的电话？

2. 林丽为什么现在喜欢看篮球比赛了？

3. 林丽为什么不能去看李明的游泳比赛，他要做什么？

2. Vocabulary

	Word	Pinyin	English equivalent
1.	体育馆	tǐyùguǎn	gymnasium; stadium
2.	比赛	bǐsài	competition; match
3.	联系	liánxì	contact
4.	急	jí	worried
5.	响	xiǎng	ring; sound
6.	赢	yíng	win
7.	输	shū	lose
8.	紧张	jǐnzhāng	nervous
9.	篮球队	lánqiúduì	basketball team
10.	支持	zhīchí	support
11.	长	zhǎng	appear; look
12.	帅	shuài	good-looking; handsome
13.	嗓子	sǎngzi	throat; voice
14.	喊	hǎn	yell; scream
15.	哑	yǎ	lose one's voice
16.	约	yuē	make an appointment
17.	免费	miǎnfèi	free of charge
18.	结束	jiéshù	end; finish
19.	刻	kè	quarter of an hour
20.	迟到	chídào	late

3. New Characters

Fifteen characters are introduced in this lesson. Use the following explanations to help you understand and remember the characters.

赛 队 赢 输 支 持 结 束 约 联 系 紧 喊 免 急

赛

sài
match;
competition

14 STROKES 贝 RADICAL

Useful phrases and sentences

1. 足球赛 **zúqiúsài** soccer match

   Nǐ bù xǐhuan kàn zúqiúsài ma? Nà wǒmen kàn biéde.
   你不喜欢看足球赛吗？那我们看别的。
   You don't like watching soccer match? Then let's watch something else.

2. 赛马 **sàimǎ** horse racing

   Sàimǎ shì Nèiménggǔ chuántǒngde tǐyù huódòng zhī yī.
   赛马是内蒙古传统的体育活动之一。
   Horse racing is one of the traditional sports of Inner Mongolia.

3. 竞赛 **jìngsài** competition

   Lǐ Míng měinián dōu zài shùxué jìngsàizhōng qǔdé hěn hǎode chéngjì.
   李明每年都在数学竞赛中取得很好的成绩。
   Li Ming always receives good grades in the annual math competition.

4. 比赛 **bǐsài** competition; match

   Kuài diǎnr, bǐsài èrshífēnzhōng hòu jiù kāishǐle.
   快点儿，比赛二十分钟后就开始了。
   Hurry up, the match will start in twenty minutes.

队

duì
team; group

4 STROKES 阝 RADICAL

Useful phrases and sentences

1. 排队 **páiduì** line up; queue

   Jūnjūn, nǐ kàn dàjiā dōu zài páiduì, wǒmen yě bù néng chāduì.
   钧钧，你看大家都在排队，我们也不能插队。
   Junjun, you see that everyone is lining up. We can't cut in.

2. 球队 **qiúduì** sports team

   Měiguó Zhílán nǐ zhīchí nǎge qiúduì?
   美国职篮你支持哪个球队？
   Which NBA team do you support?

3. 队长 **duìzhǎng** captain (of a sports team)

   Wǒ mèimei shì xuéxiào wǎngqiú duìde duìzhǎng.
   我妹妹是学校网球队的队长。
   My younger sister is the captain of the school tennis team.

4. 队员 **duìyuán** team member

   Bīngqiúduìde duìyuán měitiān yào xùnliàn sānge zhōngtóu.
   冰球队的队员每天要训练三个钟头。
   The hockey team trains three hours a day.

赢

yíng
win

17 STROKES 贝 RADICAL

Useful phrases and sentences

1. 赢 **yíng** win

   Zuówǎnde gǎnlǎnqiú bǐsài nǎge duì yíngle?
   昨晚的橄榄球比赛哪个队赢了？
   Which team won the football game last night?

2. 双赢 **shuāngyíng** a win-win situation

   Liǎngxiào hézuò shì yíjiàn shuāngyíngde shìqing, wǒmen yīnggāi jìxù jìnxíng xiàqu.
   两校合作是一件双赢的事情，我们应该继续进行下去。
   It is a win-win situation for our two schools to collaborate. We should continue.

3. 赢得 **yíngdé** won

   Hǎo Shuàide jīngcǎi biǎoyǎn yíngdéle guānzhòng rèliède zhǎngshēng.
   郝帅的精彩表演赢得了观众热烈的掌声。
   Hao Shuai's excellent performance won warm applause from the audience.

4. 输赢 **shūyíng** outcome (of a game)

   Wǒ bú zàihu bǐsàide shūyíng, gèng xiǎngshòu bǐsàide guòchéng.
   我不在乎比赛的输赢，更享受比赛的过程。
   I don't care about the outcome of the game. I enjoy the process more.

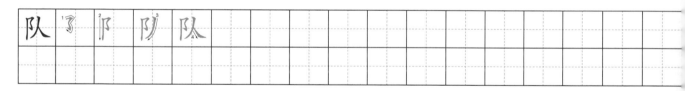

输

shū
to lose

Useful phrases and sentences

1. 输 **shū** to lose

   Tā jīntiān shūle qiú, xīnqíng hěn bù hǎo.
   他今天输了球，心情很不好。
   He lost the ball game today and is in a bad mood.

2. 认输 **rènshū** concede; admit defeat

   Suīrán chàngyè shībàile, kěshì tā bú rènshū, juédìng chóngxīn kāishǐ.
   虽然创业失败了，可是他不认输，决定重新开始。
   Although his start-up failed, he didn't concede. He decided to start again.

3. 输入 **shūrù** enter; log in

   Yào dēnglù zhège wǎngzhàn, qǐng xiān shūrù nǐde yònghùmíng hé mìmǎ.
   要登陆这个网站，请先输入你的用户名和密码。
   If you want to get access to this website, you need to enter your username and password.

4. 运输 **yùnshū** transportation

   Zhèlǐ shì shānqū, jiāotōng yùnshū fēicháng bù fāngbiàn.
   这里是山区，交通运输非常不方便。
   This is a mountainous area, so transportation is quite inconvenient.

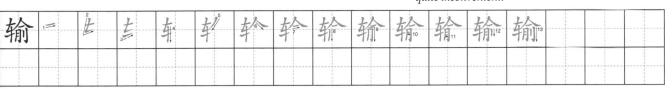

支

zhī
support; measure word for pens

Useful phrases and sentences

1. 支 **zhī** measure word for pens

   Kěyǐ gēn nǐ jiè yìzhī bǐ ma?
   可以跟你借一支笔吗？
   Can I borrow a pen?

2. 支持 **zhīchí** support

   Fùmǔ hěn zhīchí wǒ dàxué bìyè hòu jìxù dú yánjiūshēng.
   父母很支持我大学毕业后继续读研究生。
   My parents support my plan to continue studying at graduate school after college.

3. 支票 **zhīpiào** check

   Qǐng wèn, jiāo fángzū kěyǐ yòng zhīpiào ma?
   请问，交房租可以用支票吗？
   Excuse me, can I use a check to pay the rent?

4. 支出 **zhīchū** expense; cost

   Duì hěnduō Měiguó jiātíng láishuō, měige yuède yīliáo bǎoxiǎn shì hěn dà yìbǐ zhīchū.
   对很多美国家庭来说，每个月的医疗保险是很大一笔支出。
   Medical insurance is a big portion of the monthly expense for many American households.

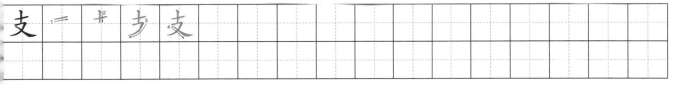

持

chí
to hold

Useful phrases and sentences

1. 坚持 **jiānchí** insist; persist

   Xuéxí gōngfu suīrán hěn lèi, dànshì wǒ jiānchí jìxù.
   学习功夫虽然很累，但是我坚持继续。
   Although learning kungfu is tiring, I insist on continuing.

2. 保持 **bǎochí** keep; maintain

   Wǒmen bǎochí liánxì. Wēixìn, LINE, WhatsApp, diànyóu dōu kěyǐ.
   我们保持联系。微信、LINE、WhatsApp、电邮都可以。
   Let's keep in touch by WeChat, LINE, WhatsApp or email.

3. 主持 **zhǔchí** host

   Míngtiānde huìyì shéi lái zhǔchí?
   明天的会议谁来主持？
   Who is hosting the meeting tomorrow?

4. 持续 **chíxù** continue

   Gāowēn tiānqì chíxùle chàbùduō yǒu bànge yuè, jīntiān zhōngyú xiàyǔle.
   高温天气持续了差不多有半个月，今天终于下雨了。
   High temperatures have continued for half a month. Finally it is raining today.

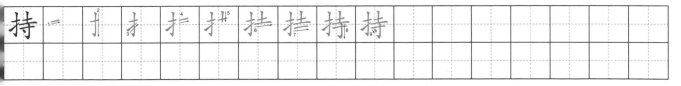

结

jiē/jié
to bear fruit/
to conclude

Useful phrases and sentences

9 STROKES ⸌ **RADICAL**

1. 结果子 **jiē guǒzi** to bear fruit

Zhèkē shù wǒ píngshí méi hǎohao zhàogù, méi xiǎngdào hái jiēle guǒzi.
这棵树我平时没好好照顾，没想到还结了果子。
I didn't have time to take care of this tree, but to my surprise it still bore fruit.

2. 结实 **jiēshi** sturdy

Zhèshuāng xié hěn jiēshi, kěndìng kěyǐ chuān hǎo jǐnián.
这双鞋很结实，肯定可以穿好几年。
This pair of shoes is sturdy. You can wear them for several years.

3. 结构 **jiégòu** structure

Zhèpiān wénzhāngde jiégòu bú tài qīngchǔ, xūyào gǎigai.
这篇文章的结构不太清楚，需要改改。
The structure of this article is unclear. It needs revision.

4. 结论 **jiélùn** conclusion

Zhōngměi guānxì yǐhòu huì zěnme fāzhǎn, xiànzài méiyǒu rén néng gěi yíge jiélùn.
中美关系以后会怎么发展，现在没有人能给一个结论。
No one can draw conclusions about the development of China-U.S. relations.

束

shù
to bundle

Useful phrases and sentences

7 STROKES 木 **RADICAL**

1. 束 **shù** bouquet

Nǐ kàn nàshù méiguīhuā, zhēn hǎokàn.
你看那束玫瑰花，真好看。
Look at that rose bouquet. How pretty!

2. 结束 **jiéshù** over; end

Qīmò kǎoshì jiéshù yǐhòu wǒ zài yuē nǐ chūqu.
期末考试结束以后我再约你出去。
Let's go out once the final exams are over.

3. 约束 **yuēshù** restrict

Yǒu xiǎngfǎ jiù nǔlì qù shìshi, bié tài yuēshù zìjǐ.
有想法就努力去试试，别太约束自己。
Just try if you have any thoughts. Don't restrict yourself.

4. 拘束 **jūshù** constrained; not at ease

Dàjiā bié jūshù, zài wǒmen jiā jiù xiàng zài zìjǐ jiā yíyàng.
大家别拘束，在我们家就像在自己家一样。
Please set yourself at ease, as if you were at home.

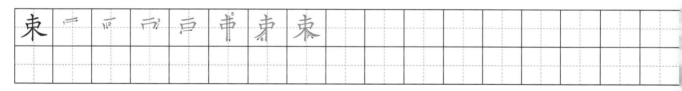

约

yuē
make an
appointment;
invite

Useful phrases and sentences

6 STROKES ⸌ **RADICAL**

1. 约 **yuē** make an appointment

Liào Jīnglǐ, kěyǐ gēn nín yuēge shíjiān liáoliáo ma?
廖经理，可以跟您约个时间聊聊吗？
Manager Liao, can I make an appointment with you to discuss something?

2. 大约 **dàyuē** approximately; about

Zuótiān dàyuē yǒu liǎngbǎi rén cānjiāle bìyè wǎnyàn.
昨天大约有两百人参加了毕业晚宴。
There were approximately two hundred people attending the graduation dinner yesterday.

3. 预约 **yùyuē** reservation

Zhōumò rén bǐjiào duō, nǐ zuìhǎo tíqián dǎ diànhuà yùyuē.
周末人比较多，你最好提前打电话预约。
There are more people on the weekend. You'd better call and make a reservation.

4. 约会 **yuēhuì** date; appointment

Nǐ gēn nǚpéngyou chángcháng qù nǎr yuēhuì?
你跟女朋友常常去哪儿约会？
Where do you and your girlfriend go when on dates?

联

lián
unite; contact

Useful phrases and sentences

1. 联系 **liánxì** contact

   Hǎojiǔ méi liánxìle, nǐ zuìjìn máng shénme ne?
   好久没联系了，你最近忙什么呢？
   I haven't contacted you for a while. What have you been up to?

2. 互联网 **hùliánwǎng** internet

   Hùliánwǎng gǎibiànle rénmende shēnghuó fāngshì.
   互联网改变了人们的生活方式。
   The internet has changed the way people live.

3. 联合国 **Liánhéguó** United Nations

   Liánhéguóde zǒngbù zài Měiguó Niǔyuē.
   联合国的总部在美国纽约。
   The United Nations is headquartered in New York City.

4. 春联 **chūnlián** Chinese New Year couplet

   Guò chūnjiéde shíhou, jiājiāhùhù dōu yào tiē chūnlián.
   过春节的时候，家家户户都要贴春联。
   Every family posts couplets during the Chinese New Year.

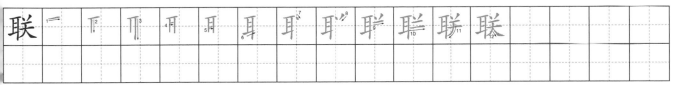

系

xì/xi
to maintain

Useful phrases and sentences

1. 维系 **wéixì** to maintain

   Fēnjū liǎngdì yào wéixì gǎnqíng bù róngyì.
   分居两地要维系感情不容易。
   It's not easy to maintain a relationship when two people are in different places.

2. 关系 **guānxi** relationship

   Nǐ gēn Qín Tiān shì shénme guānxi? Tóngshì? Péngyou? Hǎo péngyou?
   你跟秦天是什么关系？同事？朋友？好朋友？
   What is the relationship between you and Qing Tian? Are you colleagues, acquaintances or close friends?

3. 没关系 **méiguānxi** that's alright; never mind

   Méi guānxi, nǐ míngtiān bǎ shū huángěi wǒ jiù xíng.
   没关系，你明天把书还给我就行。
   That's alright. You can return the book to me tomorrow.

4. 化学系 **huàxué xì** Department of Chemistry

   Huàxué xìde Wāng Lǎoshī hěn shòu xuésheng huānyíng.
   化学系的江老师很受学生欢迎。
   Teacher Wang from the Department of Chemistry is very popular with the students.

紧

jǐn
tight; urgent

Useful phrases and sentences

1. 赶紧 **gǎnjǐn** without further delay

   Shíjiān bù zǎole, nǐ gǎnjǐn huíjiā ba.
   时间不早了，你赶紧回家吧。
   It's getting late. You should go home without further delay.

2. 紧急 **jǐnjí** urgent; emergency

   Nǐ gěi wǒ dǎle shíjǐge diànhuà, yǒu shénme jǐnjíde shìqing ma?
   你给我打了十几个电话，有什么紧急的事情吗？
   You called me several times. Anything urgent?

3. 抓紧 **zhuājǐn** grasp firmly; make the most of

   Wǒ jīntiān xiǎng zhuājǐn shíjiān xiěwán bàogào.
   我今天想抓紧时间写完报告。
   I want to make the best use of today to finish the report.

4. 不要紧 **bú yàojǐn** it is okay; doesn't matter

   Bǐsài shūle bú yàojǐn, xiàcì jìxù nǔlì.
   比赛输了不要紧，下次继续努力。
   It doesn't matter if the game is lost, try harder next time.

喊

hǎn
yell; scream

1. 喊 **hǎn** to shout; to yell
Zhèlǐ shì túshūguǎn, qǐng bú yào dàshēng hǎn.
这里是图书馆，请不要大声喊。
This is the library. Please refrain from loud shouting.

2. 大喊大叫 **dàhǎn dàjiào** to scream loudly
Wàimiàn yǒu jǐge xiǎoxuéshēng zài dàhǎn dàjiào.
外面有几个小学生在大喊大叫。
Several elementary school students are screaming loudly outside.

3. 别喊了 **bié hǎnle** don't yell
Bié hǎnle, wǒ yǐjīng tīngjiàn le.
别喊了，我已经听见了！
Don't yell. I hear you.

4. 叫喊 **jiàohǎn** shout
Xiàxuěle, háizimen xīngfènde jiàohǎnshēng bǎ dàjiā dōu chǎoxǐngle.
下雪了，孩子们兴奋的叫喊声把大家都吵醒了。
It's snowing. The children are so excited. Their shouting is waking everyone up.

免

miǎn
avoid; exempt

1. 免费 **miǎnfèi** free (of charge)
Zhèjiā kāfēiguǎn chángcháng qǐng gùkè miǎnfèi pǐncháng tiándiǎn.
这家咖啡馆常常请顾客免费品尝甜点。
This coffee shop often offers free desserts for its customers to sample.

2. 免得 **miǎndé** so as not to
Nǐ zuìhǎo xiěxiàlai, miǎnde guò jǐtiān wàngle.
你最好写下来，免得过几天忘了。
You'd better write it down so as not to forget it in the next few days.

3. 免税 **miǎnshuì** duty free
Jīchǎng yǒu miǎnshuì shāngdiàn, jiàgé piányi yìdiǎnr.
机场有免税商店，价格便宜一点儿。
There are duty free shops at the airport. Their prices are cheaper.

4. 免不了 **miǎnbuliǎo** refrain from
Chūguó shéi dōu miǎnbuliǎo huì xiǎng jiā.
出国谁都免不了会想家。
No one can refrain from being homesick when going abroad.

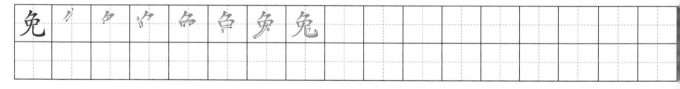

急

jí
worried; urgent

1. 急 **jí** in a rush
Zǎoshang wǒ jízhe chūmén, wàngle dài qiánbāo.
早上我急着出门，忘了带钱包。
I was in a rush heading out and forgot to bring my wallet.

2. 着急 **zháojí** to feel anxious; to worry
Nǐ bié zháojí, qǐng mànman shuō.
你别着急，请慢慢说。
Don't be anxious. Please speak slowly.

3. 急忙 **jímáng** rush
Gāo Tàitai shuō jiālǐ bèi tōule, Gāo Xiānsheng jímáng zuò chūzūchē huíjiā.
高太太说家里被偷了，高先生急忙坐出租车回家。
Mrs. Gao said that there had been a burglary at home. Mr. Gao rushed back by taxi.

4. 急诊 **jízhěn** emergency
Jízhěnshì rén hěn duō, wǒmen děngle yíge xiǎoshí cái jiàndào yīshēng.
急诊室人很多，我们等了一个小时才见到医生。
The emergency room was packed with people. We waited for one hour to see a doctor.

Lesson 14 Exercises

Part 1 Choose from the following words to fill in the blanks.

结束、约、支持、联系、免费

1. 大山回到美国以后就再也没跟我（　　　　）了。

2. 李小姐打算周末（　　　　）同事一起去看新电影。

3. 考试（　　　　）以后咱们去中国城吃饭吧。

4. 我想换一个自己更有兴趣的工作，可是我父母不太（　　　　）我的想法。

Part 2 Complete the following dialogues using Chinese characters.

1. A: 今天下午有一个冰球比赛，你想跟我一起去吗？

   B: ＿＿＿＿＿＿＿＿＿＿＿＿＿＿＿＿＿＿＿＿＿＿＿＿＿＿＿＿＿＿＿。

2. A: 你最喜欢看的体育（**tǐyù**: sports）比赛是什么？

   B: ＿＿＿＿＿＿＿＿＿＿＿＿＿＿＿＿＿＿＿＿＿＿＿＿＿＿＿＿＿＿＿。

3. A: 你有没有自己支持的球队？你为什么支持他们？

   B: ＿＿＿＿＿＿＿＿＿＿＿＿＿＿＿＿＿＿＿＿＿＿＿＿＿＿＿＿＿＿＿。

4. A: 在你的国家，年轻人比较喜欢什么运动？

   B: ＿＿＿＿＿＿＿＿＿＿＿＿＿＿＿＿＿＿＿＿＿＿＿＿＿＿＿＿＿＿＿。

5. A: 不忙的时候，你会约朋友去做什么事情？

   B: ＿＿＿＿＿＿＿＿＿＿＿＿＿＿＿＿＿＿＿＿＿＿＿＿＿＿＿＿＿＿＿。

你是学校排球队的队员，明天晚上你们有一场排球比赛。请你给朋友们写一封邮件，告诉他们比赛的时间、地点，并希望他们能来支持你们球队。

To: xuezhongwen@cmail.com ⌄

Cc:

Subject:

比赛时间：

比赛地点：

谢谢你！

祝好，

LESSON 15

Let's Go on a Picnic! 我们出去野餐吧!

1. Dialogue

Read the dialogue below and answer the questions in characters.

杨晨:	冬天终于过去了，今天阳光真好！
李竹:	是啊，难得的好天气。你听，外面都是鸟叫声。
杨晨:	我昨天路过市中心的公园，看到好多孩子在草地上游戏、放风筝，热闹极了。
李竹:	咱们也应该约个时间去公园野餐。
杨晨:	好主意！这个星期六有空吗？我记得你最近忙着找暑期实习呢。
李竹:	有空，忘了告诉你，我找到实习了，是纽约的一家科技公司。
杨晨:	太好了，那一定要给你庆祝一下！到时候咱们把朋友们都叫来。
李竹:	好啊！那我们准备点儿什么吃的呢？
杨晨:	烧烤吧！带点儿蔬菜和肉就行，我再带点儿海鲜饼。
李竹:	那我带水果，葡萄、香蕉什么的，另外再准备一些蛋糕和果汁。
杨晨:	行！对了，我新买了一台照相机，拍出来的效果特别好，到时候我们多拍点儿照片！
李竹:	真想快点儿到周六！哎，周六天气怎么样啊？
杨晨:	多亏你提醒我。我看看，哎呀，糟糕！周六下大雨！

1. 最近天气怎么样？

2. 李竹找到实习工作了吗？

3. 你觉得这个星期六他们会出去野餐吗？

2. Vocabulary

	Word	Pinyin	English equivalent
1.	终于	**zhōngyú**	finally
2.	难得	**nándé**	rare; hard to get
3.	鸟	**niǎo**	bird
4.	路过	**lùguò**	pass by
5.	草地	**cǎodì**	lawn
6.	游戏	**yóuxì**	play
7.	放风筝	**fàng fēngzhēng**	fly a kite
8.	极	**jí**	extremely
9.	野餐	**yěcān**	picnic
10.	庆祝	**qìngzhù**	celebrate
11.	烧烤	**shāokǎo**	grill
12.	蔬菜	**shūcài**	vegetable
13.	海鲜	**hǎixiān**	seafood
14.	葡萄	**pútao**	grapes
15.	香蕉	**xiāngjiāo**	bananas
16.	蛋糕	**dàngāo**	cake
17.	果汁	**guǒzhī**	fruit juice
18.	照相机	**zhàoxiàngjī**	camera
19.	拍	**pāi**	take (photos)
20.	效果	**xiàoguǒ**	effect
21.	多亏	**duōkuī**	thanks to

3. New Characters

Fifteen characters are introduced in this lesson. Use the following explanations to help you understand and remember the characters.

终　拍　戏　忘　糕　祝　海　鲜　汁　照　相　草　烧　烤　蔬

终
zhōng
end; finish

Useful phrases and sentences

1. 终于 **zhōngyú** finally
   Lǐ Wénjié zhōngyú zhǎodàole yífèn mǎnyìde gōngzuò.
   李文杰终于找到了一份满意的工作。
   Li Wenjie finally found a fulfilling job.

2. 始终 **shǐzhōng** from beginning to end; all along
   Suīrán shìle gèzhǒng bànfa, dànshì zhège wèntí shǐzhōng méiyou jiějué.
   虽然试了各种办法，但是这个问题始终没有解决。
   Although we have tried all kinds of solutions, this issue has still remained unresolved.

3. 终点 **zhōngdiǎn** finishing line
   Mǎshàng jiù pǎodào zhōngdiǎn le, nǐ zài jiānchí yíxia.
   马上就跑到终点了，你再坚持一下。
   The finishing line is coming up. Hang in there a bit longer.

4. 终止 **zhōngzhǐ** terminate
   Rúguǒ tíqián zhōngzhǐ zūfáng hétong, yào fákuǎn yìqiān kuài.
   如果提前终止租房合同，要罚款一千块。
   Early termination of the rental agreement will result in a penalty of one thousand kuai.

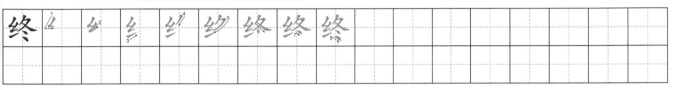

拍
pāi
pat; take

Useful phrases and sentences

1. 拍 **pāi** pat
   Bàba pāizhe wǒde jiānbǎng shuō: "Xiāngxìn nǐ kěyǐ zuòde gèng hǎo."
   爸爸拍着我的肩膀说："相信你可以做得更好"。
   My father patted me on my shoulder and said, "I believe you can do better."

2. 球拍 **qiúpāi** racket
   Zhèfù qiúpāi hěn qīng, zhìliàng yě hěn hǎo.
   这副球拍很轻，质量也很好。
   This racket is light and of high-quality.

3. 拍照片 **pāi zhàopiān** take a photo
   Tā hěn ài pāi zhàopiān, Liǎnshūshàng yígòng yǒu hǎo jǐbǎizhāng.
   他很爱拍照片，脸书上一共有好几百张。
   He loves taking photos. He has posted hundreds of photos on Facebook.

4. 拍电影 **pāi diànyǐng** make a movie
   Wǒ xiǎng pāi yíbù guānyú dàxué shēnghuóde diànyǐng.
   我想拍一部关于大学生活的电影。
   I want to make a movie about college life.

戏
xì
play; drama

Useful phrases and sentences

1. 游戏 **yóuxì** game
   Tā měitiān búshì shuìjiào jiùshì wánr diànnǎo yóuxì.
   他每天不是睡觉就是玩儿电脑游戏。
   He either sleeps or plays video games every day.

2. 戏曲 **xìqǔ** Chinese opera
   Tā yuánlái shì xué xìqǔ de, hòulái dāngle diànyǐng yǎnyuán.
   他原来是学戏曲的，后来当了电影演员。
   He used to study the Chinese opera and later became a movie actor.

3. 儿戏 **érxì** child's play; trifling matter
   Bié ná wǒde huà dāng érxì, wǒ shì rènzhēn de.
   别拿我的话当儿戏，我是认真的。
   Don't take my words as mere trifle. I am serious.

4. 戏迷 **xìmí** fan of Chinese opera
   Yéye shìge xìmí, měige zhōumò dōu qù kàn Jīngjù.
   爷爷是个戏迷，每个周末都去看京剧。
   My grandfather is a fan of the Chinese opera. He goes to the Beijing Opera every weekend.

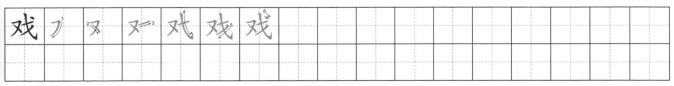

CHARACTER 214

忘
wàng
forget

7 STROKES · **心 RADICAL**

Useful phrases and sentences

1. 忘了 **wàngle** forgot
Yáng Chén yòu wàngle fù xìnyòngkǎde qián.
杨晨又忘了付信用卡的钱。
Yang Chen forgot to pay her credit card again.

2. 忘记 **wàngjì** forget
Shēnghuó zhōng yǒu hěn duō fánnǎo, wǒmen yīnggāi xuéhuì wàngjì.
生活中有很多烦恼，我们应该学会忘记。
There are many worries in life. We should learn to forget about them.

3. 难忘 **nánwàng** unforgettable
Dàxué dìyìtiānde shēnghuó zhēn ràng rén nánwàng.
大学第一天的生活真让人难忘。
The first day in college was unforgettable.

4. 忘不掉 **wàngbùdiào** cannot forget
Wǒ érzi dìyīcì jiào wǒ "bàba"de nàyītiān, wǒ yǒngyuǎn wàngbùdiào.
我儿子第一次叫我"爸爸"的那一天，我永远忘不掉。
I can never forget the day when my son called me "Daddy" the first time.

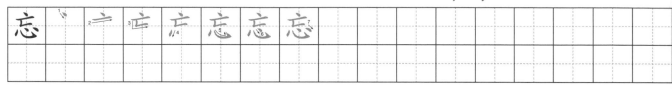

CHARACTER 215

糕
gāo
cake

16 STROKES · **米 RADICAL**

Useful phrases and sentences

1. 糟糕 **zāogāo** darn it
Zāogāo, wǒ wàngle jīntiān yǒu dàkǎo.
糟糕，我忘了今天有大考。
Darn, I forgot that I have a big exam today.

2. 年糕 **niángāo** rice cake
Zhōngguó rén guòniánde shíhou huì chī niángāo.
中国人过年的时候会吃年糕。
Chinese people eat rice cakes during the Chinese New Year.

3. 糕点 **gāodiǎn** cakes; pastries
Fènglísū shì Táiwān hěn yǒumíngde gāodiǎn.
凤梨酥是台湾很有名的糕点。
Taiwan is famous for its pineapple cakes.

4. 雪糕 **xuěgāo** popsicle
Xuěgāo nǐ yào shénme kǒuwèirde? Xiāngcǎode háishì cǎoméide?
雪糕你要什么口味儿的？香草的还是草莓的？
What flavor of popsicle would you like? Vanilla or strawberry?

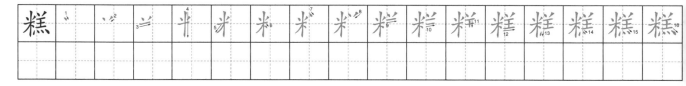

CHARACTER 216

祝
zhù
wish

9 STROKES · **礻 RADICAL**

Useful phrases and sentences

1. 祝 **zhù** wish
Zhù dàjiā xuéxí jìnbù, yíqiè shùnlì.
祝大家学习进步，一切顺利！
I wish everyone the best for your studies and that everything go smoothly.

2. 庆祝 **qìngzhù** celebrate
Jīnnián gōngsī fāzhǎnde hěn hǎo, wǒmen yīnggāi qìngzhù yíxia.
今年公司发展得很好，我们应该庆祝一下。
Our company has been doing well this year. We should celebrate.

3. 祝贺 **zhùhè** congratulations
Zhùhè nǐ shùnlì nádàole bóshì xuéwèi.
祝贺你顺利拿到了博士学位。
Congratulations on the smooth completion of your doctoral degree.

4. 祝福 **zhùfú** well wishes; blessings
Zài yīyuàn shōudào dàjiāde zhùfú hěn kāixīn! Xièxiè nǐmen.
在医院收到大家的祝福很开心！谢谢你们。
I am really happy to receive all your well wishes in the hospital. Thank you.

海

hǎi
sea

Useful phrases and sentences

10 STROKES　氵 RADICAL

1. 海 **hǎi** sea

Wǒde jiāxiāng kào hǎi, qìhou hěn shīrùn.
我的家乡靠海，气候很湿润。
My hometown by the sea has a humid climate.

2. 海关 **hǎiguān** customs

Guò hǎiguānde shíhou yào jiǎnchá xínglǐxiāng ma?
过海关的时候要检查行李箱吗？
Do they check the baggage at customs?

3. 海报 **hǎibào** flyer; poster

Zhèzhāng diànyǐng hǎibàode shèjì hěn tèbié.
这张电影海报的设计很特别。
The design of this movie flyer is unique.

4. 沿海 **yánhǎi** along the coast

Zhōngguó yánhǎi chéngshì jīngjì dōu bǐjiào fādá.
中国沿海城市经济都比较发达。
The economy of Chinese coastal cities is comparatively better.

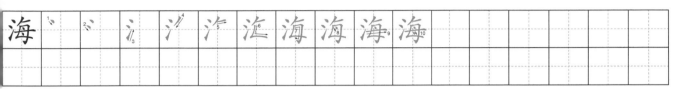

鲜

xiān
fresh

Useful phrases and sentences

14 STROKES　鱼 RADICAL

1. 鲜艳 **xiānyàn** colorful

Wǒ juéde yánsè xiānyànde yīfu gèng shìhé nǐ.
我觉得颜色鲜艳的衣服更适合你。
I feel that colorful clothes suit you better.

2. 海鲜 **hǎixiān** seafood

Lǐ Zhú duì hǎixiān guòmǐn, yúxiā dōu bù néng chī.
李竹对海鲜过敏，鱼虾都不能吃。
Li Zhu is allergic to seafood. She doesn't eat fish nor shrimp.

3. 鲜美 **xiānměi** delicious; tasty

Zhège yúpiàntāng wèidao hěn xiānměi.
这个鱼片汤味道很鲜美。
The fish fillet soup is delicious.

4. 鲜花 **xiānhuā** fresh flowers

Jīntiān shì Qíngrénjié, hěnduō rén páiduì mǎi xiānhuā.
今天是情人节，很多人排队买鲜花。
Today is Valentine's Day. Many people are lining up to buy fresh flowers.

汁

zhī
juice

Useful phrases and sentences

5 STROKES　氵 RADICAL

1. 果汁 **guǒzhī** fruit juice

Píjiǔ wǒ hēbuliǎo, hē diǎnr guǒzhī jiù xíng.
啤酒我喝不了，喝点儿果汁就行。
I don't drink beer. Fruit juice will be fine.

2. 苹果汁 **píngguǒzhī** apple juice

Wǒmen diànde píngguǒzhī dōushì yòng xīnxiān píngguǒ zhàde.
我们店的苹果汁都是用新鲜苹果榨的。
The apple juice in our store is made of freshly pressed apples.

3. 墨汁 **mòzhī** Chinese calligraphy ink

Zài Zhōngguóchéng néng mǎidào mòzhī ma?
在中国城能买到墨汁吗？
Do they have Chinese calligraphy ink in Chinatown?

4. 橙汁 **chéngzhī** orange juice

Xiǎojiě, nín yào lái yìbēi chéngzhī ma?
小姐，您要来一杯橙汁吗？
Miss, would you like a glass of orange juice?

照

zhào
take; look after

13 STROKES | **RADICAL**

Useful phrases and sentences

1. 照看 **zhàokàn** to look after

   Zhū Xiānsheng xiàge yuè yào chūchāi, tā qǐng wǒ bāngmáng zhàokàn fángzi.
   朱先生下个月要出差，他请我帮忙照看房子。
   Mr. Zhu is taking a business trip next month. He has asked me to look after his house.

2. 照顾 **zhàogù** care

   Zhècì lái Zhōngguó duōxiè nǐmende zhàogù.
   这次来中国多谢你们的照顾。
   Thank you very much for your care during my stay in China this trip.

3. 按照 **ànzhào** according to

   Ànzhào guīdìng, dàyī xīnshēng bìxū zhùzài xuéxiào sùshè.
   按照规定，大一新生必须住在学校宿舍。
   According to the school's policy, freshmen must live on campus.

4. 照相机 **zhàoxiàngjī** camera

   Zhètái zhàoxiàngjī shì wǒ dàxuéde shíhou mǎide.
   这台照相机是我大学的时候买的。
   I bought this camera when I was in college.

相

xiàng / xiāng
photo/each other

9 STROKES | 目 **RADICAL**

Useful phrases and sentences

1. 相片 **xiàngpiàn** picture; photo

   Qiángshang guàde nàzhāng xiàngpiàn shì nǐ fùmǔ ma?
   墙上挂的那张相片是你父母吗？
   Is the picture on the wall of your parents?

2. 相馆 **xiàngguǎn** photo studio

   Zhè fùjìn yǒu xiàngguǎn ma? Wǒ xūyào hùzhàode xiàngpiàn.
   这附近有相馆吗？我需要护照的相片。
   Is there a photo studio around here? I need passport photos.

3. 相互 **xiānghù** each other

   Péngyou zhījiān dāngrán yīnggāi xiānghù bāngzhù.
   朋友之间当然应该相互帮助。
   Friends should help each other.

4. 相信 **xiāngxìn** believe

   Nǐ xiāngxìn yǒu wàixīng rén ma?
   你相信有外星人吗？
   Do you believe in aliens?

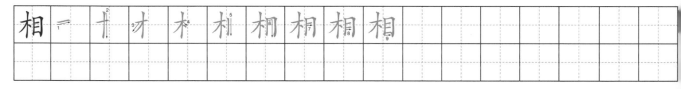

草

cǎo
grass; straw

9 STROKES | **RADICAL**

Useful phrases and sentences

1. 草 **cǎo** grass

   Huā kāile, cǎo lǜle, chūntiān láile.
   花开了，草绿了，春天来了。
   The flowers are blossoming and the grass is turning green. Spring is on its way.

2. 草莓 **cǎoméi** strawberry

   Shuǐguǒ lǐmiàn wǒ zuì xǐhuan chī cǎoméi.
   水果里面我最喜欢吃草莓。
   Strawberries are my favorite fruit.

3. 草地 **cǎodì** lawn

   Hěnduō rén tǎngzài wàimiànde cǎodìshang shài tàiyang.
   很多人躺在外面的草地上晒太阳。
   Many people are sunbathing on the lawn.

4. 潦草 **liáocǎo** illegible

   Nǐ xiěde zì tài liáocǎole. Qǐng zài xiě yībiàn.
   你写的字太潦草了。请再写一遍。
   Your handwriting is illegible. Please write it again.

10 STROKES | **火 RADICAL**

烧

shāo
burn

Useful phrases and sentences

1. 烧 **shāo** boil

Wǒmen shāo diǎn rèshuǐ, pào xiē chá hē ba.
我们烧点热水，泡些茶喝吧。
Let's boil some water and make hot tea.

2. 退烧 **tuìshāo** to reduce fever

Nǐ yǐjīng tuìshāole, kěyǐ bú yòng chīyàole.
你已经退烧了，可以不用吃药了。
Your fever has been reduced. You don't need any more medicine.

3. 烧饭 **shāofàn** cook

Zài wǒmen jiā, zuì huì shāofànde shì érzi.
在我们家，最会烧饭的是儿子。
Our son is the best cook in the family.

4. 红烧肉 **hóngshāo ròu** braised pork in brown sauce

Zhèjiā fànguǎnrde hóngshāo ròu zuì yǒumíng.
这家饭馆儿的红烧肉最有名。
This restaurant is famous for its braised pork in brown sauce.

10 STROKES | **火 RADICAL**

烤

kǎo
roast; bake

Useful phrases and sentences

1. 烤鸭 **kǎoyā** roast duck

Dàole Běijīng dāngrán yàochī kǎoyā.
到了北京当然要吃烤鸭。
You must try roast duck in Beijing.

2. 烤火 **kǎo huǒ** warm oneself up by a fire

Wàimiàn tài lěngle, kuài jìnlai kǎokao huǒ.
外面太冷了，快进来烤烤火。
It's freezing outside. Come inside to warm up by the fire.

3. 烤面包 **kǎo miànbāo** bake bread

Bù mángde shíhou, wǒ zuì xǐhuan kǎo miànbāo.
不忙的时候，我最喜欢烤面包。
I like to bake bread when I have time.

4. 烤箱 **kǎoxiāng** oven

Zhèdào cài bù nánzuò, fàngjìn kǎoxiāng wǔfēnzhōng jiù hǎole.
这道菜不难做，放进烤箱五分钟就好了。
This dish is not hard to make. Just put it into the oven for five minutes and it's ready.

15 STROKES | **艹 RADICAL**

蔬

shū
vegetable

Useful phrases and sentences

1. 蔬菜 **shūcài** vegetable

Wǒ dǎsuàn yǐhòu duō chī shūcài shǎo chī ròu.
我打算以后多吃蔬菜少吃肉。
I plan to eat more vegetables and less meat.

2. 时蔬 **shíshū** seasonal vegetable

Zhèxiē dōu shì dāngjì shíshū, nǐ láidé zhèng shì shíhòu.
这些都是当季时蔬，你来得正是时候。
These are all seasonal vegetables. You have come at the right time.

3. 蔬果 **shūguǒ** vegetables and fruit

Nàjiā nóngchǎngde shūguǒ jì xīnxiān yòu piányi.
那家农场的蔬果既新鲜又便宜。
The vegetables and fruit at that farm are fresh and cheap.

4. 蔬果汁 **shūguǒzhī** vegetable and fruit juice

Lóuxià xīnkāide diàn zhǐ mài yǒujī shūguǒzhī, chángcháng dà-pái-cháng-lóng.
楼下新开的店只卖有机蔬果汁，常常大排长龙。
The newly open store downstairs sells only organic vegetable and fruit juice. There is often a long line.

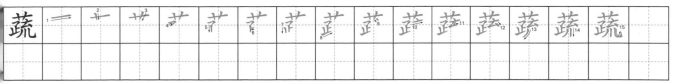

Lesson 15 Exercises

Part 1 Choose from the following words to fill in the blanks.

> 终于、祝、忘、照、烧烤

1. 先生，可以麻烦您帮我（　　　　）张相吗？

2. 你（　　　　）来了，我等了你快一个小时了。

3. 你明天再提醒下我，我担心自己（　　　　）了。

4. 新的一年（　　　　）大家身体健康，工作顺利！

Part 2 Complete the following dialogues using Chinese characters.

1. A: 天气好的时候，你会出去野餐吗？

   B: _____ 。

2. A: 要是出去野餐，你常带什么食物？

   B: _____ 。

3. A: 你最喜欢什么户外活动（**shìwài huódòng**: outdoor activities）？

   B: _____ 。

4. A: 你你喜不喜欢拍照片？

   B: _____ 。

5. A: 在你的脸书（**Liǎnshū**: Facebook）上有很多照片吗？

   B: _____ 。

Part 3 学以致用

你是学校学生会的会长，现在请你组织一个给大一学生的室外活动。这次活动主要是希望大一新生能多认识新朋友，早一点儿适应大学生活。请你写下这个活动的时间、地点以及活动的内容。

活动时间：

活动地点：

谁可以参加：

学生要准备什么？

活动那一天要做什么？

What to Do During Our Break? 假期做什么好？

1. Dialogue

Read the dialogue below and answer the questions in characters.

小江：	大海，寒假快到了，你有什么计划？会出去玩儿吗？
大海：	寒假很短，不出去了，刚好省钱。我打算上午在图书馆打工，下午去当家教挣点儿生活费。
小江：	你教什么课？
大海：	数学跟英文都教。你呢？想好做什么了吗？
小江：	我要跟学校的合唱团去澳洲演出。
大海：	真棒！现在正好是澳洲的夏天，多暖和啊！听说澳洲人很喜欢骑马和跳伞。你要去试试吗？
小江：	骑马可以，跳伞我可不敢！我怕高，对我来说简直太可怕了。我想去参观当地的博物馆和艺术馆。
大海：	澳洲的海鲜也很有名，你一定要好好品尝品尝。
小江：	哈哈，我已经预订好了要去的餐厅。
大海：	真羡慕你，希望以后我也能去世界各地看看。
小江：	以后有的是机会。
大海	那祝你在澳洲玩儿得开心。
小江：	谢谢，也祝你假期愉快！等我回来我们再聚！

1. 大海假期有什么计划？

2. 小江跟谁去澳洲？他去澳洲做什么？

3. 小江去澳洲会品尝什么美食？

2. Vocabulary

	Word	Pinyin	English equivalent
1.	寒假	**hánjià**	winter break
2.	计划	**jìhuà**	plan
3.	省钱	**shěng qián**	save money
4.	打工	**dǎgōng**	have a job outside of class time
5.	家教	**jiājiào**	tutor
6.	挣	**zhèng**	make (money)
7.	教	**jiāo**	teach
8.	短	**duǎn**	short
9.	演出	**yǎnchū**	perform; show
10.	正好	**zhènghǎo**	just in time; happen to
11.	夏天	**xiàtiān**	summer
12.	马	**mǎ**	horse
13.	跳伞	**tiàosǎn**	parachute
14.	敢	**gǎn**	dare
15.	简直	**jiǎnzhí**	simply
16.	当地	**dāngdì**	local
17.	艺术馆	**yìshùguǎn**	museum
18.	预定	**yùdìng**	reserve
19.	世界	**shìjiè**	world
20.	各地	**gèdì**	various places
21.	开心	**kāixīn**	have a good time
22.	愉快	**yúkuài**	delightful; pleasant

3. New Characters

Fifteen characters are introduced in this lesson. Use the following explanations to help you understand and remember the characters.

假　省　教　数　简　世　界　观　博　季　艺　术　演　图　定

CHARACTER 226

假

jià/jiǎ
vacation/false

11 STROKES   亻 **RADICAL**

Useful phrases and sentences

1. 假期 **jiàqī** vacation

   Wǒ hái méi xiǎnghǎo zěnme ānpai zìjǐde jiàqī.
   我还没想好怎么安排自己的假期。
   I haven't decided what to do during my vacation.

2. 暑假 **shǔjià** summer vacation

   Shǔjià kuài dàole, dàxuésheng kāishǐ zhǎo shíxíde gōngzuò.
   暑假快到了，大学生开始找实习的工作。
   Summer vacation is approaching. College students are starting to find internship opportunities.

3. 假 **jiǎ** false; fake

   Zhège xīnwén shì jiǎde, nǐ bié xiāngxìn.
   这个新闻是假的，你别相信。
   This is fake news. Don't believe it.

4. 假装 **jiǎzhuāng** pretend

   Wǒ gēn tā dǎ zhāohu, kěshì tā jiǎzhuāng méi tīngjiàn.
   我跟他打招呼，可是他假装没听见。
   I said hi to him, but he pretended that he didn't hear me.

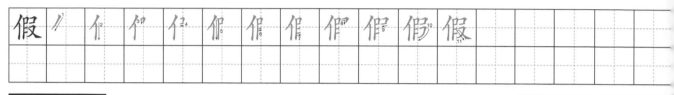

CHARACTER 227

省

shěng
save; province

9 STROKES   目 **RADICAL**

Useful phrases and sentences

1. 省 **shěng** province

   Nǐ zhùzài nǎge shěng? Nǎge shì?
   你住在哪个省？哪个市？
   Which province and which city do you live in?

2. 省会 **shěnghuì** provincial capital

   Hēilóngjiāngde shěnghuì shì Hā'ěrbīn.
   黑龙江的省会是哈尔滨。
   The provincial capital of Heilongjiang Province is Harbin.

3. 省钱 **shěng qián** to save money

   Wèile shěng qián, tā cónglái bú qù fànguǎnr chīfàn.
   为了省钱，他从来不去饭馆儿吃饭。
   To save money, he never eats at restaurants.

4. 省时间 **shěng shíjiān** to save time

   Dàhǎi gōngzuò tài mángle, wèile shěng shíjiān chángcháng chī fāngbiànmiàn.
   大海工作太忙了，为了省时间常常吃方便面。
   Dahai's job keeps him very busy. He often has instant noodles in order to save time.

CHARACTER 228

教

jiāo/jiào
teach/teaching

11 STROKES   攵 **RADICAL**

Useful phrases and sentences

1. 教 **jiāo** teach

   Nǐ kě-bùkěyi jiāo wǒ zuò mápó dòufu?
   你可不可以教我做麻婆豆腐？
   Can you teach me how to make mapo dofu?

2. 教育 **jiàoyù** education

   Měiguó jiàoyù tèbié zhòngshì xuésheng gèrénde xìngqù hé fāzhǎn.
   美国教育特别重视学生个人的兴趣和发展。
   American education puts special focus on the students' individual interests and development.

3. 教堂 **jiàotáng** church

   Zhōumò wǒmen quánjiārén dōu huì qù jiàotáng zuò lǐbài.
   周末我们全家人都会去教堂做礼拜。
   Our family goes to church every weekend.

4. 教授 **jiàoshòu** professor

   Lǐ Jiàoshòu yánjiū zuòde hěn hǎo, kè yě shàngde hěn yǒuyìsi.
   李教授研究做得很好，课也上得很有意思。
   Professor Li's research is outstanding. His lectures are also interesting.

CHARACTER 229

数

shù/shǔ
number/count

13 STROKES **攵 RADICAL**

Useful phrases and sentences

1. 数据 **shùjù** data
   Tā yánjiūde shì jìsuànjī shùjù fēnxī.
   他研究的是计算机数据分析。
   His research is about computational data analysis.

2. 数字 **shùzì** number
   Zhōngguó rén bù xǐhuan "sì" zhège shùzì, yīnwèi gēn "sǐ" de fāyīn bǐjiào xiàng.
   中国人不喜欢"四"这个数字，因为跟"死"的发音比较像。
   Chinese people don't like the number "four" as it sounds like "si" meaning "death."

3. 数一数 **shǔyishǔ** count
   Nǐ shǔyishǔ jīntiān yígòng láile duōshǎo rén.
   你数一数今天一共来了多少人。
   You should take today's attendance.

4. 数学 **shùxué** mathematics
   Dīng Xiānshengde liǎngge háizi dōu shì xué shùxué zhuānyède.
   丁先生的两个孩子都是学数学专业的。
   Both of Mr. Ding's children are majoring in mathematics.

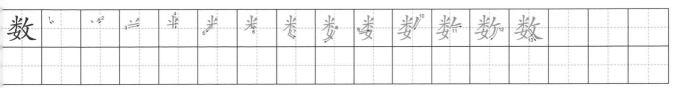

CHARACTER 230

简

jiǎn
simple

13 STROKES **竹 RADICAL**

Useful phrases and sentences

1. 简历 **jiǎnlì** curriculum vitae
   Míngtiān lái miànshì qǐng nǐ dài yífèn jiǎnlì.
   明天来面试请你带一份简历。
   Please bring your CV to your interview tomorrow.

2. 简称 **jiǎnchēng** abbreviation
   "Húnán" de jiǎnchēng shì "Xiāng".
   "湖南"的简称是"湘"。
   The abbreviated term for Hunan Province is "Xiang."

3. 简直 **jiǎnzhí** simply
   Tā fàngqìle zhème hǎode gōngzuò, wǒ jiǎnzhí bù néng lǐjiě.
   他放弃了这么好的工作，我简直不能理解。
   I simply can't understand why he gave up such a good job.

4. 简体字 **jiǎntǐzì** Simplified Chinese Character
   Wǒ huì xiě Jiǎntǐzì, yě huì rèn Fántǐzì.
   我会写简体字，也会认繁体字。
   I can write in Simplified Characters. I am also able to read Traditional Characters.

CHARACTER 231

世

shì
life; world

5 STROKES **一 RADICAL**

Useful phrases and sentences

1. 问世 **wènshì** to come out
   Nǐ zhīdao dìyītái jìsuànjī shì nǎnián wènshìde ma?
   你知道第一台计算机是哪年问世的吗？
   Do you know the year when the first computer came out?

2. 世纪 **shìjì** century
   Zhōngguó zài èrshí shìjì qīshí niándài mò shíxíngle "Gǎigé Kāifàng" zhèngcè.
   中国在二十世纪七十年代末实行了"改革开放"政策。
   China implemented the "Reform and Open Policy" by the end of 1970s.

3. 世界杯 **Shìjièbēi** World Cup
   Shìjièbēi zúqiúsài měi sìnián jǔbàn yícì.
   世界杯足球赛每四年举办一次。
   The FIFA World Cup is held every four years.

4. 世界 **shìjiè** world
   Wǒ zuìdàde mèngxiǎng jiù shì qù shìjiè gèdì lǚxíng.
   我最大的梦想就是去世界各地旅行。
   My biggest dream is to travel to various places in the world.

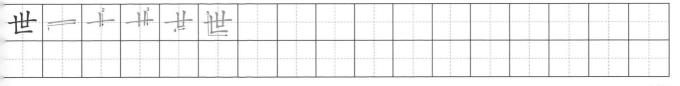

界

jiè
boundary

Useful phrases and sentences

1. 界限 **jièxiàn** boundary

Hùliánwǎng dǎpòle gōutōngde jièxiàn.
互联网打破了沟通的界限。
The internet has broken the boundaries of communication.

2. 外界 **wàijiè** outside world

Liǎngguó Zǒngtǒng hái méiyǒu duì wàijiè shuōmíng tāmende tánhuà nèiróng.
两国总统还没有对外界说明他们的谈话内容。
The two presidents have not revealed their discussions to the outside world.

3. 动物界 **dòngwùjiè** animal world

Shīzi kěyǐ shuō shì dòngwùjiè zuì xiōngměngde yěshòu.
狮子可以说是动物界最凶猛的野兽。
Lions are said to be the most ferocious beasts in the animal world.

4. 大开眼界 **dà-kāi-yǎn-jiè** eye-opening

Zhècì chūguó fǎngwèn zhēn ràng wǒ dà-kāi-yǎn-jiè, shōuhuò hěn duō.
这次出国访问真让我大开眼界，收获很多。
This visit abroad is truly eye-opening. I've learned a lot.

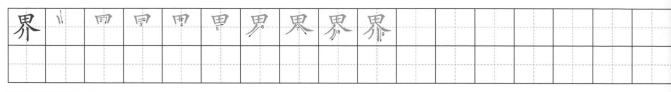

观

guān
watch;
point of view

Useful phrases and sentences

1. 观看 **guānkàn** to watch

Tīngshuō Xiàozhǎng jīntiān wǎnshang yě huì lái guānkàn wǒmende yǎnchū.
听说校长今天晚上也会来观看我们的演出。
I heard that the school president will also come to watch our performance tonight.

2. 观察 **guānchá** to observe

Dàole guówài, nǐ yīnggāi duō guānchá dāngdì rénde shēnghuó xíguàn.
到了国外，你应该多观察当地人的生活习惯。
When you are abroad, you should observe the lifestyles of the local people.

3. 观点 **guāndiǎn** point of view; viewpoint

Yǒuqián jiù děngyú kuàilè ma? Wǒ bù tóngyì zhège guāndiǎn.
有钱就等于快乐吗？我不同意这个观点。
Is being rich equal to being happy? I disagree with this viewpoint.

4. 观念 **guānniàn** concept; views

Zài guòqù, hěnduō rén yǒu zhòng-nán-qīng-nǚde guānniàn.
在过去，很多人有重男轻女的观念。
In the past, many people had a patriarchal view.

博

bó
rich; extensive

Useful phrases and sentences

1. 博学 **bóxué** knowledgeable

Gāo Zhì'ān fēicháng bóxué, jīngtōng hǎojǐguó yǔyán.
高志安非常博学，精通好几国语言。
Gao Zhi'an is knowledgeable. He is fluent in several languages.

2. 博士 **bóshì** doctoral degree; PhD

Jùshuō zài Měiguó dú bóshì xuéwèi fēicháng bù róngyì.
据说在美国读博士学位非常不容易。
I heard that it is not easy to complete a PhD in the U.S.A. .

3. 博客 **bókè** blog

Xiǎojiāng jīngcháng zài bókèshang xiě yìxiē gēn jiàoyù yǒuguānde wénzhāng.
小江经常在博客上写一些跟教育有关的文章。
Xiao Jiang often writes articles about education on her blog.

4. 赌博 **dǔbó** to gamble

Tā yuánlái hěn yǒu qián, hòulái dǔbó bǎ qián shūguāngle.
他原来很有钱，后来赌博把钱输光了。
He was rich, but he lost all his money to gambling.

CHARACTER 235

季
jì
season

8 STROKES   子 **RADICAL**

Useful phrases and sentences

1. 季节 **jìjié** season

   Qù Wēngēhuá lǚyóude huà nǎge jìjié bǐjiào hǎo?

   去温哥华旅游的话哪个季节比较好？

   What is the best season to go to Vancouver?

2. 旺季 **wàngjì** peak season

   Nǐ qiānwàn bié zài lǚyóu wàngjì qù pá Chángchéng, rén tài duōle.

   你千万别在旅游旺季去爬长城，人太多了。

   Please don't go to the Great Wall during the peak season. It's totally packed.

3. 季军 **jìjūn** third place; bronze medalist

   Xiǎo Xīn zài shèjī bǐsàizhōng huòdé jìjūn.

   小新在射击比赛中获得季军。

   Xiao Xin won third place in the shooting competition.

4. 雨季 **yǔjì** rainy season

   Zhōngguó nánfāng yǔjì yìbān shì cóng sìyuè dào jiǔyuè.

   中国南方雨季一般是从四月到九月。

   In southern China, the rainy season goes from April to September.

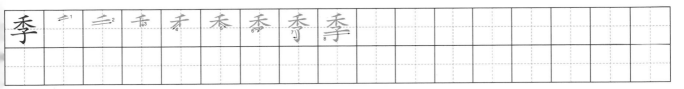

CHARACTER 236

艺
yì
skill; art

4 STROKES   艹 **RADICAL**

Useful phrases and sentences

1. 手艺 **shǒuyì** skill; craftsmanship

   Bié kàn shīfu niánqīng, kěshì zuòfànde shǒuyì hěn hǎo.

   别看师傅年轻，可是做饭的手艺很好。

   The chef may look young, but his cooking skills are very good.

2. 文艺 **wényì** literature and art

   Tā rènwéi wényì zuòpǐn bìxū yào fǎnyìng zhēnshíde shēnghuó.

   他认为文艺作品必须要反映真实的生活。

   He thinks that literature and art need to reflect genuine life.

3. 工艺品 **gōngyìpǐn** handicraft

   Zhèjiàn gōngyìpǐn hěn yǒu shǎoshù mínzú tèsè.

   这件工艺品很有少数民族特色。

   This piece of handicraft has the characteristics of minority groups.

4. 艺术 **yìshù** art; fine arts

   Jiějie cóngxiǎo xǐhuan yìshù, duì huìhuà, yīnyuè, wǔdǎo dōu hěn gǎn xìngqu.

   姐姐从小喜欢艺术，对绘画、音乐、舞蹈都很感兴趣。

   My older sister has liked the fine arts since she was young. She is interested in drawing, music, and dancing.

CHARACTER 237

shù
method; technique

5 STROKES   木 **RADICAL**

Useful phrases and sentences

1. 技术 **jìshù** technique; technology

   Zhèjiā yīyuàn zhǎngwòle zuì xiānjìnde yīliáo jìshù.

   这家医院掌握了最先进的医疗技术。

   This hospital possesses the most advanced medical technology.

2. 医术 **yīshù** medical expertise

   Wáng Dàifu yīshù hěn gāo, duì bìngrénde tàidù yě tèbié hǎo.

   王大夫医术很高，对病人的态度也特别好。

   Dr. Wang's medical expertise is very high. He has also been praised for his attitude towards patients.

3. 武术 **wǔshù** wushu (martial arts)

   Hěnduō xué wǔshùde háizi dōu xīwàng yǐhòu néng yǎn gōngfu diànyǐng.

   很多学武术的孩子都希望以后能演功夫电影。

   Many kids learning martial arts have the dream of being in a kungfu film.

4. 美术 **měishù** art; the fine arts

   Wǒ xiǎoxuéde shíhou zuì xǐhuan shàng měishù kè.

   我小学的时候最喜欢上美术课。

   I loved art class the most in elementary school.

What to Do During Our Break?   149

CHARACTER 238

演

yǎn
to act; perform

Useful phrases and sentences

1. 演出 **yǎnchū** perform

   Míngnián wǒ yào gēn xuéxiào héchàngtuán qù guówài yǎnchū.
   明年我要跟学校合唱团去国外演出。
   I am traveling with the school choir next year to perform abroad.

2. 演员 **yǎnyuán** actor; cast

   Zhèbù diànyǐngde yǎnyuán hěn niánqīng, dànshì yǎnde hěn hǎo.
   这部电影的演员很年轻，但是演得很好。
   The cast in this movie are young but they acted well.

3. 表演 **biǎoyǎn** perform

   Jīntiānde Zhōngwénkè Lǎoshī ràng wǒmen biǎoyǎn yíge xiǎopǐn.
   今天的中文课老师让我们表演一个小品。
   The teacher asked us to perform a skit in our Chinese class today.

4. 导演 **dǎoyǎn** director (film, etc.)

   Jīnnián Àosīkǎ zuìjiā dǎoyǎn huì shì shéi ne?
   今年奥斯卡最佳导演会是谁呢？
   Who is going to be the winner of the Best Director Oscar this year?

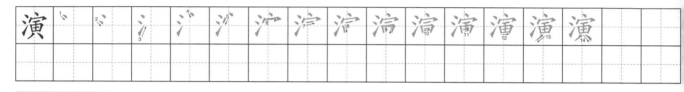

CHARACTER 239

图

tú
diagram; picture

Useful phrases and sentences

1. 图案 **tú'àn** pattern

   Nǐ T-xùshānde tú'àn hěn hǎokàn, búguò shì shénme yìsi?
   你T-恤衫的图案很好看，不过是什么意思？
   I like the pattern on your T-shirt, but what does it mean?

2. 图片 **túpiàn** photo

   Míngtiān xiàwǔ yǒu yíge gǔdài jiànzhù túpiàn zhǎn.
   明天下午有一个古代建筑图片展。
   There is a photo exhibition on ancient architecture tomorrow afternoon.

3. 图表 **túbiǎo** table; chart; diagram

   Zhèxiē shùzì zuìhǎo yòng túbiǎo biǎoshì chūlai, zhèyàng gèng qīngchǔ.
   这些数字最好用图表表示出来，这样更清楚。
   These numbers are best illustrated with diagrams. It's much clearer.

4. 图书馆 **túshūguǎn** library

   Xuéxiào túshūguǎn lǐ yǒu gèzhǒng shūjí.
   学校图书馆里有各种书籍。
   The school library has all kinds of books.

CHARACTER 240

定

dìng
to fix; decide

Useful phrases and sentences

1. 规定 **guīdìng** to stipulate; to set

   Gōngsī guīdìng, chídào shíwǔfēnzhōng fá yìbǎikuài.
   公司规定，迟到十五分钟罚一百块。
   The company has set a fine of one hundred kuai for being fifteen minutes late.

2. 肯定 **kěndìng** definitely; to be certain

   Gāng dào Zhōngguóde shíhou nǐ kěndìng hěn bù xíguàn ba?
   刚到中国的时候你肯定很不习惯吧？
   You were definitely not used to it when you just arrived in China, right?

3. 一定 **yídìng** must; be sure to

   Yǒu rènhé wèntí yídìng yào ràng wǒ zhīdao.
   有任何问题一定要让我知道。
   You must let me know if you have any questions.

4. 不确定 **bú quèdìng** uncertain

   Wáng Xiānsheng bú quèdìng néng-bùnéng cānjiā wǒmen bāyuède jùhuì.
   王先生不确定能不能参加我们八月的聚会。
   Mr. Wang is uncertain if he can join our gathering in August.

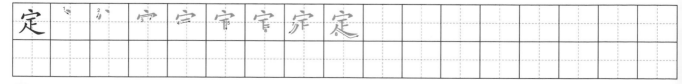

Part 1 Choose from the following words to fill in the blanks.

参观、省钱、教、演、一定

1. 这个电影的故事不太好，可是演员（　　　　　）得还不错。

2. 这次你帮了我这么大的忙，（　　　　　）让我请你吃顿饭。

3. 为了（　　　　　），她总是在打折的时候买东西。

4. 你能（　　　　　）我怎么用这个新手机吗？

Part 2 Complete the following dialogues using Chinese characters.

1. A: 你最近有没有假期？

   B: _____ 。

2. A: 一般来说，你怎么安排自己的假期？

   B: _____ 。

3. A: 你有没有去过别的国家演出？

   B: _____ 。

4. A: 你在假期打过工吗？你觉得在图书馆打工有意思吗？

   B: _____ 。

5. A: 你当过家教吗？你教谁？教什么课？

   B: _____ 。

Part 3 学以致用

暑假到了，你准备开始安排你的假期生活。下面有四个选择，请选择一个你觉得适合你做的，并说说为什么。

1. 去社区图书馆打工　　　　2. 去国外旅游　　　　3. 去饭馆儿打工　　　　4. 去当志愿者

LESSON 17

Studying Abroad 出国留学

1. Dialogue

Read the dialogue below and answer the questions in characters.

李想:	陈彬，这是上次借你的书，谢谢！
陈彬:	不客气。对了，你在微信上说申请上了美国大学的研究生院，恭喜你啊！
李想:	谢谢，运气不错，比想象的顺利多了。
陈彬:	我在网上看了你们学校的照片，绿树、蓝天、白房子，景色很美。那你什么时候出发？
李想:	我打算七月走，最近忙着办护照，申请签证什么的。
陈彬:	你现在一定很期待吧！
李想:	说实话，压力挺大的。一是担心我的口语不够好，怕讲话别人听不明白。二是留学费用太高，一年好几十万。还有，到了国外，得学会独立，不像现在，有家人在身边。
陈彬:	国外生活方式跟中国确实很不一样，但是相信你会很快适应的。如果你心情不好，记得给我打电话。对了，我们有多少个小时的时差？
李想:	十二个。
陈彬:	知道了，那你快去忙吧。你走之前我们再吃个饭聊聊。
李想:	好的，再联系！

1. 李想要去哪儿留学？他申请研究生院顺利吗？

2. 李想最近在忙什么？

3. 李想为什么觉得出国留学压力很大？

2. Vocabulary

	Word	Pinyin	English equivalent
1.	借	**jiè**	lend; borrow
2.	微信	**Wēixìn**	WeChat
3.	研究生院	**yánjiūshēngyuàn**	graduate school
4.	运气	**yùnqì**	luck
5.	想象	**xiǎngxiàng**	imagine
6.	树	**shù**	tree
7.	蓝	**lán**	blue
8.	景色	**jǐngsè**	scenery
9.	护照	**hùzhào**	passport
10.	申请	**shēnqǐng**	apply
11.	期待	**qīdài**	expect
12.	压力	**yālì**	pressure; stress
13.	口语	**kǒuyǔ**	spoken language
14.	讲话	**jiǎnghuà**	talk
15.	留学	**liúxué**	study abroad
16.	万	**wàn**	ten thousand
17.	独立	**dúlì**	independent
18.	方式	**fāngshì**	style; way
19.	确实	**quèshí**	indeed
20.	适应	**shìyìng**	adapt; get used to
21	如果	**rúguǒ**	if
22.	时差	**shíchā**	jet lag

3. New Characters

Fifteen characters are introduced in this lesson. Use the following explanations to help you understand and remember the characters.

留　护　式　申　签　证　如　独　立　景　适　树　蓝　压　讲

留

liú
to stay; leave

10 STROKES   田 **RADICAL**

Useful phrases and sentences

1. 留 **liú** to leave (something)

   Bīngxiānglǐ nà iǎngkuài dàngāo shì wǒ liúgěi nǐ de.
   冰箱里那两块蛋糕是我留给你的。
   I left you two pieces of cakes in the fridge.

2. 留学 **liúxué** to study abroad

   Qù Yīngguó liúxué yìnián dàgài yào huā duōshǎo qián?
   去英国留学一年大概要花多少钱?
   How much does it cost annually to study in the U.K.?

3. 挽留 **wǎnliú** keep

   Jìrán nín hái yǒu biéde shì, wǒ jiù bù wǎnliú nín le.
   既然您还有别的事, 我就不挽留您了。
   Since you still have other things to do, I will not keep you any longer.

4. 保留 **bǎoliú** to retain; to maintain

   Zhège xiǎozhènde jūmín bǎoliúle hěnduō chuántǒngde fēngsú xíguàn.
   这个小镇的居民保留了很多传统的风俗习惯。
   The residents of this small town retain many traditional customs.

护

hù
protect

7 STROKES   扌 **RADICAL**

Useful phrases and sentences

1. 保护 **bǎohù** protect

   Mùqián hěnduō yěshēng dòngwù dōu débudào bǎohù.
   目前很多野生动物都得不到保护。
   Many wild animals are still not protected.

2. 护照 **hùzhào** passport

   Zāogāo, wǒde hùzhào bú jiànle. Kànyīxià shì-búshì zài nǐde bèibāo?
   糟糕, 我的护照不见了。看一下是不是在你的背包?
   Darn, I can't find my passport. Can you check your backpack?

3. 救护车 **jiùhùchē** ambulance

   Jiùhùchē yǐjīng zài lùshàngle, mǎshàng jiù dào.
   救护车已经在路上了, 马上就到。
   The ambulance is already on the way and will be here soon.

4. 护士 **hùshì** nurse

   Hùshì nǐ hǎo, Xú Yīshēng zài nǎge bàngōngshì?
   护士你好, 徐医生在哪个办公室?
   Excuse me, Nurse, where is Dr. Xu's office?

式

shì
pattern; style

6 STROKES   弋 **RADICAL**

Useful phrases and sentences

1. 样式 **yàngshì** style

   Nǐ kàn, nàjiàn yīfude yàngshì hěn tèbié.
   你看, 那件衣服的样式很特别。
   Look, the style of that dress is special.

2. 开幕式 **kāimùshì** opening ceremony

   Huìyìde kāimùshì wǎnshàng qīdiǎnbàn kāishǐ.
   会议的开幕式晚上七点半开始。
   The opening ceremony of the conference begins at 7.30 pm.

3. 形式 **xíngshì** format

   Lǎoshī, wǒmen qīmò kǒushìde xíngshì shì shénme?
   老师, 我们期末口试的形式是什么?
   Teacher, what is the format of our final oral exam?

4. 正式 **zhèngshì** formal

   Zhèpiān wénzhāngde yǔyán fēicháng zhèngshì, bú tài róngyì dǒng.
   这篇文章的语言非常正式, 不太容易懂。
   The language of this article is very formal. It's not easy to understand.

CHARACTER 244

申

shēn
to state; to extend

5 STROKES | 田 RADICAL

Useful phrases and sentences

1. 申请 **shēnqǐng** apply

Chén Bīn zuìjìn mángzhe shēnqǐng xīn gōngzuò.
陈彬最近忙着申请新工作。
Chen Bin is busy applying for new jobs recently.

2. 申办 **shēnbàn** bid for

Mùqián yǒu sānge chéngshì yào shēnbàn Àoyùnhuì.
目前有三个城市要申办奥运会。
At this point, three cities are bidding to host the Olympic Games.

3. 申诉 **shēnsù** appeal

Rúguǒ nǐ juéde bù gōngpíng, kěyǐ jìxù shēnsù.
如果你觉得不公平，可以继续申诉。
If you think this is unfair, you can file an appeal.

4. 申城 **Shēnchéng** Shencheng

Shànghǎi yě bèi jiàozuò "Shēnchéng."
上海也被叫做"申城"。
Shanghai is also called "Shencheng."

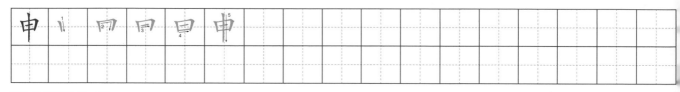

CHARACTER 245

签

qiān
sign one's name

13 STROKES | 竹 RADICAL

Useful phrases and sentences

1. 签证 **qiānzhèng** visa

Xiàge yuè dàgē yào dào Chéngdū qù bàn Měiguóde qiānzhèng.
下个月大哥要到成都去办美国的签证。
My older brother is going to Chengdu next month to apply for a U.S. visa.

2. 签名 **qiānmíng** one's signature

Nǐ kàn, zhè shàngtou yǒu Zǒngtǒngde qiānmíng.
你看，这上头有总统的签名。
Look, the president's signature is on it.

3. 签字 **qiānzì** sign one's name

Xiānsheng, qǐng nín zài zhèzhāng fāpiàoshang qiānzì.
先生，请您在这张发票上签字。
Sir, please sign your name on this receipt.

4. 签约 **qiānyuē** sign a contract

Wǒ yǐjīng gēn yìjiā shípǐn gōngsī qiānyuēle.
我已经跟一家食品公司签约了。
I've signed a contract with a food company.

CHARACTER 246

证

zhèng
to prove;
certificate

7 STROKES | 讠 RADICAL

Useful phrases and sentences

1. 保证 **bǎozhèng** promise; guarantee

Lǐ Xiānsheng xiàng qīzi bǎozhèng, cóng míngtiān qǐ zài yě bù chōuyānle.
李先生向妻子保证，从明天起再也不抽烟了。
Mr. Li promised his wife that he would never smoke again from tomorrow onward.

2. 证明 **zhèngmíng** proof

Kǎoshì chéngjì hǎo bù néng zhèngmíng yígè rénde gōngzuò nénglì qiáng.
考试成绩好不能证明一个人的工作能力强。
Good grades on tests are not a proof of a person's working ability.

3. 证书 **zhèngshū** certificate

Lǐ Xiǎng sùshè qiángshang guàzhe tā shùxué bǐsàide huòjiǎng zhèngshū.
李想宿舍墙上挂着他数学比赛的获奖证书。
An award certificate from a math competition is hanging on the wall of Li Xiang's dormitory.

4. 证件 **zhèngjiàn** permit; identification

Qǐng chūshì nínde zhèngjiàn, fǒuzé bù néng jìnrù.
请出示您的证件，否则不能进入。
Please show your identification. Otherwise you cannot enter.

CHARACTER 247

如

rú
if; as

Useful phrases and sentences

1. 如果 rúguǒ if

Rúguǒ wǒ qùwǎnle, nǐmen xiān chīfàn, bú yào děng wǒ.
如果我去晚了，你们先吃饭，不要等我。
If I am late, you eat first. Don't wait for me.

2. 假如 jiǎrú if; hypothetically

Jiǎrú wǒ yǒu mófǎ, wǒ xīwàng zìjǐ huì shuō hěnduōzhǒng yǔyán.
假如我有魔法，我希望自己会说很多种语言。
If I could use magic, I would use it to be able to speak in many languages.

3. 比如 bǐrú such as

Tā yǒu hěnduō àihào, bǐrú yóuyǒng hé dúshū.
她有很多爱好，比如游泳和读书。
She has many hobbies, such as swimming and reading.

4. 不如 bùrú not as good as

Qù xuéxiào shítáng chīfàn bùrú zìjǐ zuò, jì piányi yòu hǎochī.
去学校食堂吃饭不如自己做，既便宜又好吃。
Eating at the school's cafeteria is not as good as cooking on your own. It's cheaper and tasty.

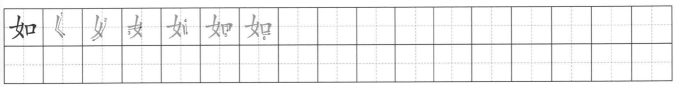

CHARACTER 248

独

dú
alone; independent

Useful phrases and sentences

1. 独立 dúlì independent

Nǐ yǐjīng dàxué bìyèle, yīnggāi xuéhuì dúlì shēnghuó.
你已经大学毕业了，应该学会独立生活。
You've graduated from college. You should learn to live independently.

2. 单独 dāndú alone

Wǒ xiǎng gēn nǐ dāndú jiàngemiàn, bú yào jiào qítā rén.
我想跟你单独见个面，不要叫其他人。
I would like to meet you alone. Do not invite other people.

3. 独特 dútè unique

Zhège tǐyùguǎnde shèjì hěn dútè, xiàng yīge niǎocháo.
这个体育馆的设计很独特，像一个鸟巢。
The design of this gymnasium is unique. It looks like a bird's nest.

4. 孤独 gūdú lonely

Wáng Tàitaide háizi dōu zài guówài gōngzuò, tā yíge rén shēnghuó hěn gūdú.
王太太的孩子都在国外工作，她一个人生活很孤独。
Mrs. Wang's children are all abroad. She feels lonely living by herself.

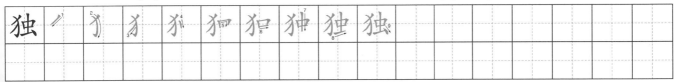

CHARACTER 249

lì
to stand

Useful phrases and sentences

1. 立刻 lìkè immediately

Lǎobǎn shuō yǒu jíshì, jiào wǒ lìkè qù zhǎo tā.
老板说有急事，叫我立刻去找他。
My boss asked me to go to him immediately for something urgent.

2. 立场 lìchǎng position; standpoint

Nǐ shì wǒmen gōngsīde rén, zěnme néng zhànzài duìfāngde lìchǎng?
你是我们公司的人，怎么能站在对方的立场？
You are from our company. How can you take the other side's position?

3. 立体 lìtǐ 3D; three dimensional

Nǐ liǎojiě 3D lìtǐ dǎyìn jìshù ma?
你了解3D立体打印技术吗？
Do you know the engineering for 3D printing?

4. 立足 lìzú to stand; establish

Rújīn, yíge rén yàoshì méiyǒu hěn hǎode jiàoyù bèijǐng, jiù hěn nán zài shèhuì lìzú.
如今，一个人要是没有很好的教育背景，就很难在社会立足。
Nowadays if a person does not have a good educational background, he will find it hard to establish himself in society.

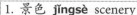

CHARACTER 250

景

jǐng
scenery

12 STROKES · 日 RADICAL

Useful phrases and sentences

1. 景色 **jǐngsè** scenery

   Nǐ chuāngwàide jǐngsè zhēn měi.
   你窗外的景色真美。
   The scenery outside your window is so beautiful.

2. 景物 **jǐngwù** landscape

   Jǐngwù huà hé rénwù huà, nǐ nǎge huàdehǎo?
   景物画和人物画，你哪个画得好？
   Landscape paintings and figure paintings, which do you do better?

3. 景点 **jǐngdiǎn** scenic spots

   Jiùjīnshān yǒu nǎxiē zhùmíngde jǐngdiǎn?
   旧金山有哪些著名的景点？
   What are some famous scenic spots in San Francisco?

4. 背景 **bèijǐng** background

   Hán Fēngde jiàoyù bèijǐng hěn hǎo, zhǎodào gōngzuò bìng bù nán.
   韩峰的教育背景很好，找到工作并不难。
   Han Feng's educational background is good. It's not difficult for him to find a job.

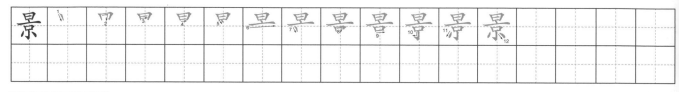

CHARACTER 251

适

shì
to fit

9 STROKES · 辶 RADICAL

Useful phrases and sentences

1. 适合 **shìhé** suit; fit

   Dìdi hái méi xiǎnghǎo shénme zhuānyè bǐjiào shìhé zìjǐ.
   弟弟还没想好什么专业比较适合自己。
   My younger brother hasn't decided which major is more suitable for him.

2. 适应 **shìyìng** adapt

   Xīwàng nǐ jìnkuài shìyìng dàxuéde shēnghuó.
   希望你尽快适应大学的生活。
   I hope that you will adapt to your college life quickly.

3. 合适 **héshì** appropriate

   Jīntiānde wǎnyàn bǐjiào zhèngshì, chuān niúzǎikù qù bú tài héshì.
   今天的晚宴比较正式，穿牛仔裤去不太合适。
   Today's banquet is formal. Wearing jeans is not appropriate.

4. 适当 **shìdàng** suitable; appropriate

   Tāmen zhījiān yǒu wùjiě, yīnggāi zhǎoge shìdàngde jīhuì tántán.
   他们之间有误解，应该找个适当的机会谈谈。
   There are misunderstandings between them. They need to find a suitable opportunity to talk.

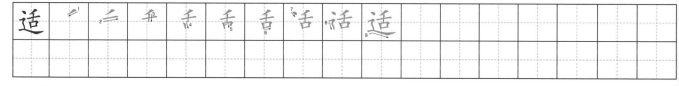

CHARACTER 252

树

shù
tree

9 STROKES · 木 RADICAL

Useful phrases and sentences

1. 树 **shù** tree

   Wǒ tèbié xǐhuān sùshè lóu ménkǒude nàjǐkē shù.
   我特别喜欢宿舍楼门口的那几棵树。
   I especially like the trees in front of our dormitory.

2. 种树 **zhòng shù** plant a tree

   Bàba zài hòuyuàn zhòngle jǐkē píngguǒ shù.
   爸爸在后院种了几棵苹果树。
   My father planted a few apple trees in the backyard.

3. 树枝 **shùzhī** branch

   Jǐzhī sōngshǔ zài shùzhīshang tiàolái tiàoqù.
   几只松鼠在树枝上跳来跳去。
   Several squirrels are jumping around the branches.

4. 树林 **shùlín** forest

   Zhèpiān shùlínlǐ yǒu hěnduō dòngwù, xiàng húlí, láng shénmede.
   这片树林里有很多动物，像狐狸、狼什么的。
   There are many animals in this forest, such as foxes and coyotes.

CHARACTER 253

蓝

lán
blue

13 STROKES   ^艹 **RADICAL**

Useful phrases and sentences

1. 蓝莓 **lánméi** blueberry

   Lánméi shì zhèrde tèchǎn, wèidao tèbié hǎo.
   蓝莓是这儿的特产，味道特别好。
   Blueberries are a special local product here. They taste amazing.

2. 蓝领 **lánlǐng** blue collar; common laborer

   Tīngshuō zài Àozhōu lánlǐngde gōngzī yě fēicháng gāo.
   听说在澳洲蓝领的工资也非常高。
   I heard that blue collar workers in Australia are also well-paid.

3. 蓝牙 **lányá** Bluetooth

   Xièxie nǐ sònggěi wǒde lányá ěrjī, tèbié hǎo yòng.
   谢谢你送给我的蓝牙耳机，特别好用。
   Thank you for the Bluetooth earphones you gave me. They are great.

4. 蓝色 **lánsè** blue

   Zhèjiàn lánsède wàitào gèng piàoliang yìxiē.
   这件蓝色的外套更漂亮一些。
   This blue jacket is prettier.

CHARACTER 254

压

yā
to press

6 STROKES   厂 **RADICAL**

Useful phrases and sentences

1. 压力 **yālì** pressure

   Měiguóde gāozhōngshēng xuéxí yālì yě fēicháng dà.
   美国的高中生学习压力也非常大。
   American high school students also have a great deal of study pressure.

2. 血压 **xuèyā** blood pressure

   Xǔ Māmā, nínde xuèyā dōu hěn zhèngcháng, méi shénme dàshì.
   许妈妈，您的血压都很正常，没什么大事。
   Mrs. Xu, your blood pressure is normal. You should be okay.

3. 气压 **qìyā** atmospheric pressure

   Shānshàng qìyā bǐjiào dī, zhùyìyīxià hūxī.
   山上气压比较低，注意一下呼吸。
   Atmospheric pressure is lower in the mountains. Pay attention to your breathing.

4. 压岁钱 **yāsuìqián** money given to children as a New Year's present

   Háizimen nádào yāsuìqián dōu hěn kāixīn.
   孩子们拿到压岁钱都很开心。
   Children are all very happy to receive money for the New Year.

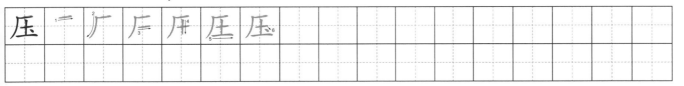

CHARACTER 255

讲

jiǎng
to talk; tell

6 STROKES   讠 **RADICAL**

Useful phrases and sentences

1. 讲 **jiǎng** tell

   Lǎoshī cháng gēn wǒmen jiǎng xuéxí wàiyǔde zhòngyàoxìng.
   老师常跟我们讲学习外语的重要性。
   The teacher often tells us the importance of learning foreign languages.

2. 讲话 **jiǎnghuà** talk

   Qǐng bú yào jiǎnghuàle, wǒmen zhǔnbèi shàngkèle.
   请不要讲话了，我们准备上课了。
   Please stop talking. The class is about to start.

3. 讲故事 **jiǎng gùshì** tell a story

   Wǒ měige zhōumò qù shèqū túshūguǎn gěi xiǎopéngyou jiǎng Zhōngwén gùshì.
   我每个周末去社区图书馆给小朋友讲中文故事。
   I go to the community library every weekend to tell Chinese stories to small kids.

4. 演讲 **yǎnjiǎng** speech

   Zhècì yǎnjiǎng bǐsàide tímù shì "Chéngshì Fāzhǎn yǔ Huánjìng Bǎohù."
   这次演讲比赛的题目是"城市发展与环境保护"。
   The topic of this speech contest is "Urban Development and Environmental Protection."

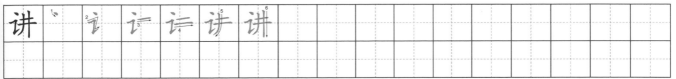

Lesson 17 Exercises

Part 1 Choose from the following words to fill in the blanks.

留学、独立、申请、讲、压力

1. 最近有好几个面试，我的（　　　　　）很大。

2. 高中毕业以后我就（　　　　　）生活了，没跟父母要过钱。

3. 小张，你在英国（　　　　　）那几年习惯那儿的生活吗？

4. 妹妹（　　　　　）了好几所大学，可是到现在还没有消息。

Part 2 Complete the following dialogues using Chinese characters.

1.　A: 你有没有留过学？要是有，你喜欢留学生活吗？

　　B: _____ 。

2.　A: 如果你有机会出国留学，你会选择哪个国家？

　　B: _____ 。

3.　A: 在你学校或者你住的城市，外国留学生多吗？

　　B: _____ 。

4.　A: 如果外国人去你的国家留学，你觉得什么比较难习惯？

　　B: _____ 。

5.　A: 你学习或者工作压力很大的时候，常常会怎么办？

　　B: _____ 。

Part 3 学以致用

一个外国学生准备去你的大学留学了，可是他担心习惯不了当地的生活。请你给他几点建议，帮助他早点适应新的留学生活。

1. _____

2. _____

3. _____

4. _____

LESSON 18

The Environment 环境问题

1. Dialogue

Read the dialogue below and answer the questions in characters.

张川：	你怎么戴着口罩？生病了吗？
安明：	没有，今天空气质量太差了，戴口罩是为了身体健康。你看，我在外面走了一天，口罩都变黑了。
张川：	唉，空气污染的问题真是越来越严重了，我感觉已经有很长时间没有看到太阳和蓝天了。
安明：	除了空气污染，城市交通问题也很严重，经常堵车，地铁、公交也总是挤满了人。政府也想了一些办法希望解决这些问题，可是好像作用不大。
张川：	其实，保护环境也不能只靠政府，我们大家都应该多注意。比方说在生活上，不要浪费水、电，也不要乱扔垃圾。
安明：	我同意你的看法，可回收垃圾和不可回收的一定要分开，要不然会造成更严重的浪费。
张川：	以前觉得环保问题离我们很远，现在才发现，没有好的环境就没有好的生活。

1. 安明为什么戴口罩？他生病了吗？

2. 环境问题越来越严重，都有哪些问题呢？

3. 安明觉得人们在生活上应该注意什么？

2. Vocabulary

	Word	Pinyin	English equivalent
1.	戴	dài	wear; put on
2.	口罩	kǒuzhào	face mask
3.	质量	zhìliàng	quality
4.	差	chà	bad; poor
5.	健康	jiànkāng	health
6.	黑	hēi	black; dark
7.	空气	kōngqì	air
8.	污染	wūrǎn	pollution
9.	太阳	tàiyang	sun
10.	交通	jiāotōng	traffic
11.	堵车	dǔchē	traffic jam
12.	地铁	dìtiě	subway
13.	公交	gōngjiāo	public transport
14.	挤	jǐ	packed; crowded
15.	政府	zhèngfǔ	government
16.	作用	zuòyòng	effect; impact
17.	环境	huánjìng	environment
18.	靠	kào	rely on
19.	更	gèng	even more
20.	浪费	làngfèi	waste
21.	垃圾	lājī	trash
22.	分开	fēnkāi	separate
23.	造成	zàochéng	result in
24.	发现	fāxiàn	realize; discover
25.	生活	shēnghuó	life

3. New Characters

Fifteen characters are introduced in this lesson. Use the following explanations to help you understand and remember the characters.

环　境　活　注　差　空　通　浪　污　染　挤　健　黑　垃　圾

CHARACTER 256

环

huán
to surround; ring

8 STROKES   **王 RADICAL**

Useful phrases and sentences

1. 环境 **huánjìng** environment

Wǒmen dōu yīnggāi zhòngshì huánjìng bǎohùde wèntí.

我们都应该重视环境保护的问题。

We should all face the issue of environmental protection.

2. 连环画 **liánhuánhuà** the comics

Xiǎoshíhou wǒ zuì xǐhuan kàn bàozhǐshàngde liánhuánhuà.

小时候我最喜欢看报纸上的连环画。

I loved the comics in the newspaper when I was little.

3. 环球 **huánqiú** around the world; worldwide

Tā zuìdàde mèngxiǎng jiù shì gēn qīzǐ huánqiú lǚxíng.

他最大的梦想就是跟妻子环球旅行。

His biggest dream is to travel around the world with his wife.

4. 环 **huán** component; link

Shìchǎng hé yònghù diàochá shì qǐyè fāzhǎnde zhòngyào yìhuán.

市场和用户调查是企业发展的重要一环。

Market and user surveys are an important component of business development.

CHARACTER 257

境

jìng
border

14 STROKES   **土 RADICAL**

Useful phrases and sentences

1. 边境 **biānjìng** border; frontier

Zhèliǎngge guójiā yìzhí cúnzài biānjìng wèntí.

这两个国家一直存在边境问题。

These two countries have had border issues for a long time.

2. 出境 **chūjìng** to leave a country; emigration

Chūjìng yǐhòu Zhāng Chuānde shǒujī jiù méiyǒu xìnhào le.

出境以后张川的手机就没有信号了。

Zhang Chuan lost his mobile phone signal when he left the country.

3. 境内 **jìngnèi** domestic; within the border

Zhōngguó jìngnèi yígòng yǒu duōshǎoge yěshēng dòngwùyuán?

中国境内一共有多少个野生动物园?

How many wildlife parks are there within China?

4. 入境 **rùjìng** to enter a country; immigration

Qù biéde guójiā lǚyóu, bànlǐ rùjìng shǒuxù chángcháng hěn máfan.

去别的国家旅游，办理入境手续常常很麻烦。

The process at immigration is always troublesome when you travel to other countries.

CHARACTER 258

活

huó
to live; lively

9 STROKES   **氵 RADICAL**

Useful phrases and sentences

1. 活 **huó** to live

Yéye hěn chángshòu, huódàole jiǔshíwǔsuì.

爷爷很长寿，活到了九十五岁。

My grandfather lived a long life. He lived to the age of ninety-five.

2. 活泼 **huópō** active

Māma shuō jiějie xiǎoshíhou hěn ānjìng, ér wǒ bǐjiào huópō.

妈妈说姐姐小时候很安静，而我比较活泼。

My mother said that my older sister was quiet while I was more active when we were little.

3. 干活儿 **gànhuór** to work

Ānmíng zhèng mángzhe gànhuór ne, nǐ bié dǎrǎo tā.

安明正忙着干活儿呢，你别打扰他。

Anming is busy with his work. Don't disturb him.

4. 灵活 **línghuó** flexible

Wǒde gōngzuò shíjiān hěn línghuó, kàn nín shénme shíhou fāngbiàn.

我的工作时间很灵活，看您什么时候方便。

My working schedule is flexible. Let me know when i is convenient for you.

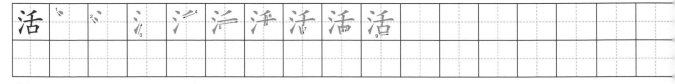

8 STROKES | 氵 RADICAL

注
zhù
pay attention;
register

Useful phrases and sentences

1. 关注 **guānzhù** follow closely

Zuìjìn dàjiā dōu zài guānzhù Zhōng-Měi màoyì wèntí.
最近大家都在关注中美贸易问题。
Everyone is closely following China-U.S. trade issues recently.

2. 注册 **zhùcè** register

Yàoshì xiǎng cānjiā wǒmende huódòng, nǐ děi tíqián zài wǎngshang zhùcè.
要是想参加我们的活动，你得提前在网上注册。
You need to register online in advance if you want to take part in our event.

3. 注重 **zhùzhòng** pay close attention to

Wǒmende Zhōngwén lǎoshī hěn zhùzhòng xùnliàn xuéshengde shēngdiào.
我们的中文老师很注重训练学生的声调。
Our Chinese teachers pay close attention to students' tones.

4. 注释 **zhùshì** notes; comments; annotation

Zhèběn cídiǎnde zhùshì suīrán jiǎndān, dànshì shuōde hěn qīngchu.
这本词典的注释虽然简单，但是说得很清楚。
The notes from this dictionary are simple but clear.

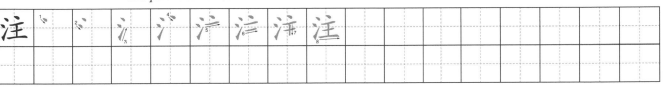

---

9 STROKES | 工 RADICAL

差
chà/chā
bad/gap

Useful phrases and sentences

1. 差 **chà** bad

Zhècì kǎoshì chéngjì tài chàle, wǒ děi hǎohao nǔlìle.
这次考试成绩太差了，我得好好努力了。
I did very badly on this test. I need to work harder.

2. 差不多 **chàbuduō** almost; about

Míngtiānde huì chàbùduō yào kāi yíge xiǎoshí.
明天的会差不多要开一个小时。
The meeting tomorrow will take about one hour.

3. 差别 **chābié** difference; distinction

Wǒ shízài kànbuchū zhèliǎngfú huàde chābié, nǐ ne?
我实在看不出这两幅画的差别，你呢？
I really can't see the difference between these two paintings. What about you?

4. 差距 **chājù** disparity; gap

Shìjièshàng hěnduō guójiā dōu yǒu yánzhòngde pínfù chājù wèntí.
世界上很多国家都有严重的贫富差距问题。
The disparity between rich and poor exists in many countries around the world.

---

8 STROKES | 穴 RADICAL

空
kōng/kòng
empty/free time

Useful phrases and sentences

1. 空 **kōng** empty

Bīngxiāng yǐjīng kōngle, wǒmen děi qù chāoshì mǎi diǎn cài le.
冰箱已经空了，我们得去超市买点菜了。
Our fridge is empty. We need to go to the supermarket to buy food.

2. 空间 **kōngjiān** space

Zhèkuǎn chē kōngjiān hěn dà, zuòzài lǐmiàn hěn shūfu.
这款车空间很大，坐在里面很舒服。
This car is spacious and is comfortable to sit in.

3. 空调 **kōngtiáo** air conditioner

Zhème rède tiān, nǐde sùshè jìngrán méiyǒu kōngtiáo?
这么热的天，你的宿舍竟然没有空调？
How come you don't have an air-conditioner in your dormitory for such a hot day?

4. 有空 **yǒukòng** have time

Nǐ shénme shíhou yǒukòng jiù lái jiālǐ zuòzuo.
你什么时候有空就来家里坐坐。
You can come to my place whenever you have time.

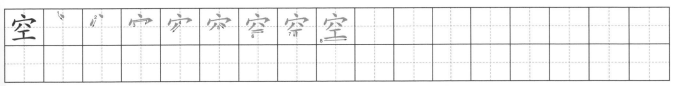

CHARACTER 262

通

tōng
to go through;
connect

10 STROKES | **辶 RADICAL**

Useful phrases and sentences

1. 通话 **tōnghuà** talk on the phone

   Bàoqiàn, wǒ zhèng gēn jiārén tōnghuà, nǐ bàngè xiǎoshí yǐhòu zài guòlái.
   抱歉，我正跟家人通话，你半个小时以后再过来。
   I am sorry. I am on the phone with my family. You can come over in half an hour.

2. 通常 **tōngcháng** usually

   Zhōngguó dàxuéshēng shǔjià tōngcháng huì qù dǎgōng huòzhě qù dāng zhìyuànzhě.
   中国大学生暑假通常会去打工或者去当志愿者。
   College students in China usually work part-time or do volunteer work in the summer.

3. 沟通 **gōutōng** to communicate

   Wǒ gēn fùmǔ gōutōng yǒu wèntí, tāmen zǒng shuō wǒde xiǎngfǎ tài tiānzhēn.
   我跟父母沟通有问题，他们总说我的想法太天真。
   I have problems communicating with my parents. They always say that I am too naïve.

4. 普通话 **pǔtōnghuà** putonghua; Mandarin Chinese

   Nǐ gēn fùmǔ shuō Pǔtōnghuà háishì Shànghǎihuà?
   你跟父母说普通话还是上海话？
   Do you speak Mandarin Chinese or Shanghainese with your parents?

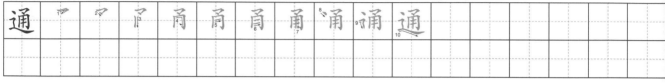

CHARACTER 263

浪

làng
wave;
unrestrained

10 STROKES | **氵 RADICAL**

Useful phrases and sentences

1. 浪费 **làngfèi** waste

   Nǐ bǎ shèngxiàde cài dǎbāo dàizǒu ba, bié làngfèile.
   你把剩下的菜打包带走吧，别浪费了。
   Please wrap up the leftovers. Don't waste them.

2. 浪漫 **làngmàn** romantic

   Zhèbù diànyǐng jiǎngle yíge làngmànde àiqíng gùshì.
   这部电影讲了一个浪漫的爱情故事。
   This movie features a romantic love story.

3. 冲浪 **chōnglàng** surf

   Chōnglàng shì yíxiàng hěn cìjide yùndòng.
   冲浪是一项很刺激的运动。
   Surfing is an exciting sport.

4. 流浪汉 **liúlànghàn** street person

   Zhège jiàotáng huì gěi liúlànghàn tígōng miǎnfèide shíwù.
   这个教堂会给流浪汉提供免费的食物。
   This church offers free food to street people.

CHARACTER 264

污

wū
dirty; corrupt

6 STROKES | **氵 RADICAL**

Useful phrases and sentences

1. 污染 **wūrǎn** pollution

   Zài chéngshì, guāng wūrǎnde wèntí biànde yuè lái yuè yánzhòng.
   在城市，光污染的问题变得越来越严重。
   Light pollution is getting worse and worse in the cities.

2. 贪污 **tānwū** corruption

   Jiāng Shìzhǎng yīngwèi tānwū zuòle shínián jiānyù.
   江市长因为贪污坐了十年监狱。
   Major Jiang was jailed ten years for corruption.

3. 污水 **wūshuǐ** sewage; polluted water

   Nàtiáo hé shínián qián shuǐ hái hěn qīng, xiànzài chàbuduō chéngle wūshuǐ.
   那条河十年前水还很清，现在差不多成了污水。
   That river was still clear ten years ago, but now it's almostly polluted.

4. 污浊 **wūzhuó** polluted and dirty

   Zhèrde kōngqì wèishénme zhème wūzhuó?
   这儿的空气为什么这么污浊？
   Why is the air here so dirty and polluted?

CHARACTER 265

染

rǎn
to infect; to dye

Useful phrases and sentences

1. 传染 chuánrǎn to infect

Wǒ déle zhòng gǎnmào, bù xiǎng chuánrǎngěi nǐ.
我得了重感冒，不想传染给你。
I have a bad flu and don't want to infect you.

2. 感染 gǎnrǎn infected

Wǒ gūjì shì gǎnrǎnle shénme bìngdú, xūyào zuò xuèyè jiǎnchá.
我估计是感染了什么病毒，需要做血液检查。
My hunch is that you are infected with some virus. You need a blood test.

3. 染发 rǎnfà to dye one's hair

Rújīn, rǎnfà zài Zhōngguó chéngle yìzhǒng shíshàng.
如今，染发在中国成了一种时尚。
Dying one's hair has become a fashion in China nowadays.

4. 染上 rǎnshàng to acquire (bad habits)

Tā shàng dàxuéde shíhou rǎnshàngle xùjiǔde huài xíguàn.
他上大学的时候染上了酗酒的坏习惯。
He acquired the bad habit of drinking alcohol when he was in college.

CHARACTER 266

挤

jǐ
to press; cram

Useful phrases and sentences

1. 挤 jǐ cram in

Dàjiā bié jǐle, qǐng páiduì shàngchē!
大家别挤了，请排队上车！
Don't cram in. Please line up to board.

2. 拥挤 yōngjǐ congested

Běijīng shàngxiàbān shíjiān jiāotōng fēicháng yōngjǐ.
北京上下班时间交通非常拥挤。
Traffic is heavily congested during rush hour in Beijing.

3. 挤满 jǐmǎn full of; packed with

Yídào zhōuwǔ wǎnshàng, zhèjiā xiǎo jiǔguǎn jiù jǐmǎnle rén.
一到周五晚上，这家小酒馆就挤满了人。
This small bar is packed with people on Fridays.

4. 挤时间 jǐ shíjiān squeeze time

Tā gōngzuò zài máng yě yào jǐ shíjiān duànliàn shēntǐ.
他工作再忙也要挤时间锻炼身体。
He squeezes time into his busy working schedule to work out.

CHARACTER 267

健

jiàn
healthy

Useful phrases and sentences

1. 健康 jiànkāng healthy

Chī tàiduō yóuzhá shípǐn bú tài jiànkāng.
吃太多油炸食品不太健康。
Eating too much fried food is unhealthy.

2. 健身中心 jiànshēn zhōngxīn gym

Xuéxiàode jiànshēn zhōngxīn zǎoshàng liùdiǎnbàn jiù kāiménle.
学校的健身中心早上六点半就开门了。
The school gym is open as early as 6.30 am.

3. 健全 jiànquán thorough; well-equipped

Zhèjiā yǎnglǎoyuànde shèshī hěn jiànquán.
这家养老院的设施很健全。
This nursing home has well-equipped facilities.

4. 健美 jiànměi bodybuilding and fitness

Liùyuè tā yào qù Fǎguó cānjiā yíge guójì jiànměi bǐsài.
六月他要去法国参加一个国际健美比赛。
He is going to France to take part in an international bodybuilding and fitness competition in June.

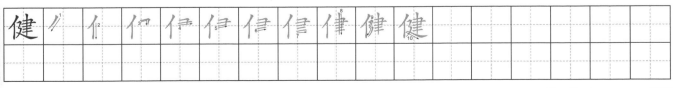

黑

hēi
black; dark

Useful phrases and sentences

1. 黑 **hēi** dark

Tiān yǐjīng hēile, zǎo diǎnr huíjiā, bié cuòguò zuìhòu yībān diànchē.
天已经黑了，早点儿回家，别错过最后一班电车。
It's getting dark. You should be going home. Don't miss the last train.

2. 黑板 **hēibǎn** blackboard

Qǐng nǐmen bǎ zìjǐde míngzi xiězài hēibǎnshàng.
请你们把自己的名字写在黑板上。
Please write your name on the blackboard.

3. 黑色 **hēisè** black

Nàge hēisède qiánbāo shì nǐde ma? Bié wàngle.
那个黑色的钱包是你的吗？别忘了。
Is that black purse yours? Don't forget it.

4. 黑色幽默 **hēisè yōumò** black humor

Zhèbù xiǎoshuō chōngmǎnle hēisè yōumò.
这部小说充满了黑色幽默。
This novel is full of black humor.

垃

lā
trash

Useful phrases and sentences

1. 垃圾 **lājī** trash

Niǔyuē yǒude jiēdào hěn zāng, dàochù dōu shì lājī.
纽约有的街道很脏，到处都是垃圾。
In New York City, some streets are very dirty with trash all over them.

2. 垃圾桶 **lājītǒng** garbage can

Zhège dìfāng lājītǒng zhēn nánzhǎo, zǒule shífēnzhōngle hái méiyǒu yīgè.
这个地方垃圾桶真难找，走了十分钟了还没有一个。
It's really hard to find a garbage can here. I still can't find one after walking for ten minutes.

3. 垃圾回收箱 **lājī huíshōuxiāng** recycling bin

Zhèxiē kōng píngzi kěyǐ fàngdào nàge lājī huíshōuxiānglǐ.
这些空瓶子可以放到那个垃圾回收箱里。
You can put these empty bottles in the recycling bin.

4. 垃圾车 **lājīchē** garbage truck

Wǒmen shèqūde lājīchē měitiān wǎnshàng bādiǎn lái shōu lājī.
我们社区的垃圾车每天晚上八点来收垃圾。
The garbage trucks will come to our community to collect trash at 8 pm every day.

圾

jī
trash; garbage

Useful phrases and sentences

1. 垃圾邮件 **lājī yóujiàn** spam email

Wèishénme wǒ měitiān dōu shōudào hǎojǐfēng lājī yóujiàn?
为什么我每天都收到好几封垃圾邮件？
Why do I receive so much spam every day?

2. 垃圾食品 **lājī shípǐn** junk food

Nǐ zhīdào nǎxiē shípǐn suàn shì lājī shípǐn ma?
你知道哪些食品算是垃圾食品吗？
Do you know what "junk food" refers to?

3. 倒垃圾 **dào lājī** dispose trash

Qǐng wèn, zhèdòng lóu dào nǎr dào lājī?
请问，这栋楼到哪儿倒垃圾？
Excuse me, where do I dispose of my trash in this building?

4. 垃圾工人 **lājī gōngrén** garbageman

Zhèrde lājī gōngrén hǎoxiàng dōu bú shì běnguó rén.
这儿的垃圾工人好像都不是本国人。
These garbagemen don't seem to be from this country.

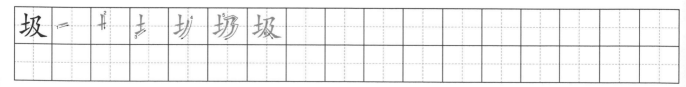

Part 1 Choose from the following words to fill in the blanks.

環境、垃圾、污染、健康、注意

1. 说中文的时候一定要（　　　　　）声调。

2. 保护（　　　　　）是我们每一个人的责任。

3. 这条河被（　　　　　）得很严重，很多鱼都死了。

4. 不吃早饭是很不（　　　　　）的生活习惯。

Part 2 Complete the following dialogues using Chinese characters.

1. A: 在你生活的城市，有没有空气污染的问题？

   B: _____ 。

2. A: 在你生活的城市，有没有堵车的问题？

   B: _____ 。

3. A: 你认为应该怎么解决交通拥挤的问题？

   B: _____ 。

4. A: 你认为还有哪些环境问题我们应该注意？

   B: _____ 。

5. A: 要解决环境问题，政府应该做哪些事情？

   B: _____ 。

你是一个环境保护组织的志愿者。请你给大家提一些建议，告诉大家在生活上应该怎么做，才能更好地保护环境。

1. _____

2. _____

3. _____

4. _____

LESSON 19

Volunteer Work 去当志愿者？

1. Dialogue

Read the dialogue below and answer the questions in characters.

艾欣:	暑假快到了，你有什么计划吗？
吴江:	我打算去南美洲当志愿者，帮助那里的人盖房子。你呢？
艾欣:	我跟你一样，也做志愿者，不过我是去中国的农村教英文。
吴江:	中国现在经济发展得这么好，农村的生活条件和教育情况应该很不错吧。
艾欣:	跟以前比确实进步了很多，但是，还有一些地方教育仍然很落后。我去的那个地方很穷，听说有的学生连本子和笔都买不起。
吴江:	那你觉得我们怎么帮他们更有效呢？他们最需要什么？
艾欣:	我们正在建一个网站，人们可以通过网站给他们捐钱、文具或者其他东西。
吴江:	捐衣服可以吗？
艾欣:	当然可以，特别是比较厚的大衣。我在网上看到那里的孩子冬天还穿着一件很薄的外套，看着就很冷，实在太可怜了。看完那些照片我难过得都想哭。
吴江:	我们应该一起想办法，使他们的生活变得好一点。哎，我好像听见你的手机响了。
艾欣:	哦，是我的，你等一下，我接个电话。
吴江:	好的！

1. 吴江暑假打算去做什么？

2. 艾欣暑假要去哪儿当志愿者？他为什么去那儿？

3. 艾欣正在建一个什么网站？

2. Vocabulary

	Word	Pinyin	English equivalent
1.	暑假	**shǔjià**	summer vacation
2.	南美洲	**Nán Měizhōu**	South America
3.	志愿者	**zhìyuànzhě**	volunteer
4.	盖	**gài**	build
5.	农村	**nóngcūn**	rural village
6.	经济	**jīngjì**	economy
7.	条件	**tiáojiàn**	condition
8.	进步	**jìnbù**	progress
9.	仍然	**réngrén**	still
10.	落后	**luòhòu**	fall behind
11.	穷	**qióng**	poor
12.	连	**lián**	even
13.	笔	**bǐ**	pen
14.	本子	**běnzi**	notebook
15.	建	**jiàn**	set up
16.	通过	**tōngguò**	through; via
17.	捐	**juān**	donate
18.	文具	**wénjù**	stationery
19.	厚	**hòu**	thick
20.	薄	**báo**	thin
21.	外套	**wàitào**	jacket
22.	可怜	**kělián**	poor; sad
23.	哭	**kū**	cry
24.	使	**shǐ**	make
25.	变	**biàn**	become
26.	响	**xiǎng**	ring

3. New Characters

Fifteen characters are introduced in this lesson. Use the following explanations to help you understand and remember the characters.

志 愿 者 暑 盖 哭 穷 连 具 笔 厚 薄 需 变 响

CHARACTER 271

zhì
will; mark

7 STROKES · **心 RADICAL**

Useful phrases and sentences

1. 杂志 **zázhì** magazine
   Zhèběn zázhì jiǎngde shì yīnggāi zěnme zhǔnbèi gōngzuò miànshì.
   这本杂志讲的是应该怎么准备工作面试。
   This magazine is about how to prepare for job interviews.

2. 标志 **biāozhì** sign; symbol
   Pīngpāng Wàijiāo shì Zhōng-Měi guānxi fāzhǎnde yígè zhòngyào biāozhì.
   乒乓外交是中美关系发展的一个重要标志。
   The Ping Pong Diplomacy was a symbol of the development of China-U.S. relations.

3. 志愿者 **zhìyuànzhě** volunteer
   Wǒ qùnián qǐ zài yīgè lǎorényuàn dāng zhìyuànzhě.
   我去年起在一个老人院当志愿者。
   I have done volunteer work at a nursing home since last year.

4. 志向 **zhìxiàng** ambition
   Wú Jiāng cóngxiǎo jiù hěn yǒu zhìxiàng, zhǎngdà yào dāng yìmíng kēxuéjiā.
   吴江从小就很有志向，长大要当一名科学家。
   Wu Jiang has been ambitious since he was young. He wants to be a scientist when he gets older.

志 一 士 士 士 志 志 志

CHARACTER 272

yuàn
to hope; willing

14 STROKES · **心 RADICAL**

Useful phrases and sentences

1. 自愿 **zìyuàn** voluntary; voluntarily
   Bāngmáng zǔzhī juānkuǎn huódòngde xuéshēng dōu shì zìyuàn láide.
   帮忙组织捐款活动的学生都是自愿来的。
   Those students who helped organize this fundraising did so voluntarily.

2. 许愿 **xǔyuàn** make a wish
   Nǐ chuī làzhúde shíhou bié wàngle xǔyuàn.
   你吹蜡烛的时候别忘了许愿！
   Don't forget to make a wish when you blow out the candles!

3. 宁愿 **nìngyuàn** would rather
   Tā nìngyuàn bù jiéhūn, yě bù xiǎng gēn bù xǐhuande rén zài yìqǐ.
   他宁愿不结婚，也不想跟不喜欢的人在一起。
   He would rather remain single than be together with someone he doesn't like.

4. 心愿 **xīnyuàn** wish; dream
   Yéye shuō tā niánqīngde shíhou zuìdàde xīnyuàn jiù shì néng shàng dàxué.
   爷爷说他年轻的时候最大的心愿就是能上大学。
   My grandfather said that his biggest wish was to attend college when he was young.

愿 一 厂 厂 厂 厂 原 原 原 原 原 原 原 愿 愿 愿

CHARACTER 273

者

zhě
person

8 STROKES 耂 **RADICAL**

Useful phrases and sentences

1. 或者 **huòzhě** or
Zhōngguó cài huòzhě Tàiguó cài wǒ dōu xǐhuan chī.
中国菜或者泰国菜我都喜欢吃。
I like Chinese food and Thai food.

2. 作者 **zuòzhě** author
Nàběn Zhōngwénde xiǎoshuōde zuòzhě yuánlái shì yíge Déguó rén.
那本中文小说的作者原来是一个德国人。
It turns out that the author for the Chinese novel is German.

3. 记者 **jìzhě** journalist
Nàwèi cóng Yīngguó láide jìzhě shuōhuà hěn zhíjiē.
那位从英国来的记者说话很直接。
That British journalist is pretty straightforward.

4. 消费者 **xiāofèizhě** consumer
Zhège zǔzhīde mùbiāo shì bǎohù xiāofèizhěde quánlì.
这个组织的目标是保护消费者的权利。
The goal of this organization is to protect consumer rights.

者 者 士 耂 者 者 者 者

CHARACTER 274

暑

shǔ
heat;
hot weather

12 STROKES 日 **RADICAL**

Useful phrases and sentences

1. 暑期 **shǔqī** summer vacation
Gāozhōngshēng cháng lìyòng shǔqī qù dāng zhìyuànzhě huò cānjiā xiàlìngyíng.
高中生常利用暑期去当志愿者或参加夏令营。
High school students often do volunteer work or go to camps during summer vacation.

2. 放暑假 **fàng shǔjià** start a summer vacation
Nǐmen shénme shíhou fàng shǔjià?
你们什么时候放暑假？
When does your summer vacation begin?

3. 中暑 **zhòngshǔ** heatstroke
Jīntiān shízài tài rèle, nǐ bié chūqùle, xiǎoxīn zhòngshǔ.
今天实在太热了，你别出去了，小心中暑。
It's really hot today. Don't go out. Be careful of getting a heatstroke.

4. 暑校 **shǔxiào** summer school
Jīnnián xiàtiān wǒ dǎsuàn zài Hāfó shǔxiào shàng yìmén Yīngwén kè.
今年夏天我打算在哈佛暑校上一门英文课。
I plan to take an English class at the Harvard Summer School this year.

暑 暑 日 旦 旦 早 星 昇 暑 暑 暑

CHARACTER 275

盖

gài
build; cover

11 STROKES 皿 **RADICAL**

Useful phrases and sentences

1. 盖 **gài** build
Shìzhǎng shuō jìhuà míngnián gài yíge xīnde gōnglì túshūguǎn.
市长说计划明年盖一个新的公立图书馆。
The mayor says that he plans to build a new public library next year.

2. 盖子 **gàizi** cover; lid
Nǐ kàndào wǒ shuǐbēide gàizi le ma?
你看到我水杯的盖子了吗？
Did you see my cup lid?

3. 盖被子 **gài bèizi** cover with a blanket
Jīntiān yìdiǎnr dōu bù lěng, wǎnshang shuìjiào bú yòng gài bèizi.
今天一点儿都不冷，晚上睡觉不用盖被子。
It's not cold at all today. You won't need a blanket tonight.

4. 膝盖 **xīgài** knee
Ài Xīnde xīgài shòushāngle, tā méi bànfǎ cānjiā zúqiú bǐsài le.
艾欣的膝盖受伤了，她没办法参加足球比赛了。
Ai Xin hurt her knees. She is unable to join the soccer game.

盖 盖 兰 兰 羊 羊 羊 盖 盖 盖 盖

Useful phrases and sentences

kū
to cry; to weep

1. 哭 **kū** to cry

Nǐ xiān bié kūle, kuài gàosù wǒ fāshēngle shénme shìqing.
你先别哭了，快告诉我发生了什么事情。
Don't just cry. Tell me what happened.

2. 哭个不停 **kūge bù tíng** can't stop crying

Zhège háizi kūge bù tíng, shì-búshì nǎr bù shūfu?
这个孩子哭个不停，是不是哪儿不舒服？
This child can't stop crying. Is he feeling unwell?

3. 大哭 **dàkū** to cry loudly

Xiǎo nǚháir kàndào qìqiú fēizǒule, dàkūqǐlái.
小女孩儿看到气球飞走了，大哭起来。
The little girl cried loudly when she saw the balloon flying away.

4. 哭声 **kūshēng** sound of crying

Wǒ hǎoxiàng tīngdàole kūshēng, nǐ tīngdàole ma?
我好像听到了哭声，你听到了吗？
I seem to hear sound of crying. Did you hear it?

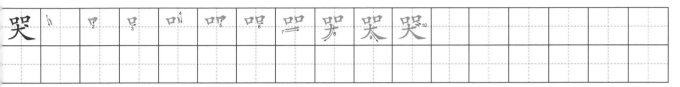

Useful phrases and sentences

穷

qióng
poor

1. 穷 **qióng** poor

Tā xiǎode shíhou jiālǐ tài qióngle, méiyǒu tiáojiàn shàngxué niànshū.
他小的时候家里太穷了，没有条件上学念书。
His family was poor when he was little. He couldn't afford to attend school.

2. 贫穷 **pínqióng** poverty

Pínqióng shì hěnduō guójiā xūyào jiějuéde wèntí.
贫穷是很多国家需要解决的问题。
Poverty is the problem that needs to be solved in many countries.

3. 穷人 **qióngrén** poor people

Zhèxiē fángzi shì zhèngfǔ gěi qióngrén miǎnfèi tígōngde.
这些房子是政府给穷人免费提供的。
These houses are offered by the government free of charge to poor people.

4. 无穷 **wúqióng** boundless; endless

Cóng zhèfú huà néng kànchū háizi wúqióngde xiǎngxiànglì.
从这幅画能看出孩子无穷的想象力。
You can see the boundless imagination of kids from this painting.

Useful phrases and sentences

连

lián
even; to link

1. 连续 **liánxù** continuous; in a row

Wǒ yǐjīng liánxù jǐtiān méi hǎohao chīfànle.
我已经连续几天没好好吃饭了。
I haven't had a proper meal for several days in a row.

2. 连...都... **lián... dōu...** even ....

Mèimei Déwén xuéle yīnián le, dànshì lián "Nǐ jiào shénme míngzì?" dōu bú huì.
妹妹德文学了一年了，但是连 "你叫什么名字？" 都不会。
My younger sister has been learning German for one year, but she doesn't even know how to say "What's your name?" in German.

3. 连贯 **liánguàn** coherent

Zhèduàn huà xiěde bú tài liánguàn, nǐ gǎigǎi ba.
这段话写得不太连贯，你改改吧。
These phrases are not coherent. Please change them.

4. 连续剧 **liánxùjù** drama series

Tāngmǔ yǒukòngde shíhou xǐhuan kàn liánxùjù xué Zhōngwén.
汤姆有空的时候喜欢看连续剧学中文。
Tom likes to watch TV dramas to learn Chinese when he is free.

CHARACTER 279

Useful phrases and sentences

具
jù
tool

1. 工具 **gōngjù** tool; instrument
   Yǔyán shì rén yǔ rén gōutōng jiāoliúde gōngjù.
   语言是人与人沟通交流的工具。
   Languages are a tool for human communication.

2. 家具 **jiājù** furniture
   Zhètào jiājù hěn yǒu Zhōngguó tèsè, yánsè yě hěn hǎokàn.
   这套家具很有中国特色，颜色也很好看。
   This set of furniture is characteristic of the Chinese style. Its colors are pretty too.

3. 具体 **jùtǐ** concrete; specific
   Nǐ qīngchu zhèdào cài jùtǐde zuòfǎ ma?
   你清楚这道菜具体的做法吗？
   Do you know the specific recipe for this dish?

4. 文具 **wénjù** stationery
   Wǒ xiǎng mǎi xiē běnzi, bù zhīdao fùjìn yǒuméiyou wénjùdiàn?
   我想买些本子，不知道附近有没有文具店？
   I like to buy some notebooks. Is there a stationery store nearby?

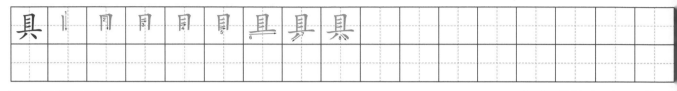

CHARACTER 280

Useful phrases and sentences

笔
bǐ
pen

1. 笔 **bǐ** pen
   Wǒ bèibāoli yǒu hóngbǐ, lánbǐ, qiānbǐ hé xiàngpícā.
   我背包里有红笔、蓝笔、铅笔和橡皮擦。
   I have red pens, blue pens, pencils and erasers in my backpack.

2. 钢笔 **gāngbǐ** fountain pen
   Zhèzhī gāngbǐ shì gāozhōng lǎoshī sòng gěi wǒde.
   这支钢笔是高中老师送给我的。
   My high school teacher gave me this fountain pen.

3. 铅笔 **qiānbǐ** pencil
   Dàjiā qǐng zhùyì, kǎoshìde shíhou bù néng yòng qiānbǐ xiě.
   大家请注意，考试的时候不能用铅笔写。
   Attention everyone, please do not use pencils on the exam.

4. 笔记本电脑 **bǐjìběn diànnǎo** laptop
   Nǐ xīn mǎide bǐjìběn diànnǎo yòngqǐlái zěnmeyàng?
   你新买的笔记本电脑用起来怎么样？
   How does your new laptop work?

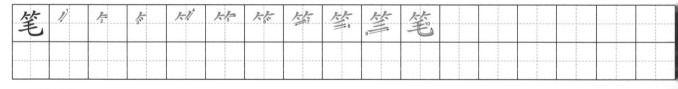

CHARACTER 281

Useful phrases and sentences

厚
hòu
thick

1. 厚 **hòu** thick
   Jīntiān hěn lěng, nǐ děi chuān hòu diǎnr.
   今天很冷，你得穿厚点儿。
   It's cold today. You need to wear more.

2. 深厚 **shēnhòu** deep; close
   Wǒ cóngxiǎo gēn nǎinai shēnghuó zài yìqǐ, wǒmende gǎnqíng fēicháng shēnhòu.
   我从小跟奶奶生活在一起，我们的感情非常深厚。
   I have lived with my grandmother since I was little. We have a very close relationship.

3. 浓厚 **nónghòu** to have a strong interest in
   Tā duì xuéxí xīfāng yìshù yǒu nónghòude xìngqù.
   她对学习西方艺术有浓厚的兴趣。
   She has a strong interest in learning Western art.

4. 厚重 **hòuzhòng** heavy; profound
   Xī'ān shì yízuò lìshǐ hòuzhòngde chéngshì, zhùmíngde bīngmǎyǒng jiù zài nàr.
   西安是一座历史厚重的城市，著名的兵马俑就在那儿。
   Xi'an is a city with a profound history. The well-known site of the terracotta soldiers is there.

Useful phrases and sentences

16 STROKES **⺿ RADICAL**

薄
báo/bó
thin/light

1. 薄 **báo** thin

Nǐ kěyǐ bǎ miànbāo qiēde báo yìdiǎnr ma?
你可以把面包切得薄一点儿吗？
Can you slice the bread a little thinner?

2. 薄片 **báopiàn** thin slice

Wǒ hěn xǐhuān huāshēng báopiàn, jiāshàng
mìxiāng hóngchá gèng hǎo.
我很喜欢花生薄片，加上蜜香红茶更好。
*I like thin toast with peanut butter. It's even better
with peach tea.*

3. 单薄 **dānbó** thin; frail

Tā yòu shòu yòu xiǎo, kànqǐlai hěn dānbó.
他又瘦又小，看起来很单薄。
He is thin and small. He looks frail.

4. 薄礼 **bólǐ** small gift; humble gift

Zhè shì wǒ zhǔnbèide bólǐ, qǐng nín shōuxià ba.
这是我准备的薄礼，请您收下吧。
This is a small gift I have prepared. Please accept it.

薄 一 ⺀ ⺿ ⺿ 声 芦 芦 芽 薄 薄 薄 蒲 蓮 薄 薄 薄

Useful phrases and sentences

14 STROKES **雨 RADICAL**

需
xū
to need

1. 需求 **xūqiú** demand; requirement

Nǐ shì chǎnpǐn jīnglǐ, yào liǎojiě xiāofèizhěde
xūqiú.
你是产品经理，要了解消费者的需求。
*You are the product manager. You need to
understand the consumers' demands.*

2. 需要 **xūyào** need

Yǒu shénme xūyào wǒ bāngmángde, qǐng nǐ
zhíshuō.
有什么需要我帮忙的，请你直说。
Please be frank if you need any help.

3. 必需品 **bìxūpǐn** necessity

Zhèlǐde jūmín tài qióngle, shènzhì lián shēnghuó
bìxūpǐn dōu mǎibuqǐ.
这里的居民太穷了，甚至连生活必需品都买不起。
*The residents here are so poor. They cannot even
afford to buy daily necessities.*

4. 急需 **jíxū** in urgent need

Bàofēngxuě guòhòu, tíngdiàn wèntí jíxū dédào
jiějué.
暴风雪过后，停电问题急需得到解决。
*The power outage needs to be fixed urgently after the
snowstorm.*

需 一 ⼁ ⼍ 而 而 雪 雪 雪 雪 雪 雪 需 需 需

Useful phrases and sentences

8 STROKES **又 RADICAL**

变
biàn
become

1. 变 **biàn** become

Àirén zǒu hòu, tā xiànzài hǎoxiàng biànde bú ài
shuōhuàle.
爱人走后，他现在好像变得不爱说话了。
*After his spouse passed away, he has become less
sociable.*

2. 变成 **biànchéng** to become

"Zhǎngdà hòu xiǎng biànchéng shénme" shì
měige rén dōu huídáguòde wèntí.
"长大后想变成什么"是每个人都回答过的问题。
*"What do you want to be when you grow up?" is a
question asked to everyone in this world.*

3. 改变 **gǎibiàn** to change

Wǒ suīrán gēn tā tánguò jǐcì, kěshì hěn nán
gǎibiàn tāde xiǎngfǎ.
我虽然跟他谈过几次，可是很难改变他的想法。
*Although I spoke with him several times, it is hard to
change his opinion.*

4. 变质 **biànzhì** (food) to go bad

Miànbāo wénqǐlái hǎoxiàng biànzhìle, nǐ zuìhǎo
bié chīle.
面包闻起来好像变质了，你最好别吃了。
This bread smells bad. You'd better not to eat it.

变 ⼂ ⼆ 亠 亦 亦 变 变

响

xiǎng
ring; sound

1. 响 **xiǎng** to ring
   Diànhuà líng xiǎngle, nǐ kuài qù jiē yíxià.
   电话铃响了，你快去接一下。
   The telephone rings. You go pick it up.

2. 反响 **fǎnxiǎng** response; feedback
   Zhèbù fǎnyìng chéngshì shēnghuóde diànshì liánxùjù fǎnxiǎng hěn hǎo.
   这部反映城市生活的电视连续剧反响很好。
   This TV drama reflecting city life has received very positive feedback.

3. 声响 **shēngxiǎng** sound; noise
   Nǐ kěyǐ zuòzài zhèr, dànshì bié fāchū shēngxiǎng.
   你可以坐在这儿，但是别发出声响。
   You can sit here, but don't make any noise.

4. 音响 **yīnxiǎng** audio; sound
   Nàjiā diànyǐngyuànde yīnxiǎng xiàoguǒ hěn bú cuò.
   那家电影院的音响效果很不错。
   The audio system in that movie theater is very good.

Lesson 19 Exercises

Part 1 Choose from the following words to fill in the blanks.

穷、改变、志愿者、需要、哭

1. 有问题我们应该想办法解决，（   ）一点儿用都没有。

2. 我认为去当（   ）是一件很有意义的事情。

3. 我现在是一个（   ）学生，根本住不起这么贵的酒店。

4. 要是你（   ）我帮你搬家，千万别客气。

Part 2 Complete the following dialogues using Chinese characters.

1. A: 你有没有当过志愿者？在什么地方当过？

   B: _____ 。

2. A: 你帮助过穷人吗？你是怎么帮助他们的？

   B: _____ 。

3. A: 你认为政府应该怎么做，才能更好地帮助穷人？

   B: _____ 。

4. A: 要是你有机会去中国农村的学校教英文，你会不会去？

   B: _____ 。

5. A: 要是你来组织一个志愿者活动，你希望做什么？帮助谁？

   B: _____ 。

Part 3 学以致用

你是一个动物保护组织的志愿者，请你给大家介绍一下 1) 你们是一个什么样的组织；2) 你们经常举办什么样的活动；3) 你希望更多的人做哪些事情来保护动物。

大家好，

我是"阳光"动物保护组织的志愿者李明。

LESSON 20

Is Chinese Difficult to Learn? 学中文难不难?

1. Dialogue

Read the dialogue below and answer the questions in characters.

陈宇：	高言，你中文学得怎么样了？
高言：	别提了，碰到很多困难，句子一长就说不流利了。
陈宇：	难在哪些地方呢？
高言：	一是声调很难，说不准有可能闹笑话；二是汉字难写难认，老师还要求我们简体字和繁体字都能认出来；还有就是一个英文词在中文里可能有好几个说法，比方说"sorry"可以是"对不起"、"抱歉"或者"不好意思"，要看情况决定用哪一个。
陈宇：	太不容易了！不过，现在网上有很多电子词典和翻译软件，这些对外语学习是不是很有帮助？
高言：	电子词典很方便，不过使用翻译软件可得小心点儿，很容易出错。另外，由于中国人说话很客气，所以说中文的时候要特别注意，要不然会显得很没有礼貌。比方说，跟很久没见的朋友打招呼可以说"你最近怎么样？"，但是遇到老师，这么说就不太好，你得说"老师您最近还好吗？"。
陈宇：	听起来好难啊！那你为什么要学呢？
高言：	虽然中文难学，但是中国文化很有意思。我觉得多了解别的国家的文化很重要。好了，不跟你多说了，我要去准备明天的小考了，上次成绩不太好。
陈宇：	你学习态度真好！那你快去忙吧，加油！

1. 高言正在学什么语言？

2. 高言为什么觉得中文很难学？

3. 高言觉得跟中国人说话要特别注意什么？

2. Vocabulary

	Word	Pinyin	English equivalent
1.	碰到	**pèngdào**	encounter
2.	困难	**kùnnan**	difficulty
3.	句子	**jùzi**	sentence
4.	流利	**liúlì**	fluent
5.	声调	**shēngdiào**	tone
6.	闹笑话	**nào xiàohuà**	make a joke
7.	要求	**yāoqiú**	require
8.	电子	**diànzǐ**	electronic
9.	词典	**cídiǎn**	dictionary
10.	翻译	**fānyì**	translate
11.	软件	**ruǎnjiàn**	software
12.	由于	**yóuyú**	due to
13.	显得	**xiǎnde**	appeal; present oneself as
14.	礼貌	**lǐmào**	well-mannered
15.	遇到	**yùdào**	bump into
16.	成绩	**chéngjì**	grade
17.	态度	**tàidù**	attitude

3. New Characters

Fifteen characters are introduced in this lesson. Use the following explanations to help you understand and remember the characters.

言　流　遇　成　绩　翻　译　词　典　于　求　碰　声　貌　态

言
yán
word; speech

1. 方言 **fāngyán** dialect

Shànghǎi huà, Sìchuān huà, Guǎngdōng huà, Húnán huà, Mǐnnán huà, zhèxiē dōu shì fāngyán.

上海话、四川话、广东话、湖南话、闽南话，这些都是方言。

Shanghainese, Sichuanese, Cantonese, Hunanese, and Southern Min are all dialects.

2. 言论 **yánlùn** speech

Nǐde guójiā yǒu-méiyou yánlùn zìyóu?

你的国家有没有言论自由？

Do you have freedom of speech in your country?

3. 三言两语 **sān-yán-liǎng-yǔ** in a few words

Zhèjiàn shì tài fùzále, sān-yán-liǎng-yǔ shuōbuqīngchu.

这件事太复杂了，三言两语说不清楚。

This matter is very complicated and cannot be clarified in a few words.

4. 留言 **liúyán** leave a message

Duìbuqǐ, wǒ xiànzài bù néng jiē diànhuà, qǐng gěi wǒ liúyán.

对不起，我现在不能接电话，请给我留言。

I am sorry that I can't pick up your phone right now. Please leave a message.

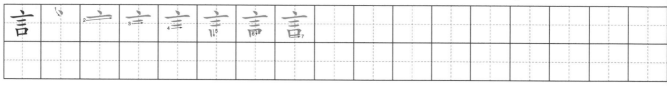

流
liú
to flow; to spread

1. 流血 **liúxuè** to bleed

Zhèr dōngtiān tài gān, wǒde bízi chángcháng liúxuè.

这儿冬天太干，我的鼻子常常流血。

The winter here is very dry. My nose often bleeds.

2. 流利 **liúlì** fluent

Nǐde Ālābó yǔ shuōde yuè lái yuè liúlì le.

你的阿拉伯语说得越来越流利了。

You are becoming more and more fluent in Arabic.

3. 流行 **liúxíng** popular; fashionable

Gēn liúxíng yīnyuè bǐ, wǒ gèng xǐhuan gǔdiǎn yīnyuè.

跟流行音乐比，我更喜欢古典音乐。

I prefer classical music to pop music.

4. 流传 **liúchuán** to circulate

Zhōngguó yìzhí liúchuánzhe Liáng Shānbó hé Zhù Yīngtáide àiqíng gùshi.

中国一直流传着梁山伯和祝英台的爱情故事。

The love story of Liang Shanbo and Zhu Yingtai has been circulating in China for a long time.

遇
yù
to encounter

1. 机遇 **jīyù** opportunity

Zài wǒ kànlái, kùnnán hé tiǎozhàn yě kěnéng dàilái jīyù.

在我看来，困难和挑战也可能带来机遇。

In my view, difficulties and challenges may also bring opportunities.

2. 遇到 **yùdào** to run into

Zhēn qiǎo! Méi xiǎngdào néng zài zhèr yùdào nǐ!

真巧！没想到能在这儿遇到你！

What a coincidence! I didn't expect to run into you here!

3. 待遇 **dàiyù** benefits

Tāmen gōngsīde dàiyù hěn hǎo, búdàn gōngzī gāo, érqiě jiàqī duō.

他们公司的待遇很好，不但工资高，而且假期多。

Their company has good benefits. Their salary is not only higher, they also have more days for personal leave.

4. 遇难 **yùnàn** to be killed

Zhècì fēijī shīshì zàochéngle shàngbǎi rén yùnàn.

这次飞机失事造成了上百人遇难。

This airplane crash killed over one hundred people.

CHARACTER 289

成

chéng
to accomplish

6 STROKES | **戈 RADICAL**

Useful phrases and sentences

1. 成功 **chénggōng** successful

Zuótiān wǎnshangde jiāoxiǎngyuè yǎnchū hěn chénggōng.
昨天晚上的交响乐演出很成功。
The orchestra performance last night was very successful.

2. 成果 **chéngguǒ** achievement

Tā zài áizhèng yánjiū fāngmiàn qǔdéle hěnduō chéngguǒ.
她在癌症研究方面取得了很多成果。
She has achieved many results in cancer research.

3. 成熟 **chéngshú** mature

Jiāyíng suīrán zhǐyǒu shí'èrsuì, kěshì tā hěn chéngshú.
佳盈虽然只有十二岁，可是她很成熟。
Although Jiaying is only twelve years old, she is quite mature for her age.

4. 成为 **chéngwéi** become

Zuìjìn zǒngtǒng xuǎnjǔ chéngwéi dàjiā zuì gǎn xìngqùde huàtí.
最近总统选举成为大家最感兴趣的话题。
The presidential election has become the most popular topic for people to talk about recently.

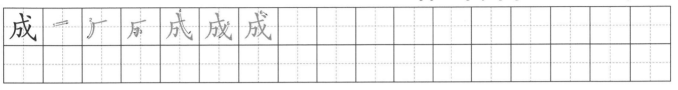

CHARACTER 290

绩

jì
merit

11 STROKES | **纟 RADICAL**

Useful phrases and sentences

1. 成绩 **chéngjì** grade

Zhào Lǎoshī, shàngge xīngqīde kǎoshì chéngjì chūláile ma?
赵老师，上个星期的考试成绩出来了吗？
Teacher Zhao, is the test result from last week available?

2. 政绩 **zhèngjì** administration accomplishment

Wáng Shìzhǎng zuìdàde zhèngjì shì jiějuéle gōngrénde shīyè wèntí.
王市长最大的政绩是解决了工人的失业问题。
The biggest accomplishment of Mayor Wang is solving the problem of unemployment among workers in his administration.

3. 业绩 **yèjì** sales

Jīnnián gōngsīde yèjì bùrú qùnián, kuīsǔnle bùshǎo qián.
今年公司的业绩不如去年，亏损了不少钱。
Our company sales this year is not as good as last year. We lost a significant amount of money.

4. 成绩单 **chéngjì dān** transcripts

Yào shēnqǐng Měiguó dàxué, nǐ děi bǎ chéngjìdān fānyìchéng Yīngwén.
要申请美国大学，你得把成绩单翻译成英文。
You need to translate your transcripts into English when applying for American colleges.

CHARACTER 291

翻

fān
to turn over;
to flip over

18 STROKES | **羽 RADICAL**

Useful phrases and sentences

1. 翻 **fān** to turn over

Tóngxuémen, qǐng bǎ shū fāndào zuìhòu yíyè.
同学们，请把书翻到最后一页。
Students, please turn your book to the last page.

2. 翻译 **fānyì** to translate

Duì wǒ láishuō, bǎ Zhōngwén fānyìchéng Yīngwén gèng róngyì yìxiē.
对我来说，把中文翻译成英文更容易一些。
It's easier for me to translate Chinese into English.

3. 翻 **fān** to overturn

Fēng tài dàle, xiǎoxīn fānchuán.
风太大了，小心船翻！
It's too windy. Be careful or the boat might overturn.

4. 翻修 **fānxiū** to renovate

Zhège lǎo fángzi fānxiū hòu gēn xīnde yíyàng.
这个老房子翻修后跟新的一样。
This old house looks new after renovation.

CHARACTER 292

译
yì
to translate

7 STROKES   **讠 RADICAL**

Useful phrases and sentences

1. 笔译 bǐyì translation

Wǒ juéde bǐyì bǐ kǒuyì gèng nán, nǐ juéde ne?
我觉得笔译比口译更难，你觉得呢？
I feel that translation is harder than interpretation. What do you think?

2. 译文 yìwén translated text

Yǒu xiē wàiguó xiǎoshuōde Zhōngwén yìwén dúqilai bú tài zìrán.
有些外国小说的中文译文读起来不太自然。
Some Chinese translated texts of foreign novels are difficult to read.

3. 译著 yìzhù translated book

Zhèjiā chūbǎnshè chūbǎnle hěnduō guówài yìzhù.
这家出版社出版了很多国外译著。
This publisher has published many translated books.

4. 口译 kǒuyì interpretation

Tā juédìng xuǎn fānyì zhuānyè, yǐhòu qù wàimào gōngsī zuò kǒuyì.
她决定选翻译专业，以后去外贸公司做口译。
She has decided to major in interpretation. She wants to work as an interpreter at a overseas trade company in the future.

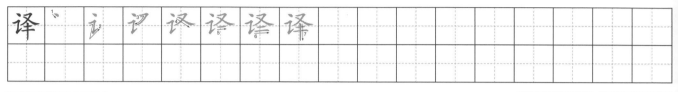

CHARACTER 293

词
cí
word

7 STROKES   **讠 RADICAL**

Useful phrases and sentences

1. 词 cí word

Jīntiānde Zhōngwén kǎoshì hěn nán, hěnduō cí wǒ dōu bù zhīdào.
今天的中文考试很难，很多词我都不知道。
The Chinese test today was hard. I don't know many words.

2. 词语 cíyǔ words and phrases

Xué wàiyǔ yīnggāi xiān xuéhuì zuì chángyòngde cíyǔ.
学外语应该先学会最常用的词语。
You should learn the most useful words and phrases when studying a foreign language.

3. 词义 cíyì meaning of a word

Wǒ zhīdào zhège cíde fāyīn, kěshì bù qīngchu tāde cíyì.
我知道这个词的发音，可是不清楚它的词义。
I know the pronunciation of this word, but I don't know its meaning.

4. 歌词 gēcí lyrics

Zhèshǒu gēde gēqǔ hé gēcí dōu hěn hǎo, shéi chàng de?
这首歌的歌曲和歌词都很好，谁唱的？
Both the melody and lyrics of this song are good. Who is the singer?

CHARACTER 294

典
diǎn
ceremony;
literary allusions

8 STROKES   **八 RADICAL**

Useful phrases and sentences

1. 词典 cídiǎn dictionary

Chén Yǔ, nǐ kěyǐ gěi wǒ tuījiàn yíbù Zhōngwén diànzǐ cídiǎn ma?
陈宇，你可以给我推荐一部中文电子词典吗？
Chen Yu, is there any Chinese e-dictionary you can recommend?

2. 典故 diǎngù allusion

Zhōngwénlǐde hěnduō chéngyǔ dōu yǒu lìshǐ diǎngù.
中文里的很多成语都有历史典故。
Many Chinese four-character idioms contain historical allusions.

3. 古典 gǔdiǎn classics

Tā shì yánjiū Zhōngguó gǔdiǎn xiǎoshuōde zhuānjiā.
他是研究中国古典小说的专家。
He is an expert on Chinese classical novels.

4. 典礼 diǎnlǐ ceremony

Wǒmen xuéxiào jīnniánde bìyè diǎnlǐ shòu yìqíng yǐngxiǎng qǔxiāole, gǎichéng wǎngshàng jìnxíng.
我们学校今年的毕业典礼受疫情影响取消了，改成网上进行。
Our graduation ceremony this year was cancelled due to the disease outbreak. It will be held online.

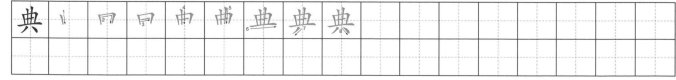

于

yú
to;
with regard to

Useful phrases and sentences

3 STROKES　　**二 RADICAL**

1. 由于 **yóuyú** due to

Yóuyú gōngzuò guānxì, tā míngnián huì bāndào Shēnzhèn.
由于工作关系，他明年会搬到深圳。
He will move to Shenzhen next year due to work.

2. 于是 **yúshì** so that; as a result

Gāo Yán dàole fànguǎnr fāxiàn méi dài qián, yǔshì zhǐhǎo huíjiā qù qǔ.
高言到了饭馆儿发现没带钱，于是只好回家去取。
Gao Yan realized at the restaurant that he hadn't brought any money, so he had no choice but to go home to fetch some.

3. 对于 **duìyú** as to; for

Duìyú háizide xuǎnzé, fùmǔ yīnggāi duō yìxiē zhīchí.
对于孩子的选择，父母应该多一些支持。
Parents should show more support for their children's choices.

4. 关于 **guānyú** with regard to

Guānyú zhǎng gōngzīde wèntí, lǎobǎn shuō xiàge xīngqī kāihuì juédìng.
关于涨工资的问题，老板说下个星期开会决定。
With regard to a salary increase, the boss says that it will be decided in the meeting next week.

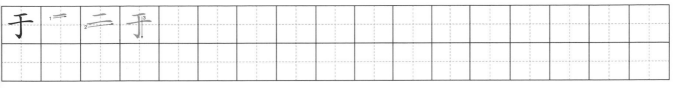

求

qiú
to seek;
to request

Useful phrases and sentences

7 STROKES　　**水 RADICAL**

1. 追求 **zhuīqiú** to pursue (a goal)

Yǒu mèngxiǎng jiù yīnggāi nǔlì qù zhuīqiú, bú yào pà shībài.
有梦想就应该努力去追求，不要怕失败。
You should pursue your dreams. Don't be afraid of failure.

2. 要求 **yāoqiú** to require

Wǒmen xuéxiào yāoqiú xuésheng bìxū shàng yìmén wàiyǔkè.
我们学校要求学生必须上一门外语课。
Students are required to take one foreign language class in our school.

3. 求学 **qiúxué** to study

Rújīn chūguó qiúxué bú zài shì yíjiàn nánshì.
如今出国求学不再是一件难事。
Studying abroad is no longer difficult.

4. 求职 **qiúzhí** to apply for jobs

Jīntiān lái gōngsī qiúzhí miànshìde dōu yǒu fēngfùde gōngzuò jīngyàn.
今天来公司求职面试的都有丰富的工作经验。
Those people who are coming to our company for job interviews today all have extensive working experience.

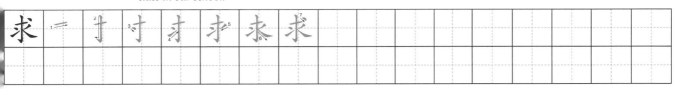

碰

pèng
to bump

Useful phrases and sentences

13 STROKES　　**石 RADICAL**

1. 碰巧 **pèngqiǎo** coincidence; perfect timing

Wǒ zhèngyào zhǎo nǐ ne, pèngqiǎo nǐ láile!
我正要找你呢，碰巧你来了！
I was about to contact you and you are already here. Perfect timing!

2. 碰 **pèng** to bump

Dìdi zǒulùde shíhou wánr shǒujī, bù xiǎoxīn bǎ tóu pèngdào ménshàng le.
弟弟走路的时候玩儿手机，不小心把头碰到门上了。
My younger brother was playing with his cell phone while walking and accidentally bumped his head on the door.

3. 碰到 **pèngdào** encounter

Zuìjìn wǒ pèngdào máfan shìr le, nǐ yídìng yào bāngbang wǒ.
最近我碰到麻烦事儿了，你一定要帮帮我。
I have been having some trouble recently. I need your help.

4. 碰见 **pèngjiàn** bump into

Zuótiān wǒ zài jiǔbā pèngjiànle Huáng Jīnglǐ.
昨天我在酒吧碰见了黄经理。
I bumped into Manager Huang at a bar yesterday.

CHARACTER 298

声

shēng
sound; voice

7 STROKES — 士 RADICAL

Useful phrases and sentences

1. 声调 **shēngdiào** tone

Yǒurén shuō guǎngdōng huà yǒu jiǔge shēngdiào, yǒurén shuō zhǐ yǒu qīge.
有人说广东话有九个声调，有人说只有七个。
Some people say that the Cantonese language has nine tones, but some say it has only seven.

2. 小声 **xiǎoshēng** in a low voice

Wǒ zhèng zài túshūguǎn, zhǐ néng xiǎoshēng shuōhuà, nǐ tīngdejiàn ma?
我正在图书馆，只能小声说话，你听得见吗？
I am in the library now and can only talk in a low voice. Can you hear me?

3. 声誉 **shēngyù** reputation

Zhèjiā jiàoyù gōngsī zài guójì shàng yǒu fēicháng hǎode shēngyù.
这家教育公司在国际上有非常好的声誉。
This educational company has a very good reputation in the world.

4. 声乐 **shēngyuè** vocal music

Nǐ shì-búshì měige xīngqī yào shàng liǎngcì shēngyuè kè?
你是不是每个星期要上两次声乐课？
You have voice classes twice a week, right?

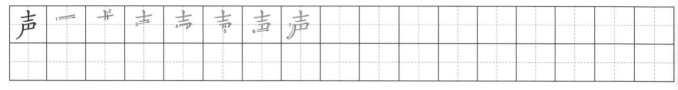

CHARACTER 299

貌

mào
appearance

14 STROKES — 豸 RADICAL

Useful phrases and sentences

1. 有礼貌 **yǒu lǐmào** well-mannered

Nǐde érzi tèbié yǒu lǐmào, měicì jiàndào wǒ dōu zhǔdòng wènhǎo.
你的儿子特别有礼貌，每次见到我都主动问好。
Your son is well-mannered. He always says hello when he sees me.

2. 美貌 **měimào** beauty

Rúguǒ měimào hé cáihuá zhǐ néng xuǎnzé yíge, nǐ huì xuǎn nǎge?
如果美貌和才华只能选择一个，你会选哪个？
If you could only choose one, would you choose beauty or talent?

3. 貌似 **màosì** appear

Tā màosì bú zàihu zhècì bǐsài, qíshí tā zhǔnbèide hěn chōngfèn.
他貌似不在乎这次比赛，其实他准备得很充分。
He appears as if he doesn't care about this game, but actually he is well-prepared.

4. 外貌 **wàimào** appearance; looks

Píngjià yíge rén dāngrán bù néng zhǐ kàn tāde wàimào.
评价一个人当然不能只看他的外貌。
You cannot evaluate a person only by his looks.

CHARACTER 300

态

tài
attitude; state

8 STROKES — 心 RADICAL

Useful phrases and sentences

1. 生态 **shēngtài** ecology

Gǎishàn yěshēng dòngwùde shēngtài huánjìng shì hěn zhòngyàode shìqing.
改善野生动物的生态环境是很重要的事情。
Improving the habitat of wild animals is important.

2. 态度 **tàidù** attitude

Zhèjiā fànguǎnr fúwùyuánde tàidù hěn chà.
这家饭馆儿服务员的态度很差。
The waiters' attitude in this restaurant is very bad.

3. 心态 **xīntài** mentality; mindset

Nǐ yào tiáozhěnghǎo zìjǐde xīntài, zuòshì bié tài zháojí.
你要调整好自己的心态，做事别太着急。
You need to adjust your mindset. Don't rush into things.

4. 状态 **zhuàngtài** state; shape

Zhèwèi xuǎnshǒu jīntiān zhuàngtài bù jiā, tài duō fēi shòupòxìng shīwù.
这位选手今天状态不佳，太多非受迫性失误。
This player in not in her best shape today. She has made too many unforced errors.

Lesson 20 Exercises

Part 1 Choose from the following words to fill in the blanks.

声调、语言、流利、翻译、碰

1. 他觉得汉语的（　　　　　　）不难学，但是汉字很难写。

2. 你能帮我把这句话（　　　　　　）成英文吗？

3. 才一年没见，没想到她的中文说得这么（　　　　　　）了。

4. 太巧了，在国外竟然（　　　　　　）到了十年没见的老同学。

Part 2 Complete the following dialogues using Chinese characters.

1. A: 你会说几种语言？

   B: _____。

2. A: 你觉得学习外语最难的是什么？

   B: _____。

3. A: 你觉得学外语最好的方法是什么？

   B: _____。

4. A: 中文跟你的母语有什么不一样？

   B: _____。

5. A: 你写简体字还是繁体字？你觉得写汉字难吗？

   B: _____。

你的好朋友艾丽下个学期想学中文，可是她听说中文很难学，所以还没决定要不要上中文课。请你给她写一封信，说说你学中文的经历，并告诉她学中文的好方法。

艾丽你好，

我听说你下个学期想上中文课，可是有点担心中文太难了。

Answers to Exercises

LESSON 1
Dialogue
1. 高山这个学期上四门课，他喜欢中国语言文化课。
2. 这个周末高山打算请几个好朋友来宿舍唱歌、跳舞。
3. 思明准备去上海学中文。

Exercise
Part 1

1. 选　　2. 准备　　3. 忙　　4. 帮忙

Part 2

1. 我最近忙毕业论文。
2. 我这个学期上三门课，中文课，数学课和国际关系课。
3. 我喜欢上数学课，因为数学课的老师教得又清楚又有意思。
4. 我的好朋友也是我的同屋，我常常找他帮忙，特别是我生病的时候。
5. 我不太喜欢开晚会。我去朋友的晚会常常带蛋糕。

LESSON 2
Dialogue
1. 妈妈要带孩子去唱歌。
2. 儿子和女儿觉得妈妈要带他们上课，他们不想上课，所以说自己病了。

Exercise
Part 1

1. 笑　　2. 身体　　3. 病　　4. 疼

Part 2

1. 我最近身体不太好，已经感冒了两个星期了。
2. 我住的地方看病不太方便，开车到医院差不多要一个小时。
3. 一个人要想少生病，一定要休息好。
4. 我申请了出国旅游的签证，可是没申请下来，真让我挺头疼的。
5. 我很喜欢给朋友讲笑话，可是我的朋友觉得我的笑话不是很好笑。

LESSON 3
Dialogue
1. 喜欢，可是她想多认识一些新朋友。
2. 小美明天想跟朋友去"好心情咖啡"喝咖啡。
3. 不远，从宿舍走过去只要十分钟。

Exercise
Part 1

1. 希望　　2. 介绍　　3. 照片　　4. 送

Part 2

1. 我最近认识了一个新朋友，是在一个晚会上认识的。
2. 我的朋友常常帮我修车。
3. 我觉得见面聊天或者用电脑聊天都很好。
4. 要是我的朋友愿意帮我的忙，我觉得他算是好朋友。
5. 要是我的朋友做了让我不高兴的事，我会跟他聊聊。

LESSON 4
Dialogue
1. 安迪不喜欢吃辣的，他点了糖醋里脊。
2. 安迪吃了米饭，喝了珍珠奶茶。
3. 糖醋里脊是用猪肉做的，味道是甜的。

Exercise
Part 1

1. 菜单　　2. 服务　　3. 辣　　4. 汤

Part 2

1. 我喜欢吃中国菜，我最喜欢吃鱼香茄子。
2. 要是我请朋友吃饭，我会带朋友去中国城的四川饭馆儿吃火锅。
3. 用中文点餐很难，因为很多菜从名字看不出来是什么菜。
4. 我不喜欢做菜，我常常自己点外卖。
5. 我早饭吃鸡蛋、面包，午饭吃米饭炒菜，晚饭比较简单，常常吃点沙拉。

LESSON 5
Dialogue
1. 陈阳想叫李真跟他去做运动。
2. 李真觉得自己太矮了，所以不打篮球，也觉得自己太胖了，不好意思去游泳。
3. 最后李真没有跟陈阳去运动。

Exercise
Part 1

1. 出汗　　2. 踢　　3. 瘦　　4. 晴

Part 2

1. 我喜欢运动，我喜欢打网球。
2. 我常常叫朋友跟我一起去运动。
3. 天气好的时候我喜欢去外面运动，天气不好的时候就去健身房运动。
4. 我喜欢看球赛，最喜欢的球队是波士顿红袜队。
5. 在我的国家，不常说别人胖了或者瘦了，可是跟家人说这样的话没问题。

LESSON 6
Dialogue
1.茱莉要去北京、杭州。
2.凯文在报纸上看到中国的高铁服务特别好。
3.朱莉这次去中国玩儿十五天。

Exercise
Part 1
1.号   2.旅游   3.报纸   4.票

Part 2
1.在我旅游过的城市，我最喜欢成都，因为成都美食多，成都人也很友好。
2.我比较喜欢自己去旅游，因为自己想去哪儿就去哪儿。
3.我的老家在哈尔滨，在中国的东北，你可以冬天来哈尔滨看冰雪节。
4.以后有机会我很想去台北玩儿。
5.对我来说，旅游最麻烦的事情就是订车票、订旅馆。

LESSON 7
Dialogue
1.晓静是在报纸上看到租房广告的。
2.这个房子有卧室、卫生间、厨房，楼下有洗衣房。这里非常安静。
3.房租一个月一千三，包括水电费。

Exercise
Part 1
1.租   2.让   3.换   4.坏

Part 2
1.我两年前租过一次房子，房东人很好，只是他说广东话，我有时候听不懂。
2.因为我不会开车，我租房子的时候一定要看附近有没有超市，最好走路能到。
3.我喜欢跟别人一起住，这样房租不会那么贵。
4.我觉得租房比较好，因为我喜欢去不同的城市工作、生活。
5.我住在广州，租房挺贵的，一个月大概需要五千块。

LESSON 8
Dialogue
1.她听说中秋节有点儿像美国的感恩节。
2.中国人中秋节跟家人一起过，而且要吃月饼。
3.带上丈夫和孩子就行，不用带别的东西。

Exercise
Part 1
1.玩   2.兴趣   3.真   4.爱

Part 2
1.我的家只有四口人，爸爸、妈妈、姐姐和我。
2.我现在因为在别的城市工作，所以很少跟家人见面，一年差不多见两三次。
3.在我的国家，春节和中秋节一定要跟家人一起过。
4.家人团聚的时候，我们常常会一起包饺子吃。
5.我知道中秋节，我吃过月饼，非常好吃。

LESSON 9
Dialogue
1.任真要搬家了，可是东西太多了。
2.任真的旧床垫会放在门口。她会去超市对面的租车公司租车。
3.思明帮任真解决了问题。

Exercise
Part 1
我的室友叫安山，他人很好，常常愿意(帮助)别人。上周五我去饭馆儿吃饭没(带)钱，他就跑来给我送钱。这个星期我病了，发高烧、咳嗽，安山就(陪)我去医院看医生，每天帮我饭，一点儿也不觉得(麻烦)。真高兴我有这么好的室友。

Part 2
1.我请朋友帮过一两次忙。
2.我会帮朋友搬家，因为请搬家公司实在太贵了。
3.如果我的朋友借的钱不是很多，我会借给朋友。
4.我会请朋友喝咖啡或者买一个小礼物谢谢他。
5.要是我碰到租房子的问题，我可能会请我的家人帮忙。

LESSON 10
Dialogue
1.小蔡工作特别忙，老板对他不满意，觉得他做事太粗心。
2.因为经济不好，小牛的公司赚不到钱，小牛担心公司关门。
3.他们下个星期要去参加乒乓球俱乐部的比赛。

Exercise
Part 1
1.担心   2.努力   3.参加   4.满意

Part 2
1.我现在在一家贸易公司工作。
2.我最近工作很忙，每天差不多睡6个钟头。
3.老板人很好，对我的工作比较满意。
4.我喜欢去公园跑步让自己放松。
5.我可能会换一个离家近一点儿的工作。

LESSON 11
Dialogue
1.夏天觉得上海有好有坏。
2.因为上下班时间交通不好，地铁里人太多了。
3.在家看电视、跟朋友逛街、逛夜市。

Exercise

Part 1

1. 习惯   2. 离   3. 热闹   4. 负担

Part 2

1. 我最喜欢的城市是青岛。
2. 我比较喜欢小一点儿的城市。
3. 住在城市的好处是生活比较方便，坏处是城市有污染的问题。
4. 交通比较方便，不过也有堵车的问题。生活负担挺重的。
5. 在我看来，一个不错的城市没有空气污染的问题。

LESSON 12

Dialogue

1. 在宿舍开一个电影晚会。
2. 宿舍很乱，厨房和卫生间都很脏。
3. 他们最后没商量怎么开电影晚会。

Exercise

Part 1

1. 特别   2. 管   3. 收拾   4. 负责

Part 2

1. 我的宿舍住三个人。
2. 我的房间非常干净、也很整齐。
3. 我每个周末花三个小时打扫房间。
4. 我给朋友在我的宿舍开过一两次生日晚会。
5. 对，开晚会以前，我会跟室友一起收拾房间。

LESSON 13

Dialogue

1. 绿茶餐厅推荐酸菜鱼和麻辣大虾。
2. 八月十八号以前去吃饭餐厅会送饮料和糖果。
3. 如果要坐靠窗的位置看夜景，最好提前打电话。

Exercise

Part 1

1. 主食   2. 座位   3. 杯   4. 酸

Part 2

1. 我差不多每个星期五都去饭馆儿吃晚饭。
2. 学校附近有一家杭州风味儿的饭馆儿，我非常喜欢。
3. 我看得懂中文菜单，用中文点菜不太难。
4. 我的饮食习惯比较清淡，所以吃不了辣的菜。
5. 在中国，特别是在大城市，有很多美国快餐店。

LESSON 14

Dialogue

1. 林丽去看篮球比赛，太吵了，没听见手机响。
2. 林丽刚认识的朋友是篮球队的，她去支持她的朋友。
3. 她要跟刚认识的朋友看音乐会、吃饭。

Exercise

Part 1

1. 联系   2. 约   3. 结束   4. 支持

Part 2

1. 不好意思，今天下午我已经约了朋友去吃饭，改天去好吗？
2. 我最喜欢看游泳比赛。
3. 我不太喜欢看球赛，所以没有特别支持的球队。
4. 在我的国家，年轻人比较喜欢足球、棒球。
5. 不忙的时候我会约朋友看电影或者一起做饭。

LESSON 15

Dialogue

1. 最近天气一直都不太好。
2. 李竹已经找到了实习工作。
3. 这个周六他们可能不会出去野餐，因为会下大雨。

Exercise

Part 1

1. 照   2. 终于   3. 忘   4. 祝

Part 2

1. 天气好的时候我会去森林里野餐。
2. 要是出去野餐，我会带面包和水果。
3. 我很喜欢去爬山，特别是到了秋天，山上风景很美。
4. 我喜欢拍照片，特别是给别人拍照片。
5. 我的脸书上有很多高中和大学时候的照片。

LESSON 16

Dialogue

1. 大海打算在图书馆打工、当家教。
2. 小江跟学校的合唱团去澳洲演出。
3. 小江去澳洲会品尝那儿的海鲜。

Exercise

Part 1

1. 演   2. 一定   3. 省钱   4. 教

Part 2

1. 下个星期就是感恩节了，我有一个星期的假期。
2. 假期我要么出去旅游要么找个实习的工作。
3. 我没有去过别的国家演出。
4. 我在假期打过工，我觉得在图书馆打工挺有意思的。
5. 我当过家教，我教几个中学生英文。

LESSON 17

Dialogue

1.李想要去美国留学，他申请研究生院很顺利。
2.李想最近忙着办护照，申请签证。
3.留学费用很高，而且在国外得学会独立生活。

Exercise

Part 1

1.压力　　2.独立　　3.留学　　4.申请

Part 2

1.我去英国留过学，我特别喜欢在英国的留学生活。
2.如果我有机会去留学，我想去新西兰。
3.在我的大学，有很多从亚洲来的留学生。
4.我觉得我们国家的气候对有些人来说比较难习惯。
5.学习压力很大的时候，我会去运动或者购物。

LESSON 18

Dialogue

1.安明没有生病，他觉得空气质量太差了，所以戴口罩。
2.空气污染问题、城市交通问题、垃圾回收问题。
3.人们在生活上不要浪费水、电，不乱扔垃圾。

Exercise

Part 1

1.注意　　2.环境　　3.污染　　4.健康

Part 2

1.我生活的城市有空气污染的问题，但是不是很严重。
2.我住的地方是一个小城，没有堵车的问题。
3.我觉得多坐公共交通是解决交通问题的好办法。
4.在很多大城市，光污染也越来越严重了。
5.政府先要重视环境问题，然后要想办法解决。

LESSON 19

Dialogue

1.吴江打算去南美洲当志愿者，帮那里的人盖房子。
2.艾欣要去农村教英文，因为那里教育很落后。
3.大家可以在这个网站上捐钱、捐东西。

Exercise

Part 1

1.哭　　2.志愿者　　3.穷　　4.需要

Part 2

1.我当过志愿者，我去老人院帮老人收拾房间。
2.我帮助过穷人，我每年都会给需要的人捐衣服。
3.政府应该在比较穷的地方建非常好的学校。
4.要是有机会，我会选择去中国农村教英文。
5.要是我组织志愿者活动，我想去帮助那些没人照顾的小动物。

LESSON 20

Dialogue

1.高言正在学中文。
2.声调很难，写汉字认汉字都很难。
3.跟不同的人说话要注意怎么说比较客气。

Exercise

Part 1

1.声调　　2.翻译　　3.流利　　4.碰

Part 2

1.我会说三种语言，西班牙文，中文和英文。
2.学外语最难的是记住生词。
3.学外语最好的方法是多说多听。
4.中文有声调，我的母语没有声调。
5.我写繁体字，我觉得汉字虽然难写，但是很漂亮。

English-Chinese Index

C

caffeine 咖啡因 **kāfēiyīn** 31

cake 糕 **gāo** 138; 蛋糕 **dàngāo** 39; 糕点 **gāodiǎn** 138

calm; serene 静 **jìng** 68

calm down 静一静 **jìngyijìng** 68; 静下来 **jìngxiàlai** 68

camera 照相机 **zhàoxiàngjī** 140

care 照顾 **zhàogù** 140

cannot bear to see 看不惯 **kànbuguàn** 103

cannot forget 忘不掉 **wàngbùdiào** 138

cannot get used to eating something 吃不惯 **chībuguàn** 103

cannot get used to living somewhere 住不惯 **zhùbuguàn** 103

can't stop crying 哭个不停 **kūge bù tíng** 175

capable 能干 **nénggàn** 110

captain (of a sports team) 队长 **duìzhǎng** 128

car 汽车 **qìchē** 57

card 卡片 **kǎpiàn** 32

care 关心 **guānxīn** 93

careful 小心 **xiǎoxīn** 93; 细心 **xìxīn** 95; 仔细 **zǐxì** 95

careless 粗 **cū** 95; 粗心 **cūxīn** 95

carry 负 **fù** 103; 提 **tí** 105

cast 演员 **yǎnyuán** 150

cause trouble to 害 **hài** 96

cautious 小心 **xiǎoxīn** 93

celebrate 庆祝 **qìngzhù** 138

cell phone 手机 **shǒujī** 30

century 世纪 **shìjì** 147

ceremony 典 **diǎn** 184; 典礼 **diǎnlǐ** 184

certificate 证 **zhèng** 156; 证书 **zhèngshū** 156

chair 椅 **yǐ** 112

change 换 **huàn** 67

change clothes 换衣服 **huàn yīfu** 67

change to 换车 **huànchē** 67

chart 图表 **túbiǎo** 150

chauffeur 司机 **sījī** 59

check 支票 **zhīpiào** 129

chef 厨师 **chúshī** 69

cheese 奶酪 **nǎilào** 38

chicken 鸡 **jī** 39; 鸡肉 **jīròu** 39

chicken wing 鸡翅 **jīchì** 39

child 孩 **hái** 74; 小孩子 **xiǎoháizi** 74

child's play 儿戏 **érxì** 137

children 孩童 **háitóng** 74

children's songs 儿歌 **érgē** 15

chili 辣椒 **làjiāo** 122

Chinese calligraphy ink 墨汁 **mòzhī** 139

Chinese New Year couplet 春联 **chūnlián** 131

Chinese opera 戏曲 **xìqǔ** 137

choir 合唱团 **héchàngtuán** 15

choose 选 **xuǎn** 12; 选择 **xuǎnzé** 12

chubby 胖 **pàng** 50; 胖乎乎 **pànghūhū** 50

church 教堂 **jiàotáng** 146

class 班级 **bānjí** 14; 班 **bān** 14

classics 古典 **gǔdiǎn** 184

clean 净 **jìng** 111; 干净 **gānjìng** 111

clear 晴 **qíng** 47

clear sky 晴天 **qíngtiān** 47

clear sky after rain 雨过天晴 **yǔguò tiānqíng** 47

climb 爬 **pá** 101

climbing stairs 爬楼梯 **pá lóutī** 101

close 深厚 **shēnhòu** 176

close to 邻近 **línjìn** 101

coarse 粗糙 **cūcāo** 95

cocktail 鸡尾酒 **jīwěijiǔ** 39

coffee 咖 **kā** 31; 啡 **fēi** 31; 咖啡 **kāfēi** 31

coffee machine 咖啡机 **kāfēijī** 31

coffee mug 咖啡杯 **kāfēibēi** 31

coffee shop 咖啡馆 **kāfēiguǎn** 31

coherent 连贯 **liánguàn** 175

coincidence 碰巧 **pèngqiǎo** 185

colorful 鲜艳 **xiānyàn** 139

comments 注释 **zhùshì** 165

commodity 商品 **shāngpǐn** 122

common 共同 **gòngtóng** 57

common laborer 蓝领 **lánlǐng** 159

communicate 打交道 **dǎjiāodào** 66

company 公司 **gōngsī** 59; 陪伴 **péibàn** 87

compassion 爱心 **àixīn** 78

competition 竞赛 **jìngsài** 128; 赛 **sài** 128; 比赛 **bǐsài** 128

complain 诉 **sù** 30; 投诉 **tóusù** 30

complete 完 **wán** 16

completely 完全 **wánquán** 16

component 环 **huán** 164

computer desktop 桌面 **zhuōmiàn** 112

computer science 计算机 **jìsuànjī** 30

concede 让步 **ràngbù** 67; 认输 **rènshū** 129

concept 观念 **guānniàn** 148

concern oneself about 管 **guǎn** 113

concern oneself about 管 **guǎn** 113

conclusion 结论 **jiélùn** 130

concrete 具体 **jùtǐ** 176

condition 条件 **tiáojiàn** 41

congested 拥挤 **yōngjǐ** 167

congratulations 祝贺 **zhùhè** 138

connect 通 **tōng** 166

considerate 懂事 **dǒngshì** 87

duck 鸭肉 **yāròu** 40
due to 由于 **yóuyú** 185
duty 义务 **yìwù** 42; 职责 **zhízé** 114
duty free 免税 **miǎnshuì** 132

E

each other 相 **xiāng** 140; 相互 **xiānghù** 140
ear 耳 **ěr** 23; 耳朵 **ěrduō** 23
earlier 早些 **zǎoxiē** 16
earphone 耳机 **ěrjī** 23
earring 耳环 **ěrhuán** 23
easy 简单 **jiǎndān** 125
eating 饮食 **yǐnshí** 121
ecology 生态 **shēngtài** 186
education 教育 **jiàoyù** 146
effective 管用 **guǎnyòng** 113
egg 蛋 **dàn** 39; 鸡蛋 **jīdàn** 39
egg drop soup 蛋花汤 **dànhuātāng** 39
egg yolk 蛋黄 **dànhuáng** 39
election 选举 **xuǎnjǔ** 12
emergency 紧急 **jǐnjí** 131; 急诊 **jízhěn** 132
emigration 出境 **chūjìng** 164
emotion 情 **qíng** 32
empty 空 **kōng** 165
encounter 碰到 **pèngdào** 185
end 结束 **jiéshù** 130; 终 **zhōng** 137
endless 无穷 **wúqióng** 175
endurance 忍让 **rěnràng** 67
engagement 安排 **ānpái** 68
enhance 提高 **tígāo** 50
enhance ability 锻炼能力 **duànliàn nénglì** 51
enough 足够 **zúgòu** 47
enter 进 **jìn** 48; 进来 **jìnlai** 48; 输入 **shūrù** 129
environment 环境 **huánjìng** 164
equip 具备 **jùbèi** 12
especially 尤其 **yóuqí** 104
establish 立足 **lìzú** 157
even.... 连...都... **lián... dōu...** 175; 连 **lián** 175
even if 哪怕 **nǎpà** 96; 虽是 **suīshì** 94
even more 更加 **gèngjiā** 94
even though 虽 **suī** 94; 虽说 **suīshuō** 94; 尽管 **jǐnguǎn** 113
exchange 交 **jiāo** 66
excited 兴奋 **xīngfèn** 77
excitement 兴 **xìng** 77
exempt 免 **miǎn** 132
exercise 锻炼 **duànliàn** 51; 锻炼身体 **duànliàn shēntǐ** 51
exercise more 多锻炼 **duō duànliàn** 51
exhausting 劳累 **láolèi** 56

expect 望 **wàng** 29
expense 支出 **zhīchū** 129
experience 经 **jīng** 77; 经验 **jīngyàn** 77; 经历 **jīnglì** 77; 体验 **tǐyàn** 20
explain 解释 **jiěshì** 85
explanation 讲解 **jiǎngjiě** 85
express thanks 答谢 **dáxiè** 13
extensive 博 **bó** 148
eye 眼 **yǎn** 21; 眼睛 **yǎnjīng** 21
eyeball 睛 **jīng** 21
eyeglasses 眼镜 **yǎnjìng** 21
eye-opening 大开眼界 **dà-kāi-yǎn-jiè** 148
eyes fixed 目不转睛 **mùbùzhuǎnjīng** 21

F

facility 设备 **shèbèi** 12
fake 假 **jiǎ** 146
false 假 **jiǎ** 146
familiar 眼熟 **yǎnshú** 21
fan of Chinese opera 戏迷 **xìmí** 137
from beginning to end; all along 始终 **shǐzhōng** 137
fans (of a singer) 歌迷 **gēmí** 15
farewell 告别 **gàobié** 29
fashionable 流行 **liúxíng** 182
fat 胖 **pàng** 50
fat or slim 胖瘦 **pàngshòu** 50
father-in-law 丈人 **zhàngren** 74
father's younger brother; uncle 叔父 **shūfù** 75
fatigued 累 **lèi** 56
fear 怕 **pà** 96
feast 大餐 **dàcān** 120
featured (dish) 特色 **tèsè** 114
fee 费 **fèi** 66
feeling 情 **qíng** 32
fever 发烧 **fāshāo** 23
figure 身材 **shēncái** 20
file a lawsuit 打官司 **dǎ guānsi** 59
film 片 **piàn** 32
final (in a competition) 决赛 **juésài** 85
finally 总算 **zǒngsuàn** 96; 终于 **zhōngyú** 137
fine arts 艺术 **yìshù** 149; 美术 **měishù** 149
finger 手指 **shǒuzhǐ** 22
finish 终 **zhōng** 137; 完 **wán** 16; 完成 **wánchéng** 16
finishing line 终点 **zhōngdiǎn** 137
fish 鱼 **yú** 40
fit 适合 **shìhé** 158
fire 火 **huǒ** 58
fishing 钓鱼 **diàoyú** 40
flexible 灵活 **línghuó** 164
flight 航班 **hángbān** 14; 飞 **fēi** 58; 飞机 **fēijī** 58

have time 有空 **yǒukòng** 165
head 头 **tóu** 22
health 健 **jiàn** 167; 身体 **shēntǐ** 20
healthy 健康 **jiànkāng** 167
heart 心 **xīn** 93; 心脏 **xīnzàng** 112
heartbroken 伤心 **shāngxīn** 93
heat 暑 **shǔ** 174
heat up 烧 **shāo** 23
heatstroke 中暑 **zhòngshǔ** 174
heavy 重 **zhòng** 10; 厚重 **hòuzhòng** 176
hectic 忙乱 **mángluàn** 15
help 帮 **bāng** 16; 助 **zhù** 83; 帮忙 **bāngmáng** 16; 帮助 **bāngzhù** 83
helping hand 帮手 **bāngshǒu** 16
hi-speed train 高铁 **gāotiě** 101
high 高 **gāo** 50
hiking 爬山 **páshān** 101
hobby 爱好 **àihào** 78
hold 举办 **jǔbàn** 86
home-style cooking 家常菜 **jiāchángcài** 42
honest 实 **shí** 104; 诚实 **chéngshí** 104
hop 跳 **tiào** 14
hope 希 **xī** 29; 希望 **xīwàng** 29
hopeful 有希望 **yǒuxīwàng** 29
horse racing 赛马 **sàimǎ** 128
horse riding 骑马 **qímǎ** 105
host 举办 **jǔbàn** 86; 主 **zhǔ** 121; 主人 **zhǔrén** 121; 主持 **zhǔchí** 129
host 主 **zhǔ** 121
hot 辣 **là** 122
hot and numbing 麻辣 **málà** 86
hot drink 热饮 **rèyǐn** 125
hot pepper 辣椒 **làjiāo** 122
hot pot 火锅 **huǒguō** 58
hot weather 暑 **shǔ** 174
household chore 家务 **jiāwù** 42
how many children 几个孩子 **jǐgeháizi** 74
how many legs 几条腿 **jǐtiáotuǐ** 48
humble abode 寒舍 **hánshè** 110
humble gift 薄礼 **bólǐ** 177
humidity 湿度 **shīdù** 24
humorous 风趣 **fēngqù** 77
hungry 饿 **è** 95
husband 丈 **zhàng** 74; 夫 **fū** 74; 丈夫 **zhàngfu** 74
husband and wife 夫妻 **fūqī** 74
husband of mother's sister; uncle 姨丈 **yízhàng** 76
husband of paternal aunt 姑丈 **gūzhàng** 74
hustle and bustle 热闹 **rènào** 102
hygiene 卫生 **wèishēng** 69
hypothetically 假如 **jiǎrú** 157

I

ice 冰 **bīng** 120
ice cold 冰凉 **bīngliáng** 120
ice skating 滑冰 **huábīng** 120
ice water 冰水 **bīngshuǐ** 120
iced coffee 冰咖啡 **bīngkāfēi** 31
idea 意 **yì** 93; 主意 **zhǔyì** 121
identification 证件 **zhèngjiàn** 156
idiot 傻瓜 **shǎguā** 39
if 如 **rú** 157; 如果 **rúguǒ** 157; 假如 **jiǎrú** 157
illegal 非法 **fēifǎ** 56
illegible 潦草 **liáocǎo** 140
illness 病 **bìng** 20; 疾病 **jíbìng** 20
immediately 立刻 **lìkè** 157
immigration 入境 **rùjìng** 164
impatient 不耐烦 **búnàifán** 87
import 进口 **jìnkǒu** 48
important 重要 **zhòngyào** 104
important point 重点 **zhòngdiǎn** 104
in a few words 三言两语 **sān-yán-liǎng-yǔ** 182
in a low voice 小声 **xiǎoshēng** 186
in a row 连续 **liánxù** 175
in a rush 急 **jí** 132
in accumulaton 累计 **lěijì** 56
in advance 提前 **tíqián** 105
in detail 详细 **xiángxì** 95
in progress 进行 **jìnxíng** 48
in return 回报 **huíbào** 13
in the end 算 **suàn** 96
in total 一共 **yígòng** 57; 总共 **zǒnggòng** 57
in urgent need 急需 **jíxū** 177
include 包括 **bāokuò** 42
income 收入 **shōurù** 113
increase 增加 **zēngjiā** 94; 提高 **tígāo** 50
indeed 确实 **quèshí** 104
independent 独 **dú** 157; 独立 **dúlì** 157
infected 感染 **gǎnrǎn** 167
ingredients 材料 **cáiliào** 125
innards 内脏 **nèizàng** 112
insist 坚持 **jiānchí** 129
instrument 工具 **gōngjù** 176
interact 交流 **jiāoliú** 66
interest 兴趣 **xìngqù** 77
interesting 趣 **qù** 77; 趣味 **qùwèi** 77
interesting thing 趣事 **qùshì** 77
internet 互联网 **hùliánwǎng** 131
interprete 口译 **kǒuyì** 184
interrupt 插嘴 **chāzuǐ** 24
intermediary 中介 **zhōngjiè** 33
intervene 介入 **jièrù** 33

manage 管理 **guǎnlǐ** 113

mark 志 **zhì** 173

market 菜市场 **càishìchǎng** 42; 市场 **shìchǎng** 31

married couple 夫妻 **fūqī** 74

martial art 功夫 **gōngfu** 74

match 赛 **sài** 128; 比赛 **bǐsài** 128

material 料 **liào** 125; 资料 **zīliào** 125

maternal grandfather 姥爷 **lǎoyé** 75

mathematics 数学 **shùxué** 147

mature 成熟 **chéngshú** 183

meaning 意 **yì** 93; 意思 **yìsi** 93

meaning of a word 词义 **cíyì** 184

measure word for long thin objects 条 **tiáo** 41

meal 餐 **cān** 120

measure word for mountains 座 **zuò** 119

measure word for pens 支 **zhī** 129

measure word for people 位 **wèi** 119

meat 肉 **ròu** 40

medical expertise 医术 **yīshù** 149

melon 瓜 **guā** 39

melon and fruit 瓜果 **guāguǒ** 39

member 会员 **huìyuán** 43

memorandum 备忘录 **bèiwànglù** 12

memory 回忆 **huíyì** 13

menu 菜单 **càidān** 125

mentality 心态 **xīntài** 186

merit 绩 **jì** 183

mess up 弄乱 **nòngluàn** 111

messy 乱 **luàn** 111; 脏乱 **zāngluàn** 112

method 术 **shù** 149

milk 奶 **nǎi** 38; 牛奶 **niúnǎi** 38

milk tea 奶茶 **nǎichá** 38

mind 介意 **jièyì** 33; 心 **xīn** 93

mindset 心态 **xīntài** 186

money given to children as a New Year's present 压岁钱 **yāsuìqián** 159

mood 心情 **xīnqíng** 32

more 越 **yuè** 114

more and more... 越来越... **yuè lái yuè...** 114

mother's sister 姨妈 **yímā** 76

mother's youngest sister 小姨 **xiǎoyí** 76

motel 汽车旅馆 **qìchē lǚguǎn** 57

mountain climbing 爬山 **páshān** 101

mouth 嘴 **zuǐ** 24; 嘴巴 **zuǐbā** 24

move 搬 **bān** 85; 搬家 **bānjiā** 85

move in 搬进来 **bānjìnlai** 85

muscles 肌肉 **jīròu** 40

must 一定 **yídìng** 150

mutton 羊肉 **yángròu** 40

N

napkin 餐巾纸 **cānjīnzhǐ** 60

nasal mucus 鼻涕 **bíti** 23

nearby 邻近 **línjìn** 101

nearsighted 近视眼 **jìnshìyǎn** 21

necessity 必需品 **bìxūpǐn** 177

necktie 领带 **lǐngdài** 84

need 需 **xū** 177; 需要 **xūyào** 177

neighbor 邻 **lín** 101; 邻居 **línju** 101

net 净 **jìng** 111

net income 净收入 **jìngshōurù** 111

never mind 没关系 **méiguānxi** 131

new residence 新居 **xīnjū** 102

news 一条新闻 **yìtiáoxīnwén** 41

newspaper 报 **bào** 60; 报纸 **bàozhǐ** 60

no hope 没希望 **méixīwàng** 29

nod 点头 **diǎntóu** 22

noise 声响 **shēngxiǎng** 178

noisy 吵 **chǎo** 68

nose 鼻 **bí** 23; 鼻子 **bízi** 23

not 非 **fēi** 56

not as good as 不如 **bùrú** 157

not at ease 拘束 **jūshù** 130

note 条子 **tiáozi** 41

notes 注释 **zhùshì** 165

nothing other than 非要 **fēiyào** 56

numb 麻 **má** 86

number 号 **hào** 59; 号码 **hàomǎ** 59; 数 **shǔ** 147; 数字 **shùzì** 147

numbing 麻 **má** 86

nurse 护士 **hùshì** 155

nursery rhymes 儿歌 **érgē** 15

O

obesity 肥胖 **féipàng** 50

occasion 场合 **chǎnghé** 31

office building 办公楼 **bàngōnglóu** 102

often 经常 **jīngcháng** 77

older brother 兄 **xiōng** 76; 兄长 **xiōngzhǎng** 76

older brother's wife 兄嫂 **xiōngsǎo** 76

older brother and younger sister 兄妹 **xiōngmèi** 76

on break 放假 **fàngjià** 84

on fire 着火 **zháohuǒ** 58

on purpose 故意 **gùyì** 93

on time (transportation) 准点 **zhǔndiǎn** 12

on time 准时 **zhǔnshí** 12

one chair 一把椅子 **yìbǎ yǐzi** 112

one's signature 签名 **qiānmíng** 156

only 非要 **fēiyào** 56

only if... 除非 **chúfēi** 56

purifier 净化器 **jìnghuàqì** 111

put 放 **fàng** 84

putonghua; Mandarin Chinese 普通话 **pǔtōnghuà** 166

Q

Q&A 提问 **tíwèn** 105

quarrel 吵架 **chǎojià** 68

queue 排队 **páiduì** 128

quiet 安静 **ānjìng** 68

R

racket 球拍 **qiúpāi** 137

rainy season 雨季 **yǔjì** 149

randomly 乱 **luàn** 111

rap 说唱 **shuōchàng** 15

raw materials 原料 **yuánliào** 125

reaction 反应 **fǎnyìng** 83

real 实 **shí** 104

reality show 真人秀 **zhēnrénxiù** 78

really 真 **zhēn** 78; 实在 **shízài** 104

receive 收 **shōu** 113; 收到 **shōudào** 113

(vinyl) records 唱片 **chàngpiān** 15

rectangle 长方形 **chángfāngxíng** 58

recycle 回收 **huíshōu** 113

recycling bin 垃圾回收箱 **lājī huíshōuxiāng** 168

refer 参考 **cānkǎo** 94

reference 参考 **cānkǎo** 94

referral 介绍人 **jièshàorén** 33

refrain from 免不了 **miǎnbuliǎo** 132

refrigerator 冰箱 **bīngxiāng** 57

register 注 **zhù** 165; 注册 **zhùcè** 165

registration 挂号 **guàhào** 59

relationship 关系 **guānxi** 131

relax 放松 **fàngsōng** 84

remind 提醒 **tíxǐng** 105

rent 房租 **fángzū** 65

rental fee 租金 **zūjīn** 65

reply 答 **dá** 13; 答复 **dáfù** 13

report 报 **bào** 60; 告 **gào** 29; 报告 **bàogào** 29

report to police 报警 **bàojǐng** 60

reptile 爬行动物 **páxíng dòngwù** 101

reputation 声誉 **shēngyù** 186

requirement 需求 **xūqiú** 177

reservation 预约 **yùyuē** 130

reside 居住 **jūzhù** 102

residence 舍 **shè** 110; 居住 **jūzhù** 102

respond 回 **huí** 13; 答复 **dáfù** 13

response; feedback 反响 **fǎnxiǎng** 178

responsible; in charge of 负责 **fùzé** 103

responsibility 义务 **yìwù** 42; 责 **zé** 114; 职责 **zhízé** 114

rest assured 放心 **fàngxīn** 84

restaurant 餐厅 **cāntīng** 120

restrict 约束 **yuēshù** 130

restroom 卫生间 **wèishēngjiān** 69; 洗手间 **xǐshǒujiān** 69

respond 回 **huí** 13

return to one's country 回国 **huíguó** 13

rice 米 **mǐ** 41; 米饭 **mǐfàn** 41

rice cake 年糕 **niángāo** 138

ride 骑 **qí** 105

ride a bicycle 骑自行车 **qí zìxíngchē** 105

ride a scooter 骑摩托车 **qí mótuōchē** 105

right and wrong 是非 **shìfēi** 56

rich 博 **bó** 148

ring 环 **huán** 164; 响 **xiǎng** 178

rise 兴 **xīng** 77; 兴起 **xīngqǐ** 77

roast 烤 **kǎo** 141

roast duck 烤鸭 **kǎoyā** 141

robot 机器人 **jīqìrén** 30

rocking chair 摇椅 **yáoyǐ** 112

romance 爱情 **àiqíng** 78

romantic 浪漫 **làngmàn** 166

room and board 食宿 **shísù** 110

rough 粗糙 **cūcāo** 95

rude 粗鲁 **cūlǔ** 95

run out 用完 **yòngwán** 16

rush 急忙 **jímáng** 132

S

sad 心酸 **xīnsuān** 121; 伤心 **shāngxīn** 93

safe 安 **ān** 68; 安全 **ānquán** 68

sales 业绩 **yèjì** 183

salesperson 售货员 **shòuhuòyuán** 43

sanitation 卫生 **wèishēng** 69

satisfied 满意 **mǎnyì** 93

save 省 **shěng** 146

scan 扫描 **sǎomiáo** 111

scary 可怕 **kěpà** 96

scenery 景 **jǐng** 158; 景色 **jǐngsè** 158

scenic spots 景点 **jǐngdiǎn** 158

school building 校舍 **xiàoshè** 110

scream 喊 **hǎn** 132

sea 海 **hǎi** 139

seafood 海鲜 **hǎixiān** 139

season 季 **jì** 149; 季节 **jìjié le** 149

seasonal vegetable 时蔬 **shíshū** 141

seat 座 **zuò** 119; 座位 **zuòwèi** 119

section 班 **bānjí** 14

see (someone) off 送（人）**sòng (rén)** 32

steam 汽 **qì** 57
steel 钢铁 **gāngtiě** 101
stingy person 铁公鸡 **tiěgōngjī** 101
stomach 肚 **dù** 22; 肚子 **dùzi** 22
stomachache 闹肚子 **nàodùzi** 22
straw 草 **cǎo** 140
strawberry 草莓 **cǎoméi** 140
stretch legs 踢腿 **tītuǐ** 47
street 街 **jiē** 103
street person 流浪汉 **liúlànghàn** 166
strength 力 **lì** 92
structure 结构 **jiégòu** 130
study hard 努力学习 **nǔlì xuéxí** 92
sturdy 结实 **jiēshi** 130
style 体 **tǐ** 20; 式 **shì** 155; 样式 **yàngshì** 155
subway 地铁 **dìtiě** 101
successful 成功 **chénggōng** 183
such 其 **qí** 104
such as 比如 **bǐrú** 157
sue 诉 **sù** 30
suffer hunger 挨饿 **ái'è** 95
sufficient 足 **zú** 47; 充足 **chōngzú** 47
suit 适合 **shìhé** 158
suitable 适当 **shìdàng** 158
summer school 暑校 **shǔxiào** 174
summer vacation 暑假 **shǔjià** 146; 暑期 **shǔqī** 174
sunny 晴朗 **qínglǎng** 47
sunny turns into cloudy 晴转多云 **qíngzhuǎnduōyún** 47
support 支 **zhī** 129; 支持 **zhīchí** 129
surf 冲浪 **chōnglàng** 166
surgery 手术 **shǒushù** 22
surpass 超越 **chāoyuè** 114
sweat 汗 **hàn** 49; 汗珠 **hànzhū** 49
sweep 扫 **sǎo/sào** 111
sweep the floor 扫地 **sǎodì** 111
sweet 甜 **tián** 122; 甜蜜 **tiánmì** 122
sweet words 甜言蜜语 **tián-yán-mì-yǔ** 122
swim 泳 **yǒng** 49; 游泳 **yóuyǒng** 49
swim the breaststroke 蛙泳 **wāyǒng** 49
swimming pool 游泳池 **yóuyǒngchí** 49
symbol 标志 **biāozhì** 173
system 制度 **zhìdù** 24

T
table 图表 **túbiǎo** 150; 桌 **zhuō** 112
table and chair (seats) 桌椅 **zhuōyǐ** 112
table tennis 桌球 **zhuōqiú** 112
take 拍 **pāi** 137; 会 **ná** 84; 选 **xuǎn** 12; 照 **zhào** 140
take (classes) 选修 **xuǎnxiū** 12
take a photo 拍照片 **pāi zhàopiān** 137

take away 拿走 **názǒu** 84
take charge of 司 **sī** 59
take off 起飞 **qǐfēi** 58
talk 倾诉 **qīngsù** 30; 讲话 **jiǎnghuà** 159
talk big 吹牛 **chuīniú** 38
talk on the phone 通话 **tōnghuà** 166
tall 高 **gāo** 50
tap dance 踢踏舞 **tītàwǔ** 47
task 任务 **rènwù** 42
tasty 鲜美 **xiānměi** 139
taxi 出租车 **chūzūchē** 65
tea cup 茶杯 **chábēi** 120
teach 教 **jiāo** 146
teaching 教 **jiào** 146
team 队 **duì** 128
team member 队员 **duìyuán** 128
tears 眼泪 **yǎnlèi** 21
technique 术 **shù** 149; 技术 **jìshù** 149
technology 技术 **jìshù** 149
tell a story 讲故事 **jiǎng gùshì** 159
tell 讲 **jiǎng** 159; 告 **gào** 29; 诉 **sù** 30; 告诉 **gàosù** 29
temperature 温度 **wēndù** 24
tennis court 网球场 **wǎngqiúchǎng** 31
terminate 终止 **zhōngzhǐ** 137
terrible 可怕 **kěpà** 96
terrific 厉害 **lìhai** 96
test 考题 **kǎotí** 13
that 其 **qí** 104
that's alright 没关系 **méiguānxi** 131
the comics 连环画 **liánhuánhuà** 164
theme 主题 **zhǔtí** 13
thick 厚 **hòu** 176; 粗 **cū** 95
third place 季军 **jìjūn** 149
thin 薄 **báo** 177; 单薄 **dānbó** 177; 瘦 **shòu** 51; 细 **xì** 95
thin/light 薄 **báo/bó** 177
thin and small 瘦小 **shòuxiǎo** 51
thin piece 片 **piàn** 32
thin slice 薄片 **báopiàn** 177
thorough 真正 **zhēnzhèng** 78; 健全 **jiànquán** 167
though 虽 **suī** 94
thoughtful 懂事 **dǒngshì** 87
thousand 千 **qiān** 67
three dimensional 立体 **lìtǐ** 157
thriving 兴隆 **xīnglóng** 77
ticket 票 **piào** 59; 门票 **ménpiào** 59
ticket price 票价 **piàojià** 59
tight 紧 **jǐn** 131
tip 小费 **xiǎofèi** 66

tired 累 **lèi** 56
to give 给 **gěi** 33; 于 **yú** 185
to accomplish 成 **chéng** 183
to acquire (bad habits) 染上 **rǎnshàng** 167
to act 演 **yǎn** 150
to allow 准 **zhǔn** 12
to answer 回答 **huídá** 13
to apply for jobs 求职 **qiúzhí** 185
to assume the office of 担任 **dānrèn** 92
to be certain 肯定 **kěndìng** 150
to be killed 遇难 **yùnàn** 182
to bear fruit 结 **jiē/jié** 130; 结果子 **jiē guǒzi** 130
to become 变成 **biànchéng** 177
to blame 责 **zé** 114
to bleed 流血 **liúxuè** 182
to break 弄坏 **nònghuài** 66
to bump 碰 **pèng** 185; 碰见 **pèngjiàn** 185
to bundle 束 **shù** 130
to change 改变 **gǎibiàn** 177
to circulate 流传 **liúchuán** 182
to clean 收拾 **shōushi** 113
to come out 问世 **wènshì** 147
to comfort 安慰 **ānwèi** 68
to communicate 沟通 **gōutōng** 166
to conclude 结 **jiē/jié** 130
to crouch 卧 **wò** 65
to cry 哭 **kū** 175
to cry loudly 大哭 **dàkū** 175
to decide 决 **jué** 85
to discipline 锻 **duàn** 51
to do 干 **gàn** 110; 办 **bàn** 86
to drink 饮 **yǐn** 125
to dye 染 **rǎn** 167
to dye one's hair 染发 **rǎnfà** 167
to encounter 遇 **yù** 182
to enter a country 入境 **rùjìng** 164
to explain 解 **jiě** 85
to extend 申 **shēn** 156
to feel anxious 着急 **zháojí** 132
to fit 适 **shì** 158
to fix 定 **dìng** 150
to flip over 翻 **fān** 183
to flow 流 **liú** 182
to forge 锻 **duàn** 51
to gamble 赌博 **dǔbó** 148
(food) to go bad 变质 **biànzhì** 177
to go downstairs 下楼 **xiàlóu** 102
to go through 通 **tōng** 166
to guard 卫 **wèi** 69
to have a baby 生孩子 **shēngháizi** 74

to have a strong interest in 浓厚 **nónghòu** 176
to hold 持 **chí** 129
to hope 愿 **yuàn** 173
to infect 染 **rǎn** 167; 传染 **chuánrǎn** 167
to joke 开玩笑 **kāiwánxiào** 78
to know 解 **jiě** 85
to leave 留 **liú** 155
to leave a country 出境 **chūjìng** 164
to leave (something) 留 **liú** 155
to lie 卧 **wò** 65
to link 连 **lián** 175
to live 活 **huó** 164
to look after 照看 **zhàokàn** 140
to lose 输 **shū** 129
to maintain 保留 **bǎoliú** 155; 系 **xì/xi** 131; 维系 **wéixì** 131
to manage 办 **bàn** 86
to observe 观察 **guānchá** 148
to one's surprise 居然 **jūrán** 102
to order (food) 点菜 **diǎncài** 42
to overturn 翻 **fān** 183
to perspire 出汗 **chūhàn** 49
to press 压 **yā** 159; 挤 **jǐ** 167
to propose a toast 干杯 **gānbēi** 110
to prove 证 **zhèng** 156
to pursue (a goal) 追求 **zhuīqiú** 185
to reduce fever 退烧 **tuìshāo** 141
to refine 炼 **liàn** 51
to renovate 翻修 **fānxiū** 183
to rent 租 **zū** 65; 租房 **zūfáng** 65
to require 要求 **yāoqiú** 185
to request 求 **qiú** 185
to reside 居 **jū** 102
to retain 保留 **bǎoliú** 155
to ring 响 **xiǎng** 178
to ruin 弄坏 **nònghuài** 66
to run into 遇到 **yùdào** 182
to sample 品 **pǐn** 122; 品尝 **pǐncháng** 122
to save money 省钱 **shěng qián** 146
to save time 省时间 **shěng shíjiān** 146
to scream loudly 大喊大叫 **dàhǎn dàjiào** 132
to seek 求 **qiú** 185
to set 规定 **guīdìng** 150
to smile 笑 **xiào** 21
to spread 流 **liú** 182; 广 **guǎng** 65
to stand 立 **lì** 157; 立足 **lìzú** 157
to state 申 **shēn** 156
to stay 留 **liú** 155
to stipulate 规定 **guīdìng** 150
to strive 努 **nǔ** 92